A CELEBRATION
OF POETS

EAST K-3
SPRING 2008

creativeCOMMUNICATION
A CELEBRATION OF TODAY'S WRITERS

A CELEBRATION OF POETS
EAST K-3
SPRING 2008

AN ANTHOLOGY COMPILED BY CREATIVE COMMUNICATION, INC.

Published by:

creativeCOMMUNICATION
A CELEBRATION OF TODAY'S WRITERS

1488 NORTH 200 WEST • LOGAN, UTAH 84341
TEL. 435-713-4411 • WWW.POETICPOWER.COM

ISBN: 978-1-60050-185-2

FOREWORD

This edition of our poetry anthology is an important transition for Creative Communication. Since our beginning in 1993, we have called our contest "A Celebration of Young Poets." Having worked with student poets for over 15 years, we realized that the writers who have been accepted to be published are not "young" poets. They are poets. Young or old, they are writers who have proven their worth as poets. These are the poets we celebrate.

We also start this year with a new cover for the anthologies. We are excited about this new look and our new logo of a hand releasing stars. Our logo can represent different things. It could be a teacher or mentor releasing a writer to the world through our publication. It could represent the fact that the stars are limitless and these writers are just starting to shine with their potential. We have become the starting point for thousands of writers and we hope each poet continues to make writing a part of their lives.

What is recorded between these pages is unique. It exists nowhere else in the world and is now recorded forever. Take the time to read what these poets have shared. A part of themselves and their world exists in each poem. Savor it. Enjoy.

Sincerely,
Thomas Kenne Worthen, Ph.D.
Editor
Creative Communication

WRITING CONTESTS!

Enter our next POETRY contest!
Enter our next ESSAY contest!

Why should I enter?

Win prizes and get published! Each year thousands of dollars in prizes are awarded in each region and tens of thousands of dollars in prizes are awarded throughout North America. The top writers in each division receive a monetary award and a free book that includes their published poem or essay. Entries of merit are also selected to be published in our anthology.

Who may enter?

There are four divisions in the poetry and essay contests. The divisions are grades K-3, 4-6, 7-9, and 10-12.

What is needed to enter the contest?

To enter the poetry contest send in one original poem, 21 lines or less. To enter the essay contest send in one original essay, 250 words or less, on any topic. Each entry must include the student's name, grade, address, city, state, and zip code, and the student's school name and school address. Students who include their teacher's name may help the teacher qualify for a free copy of the anthology.

How do I enter?

Enter a poem online at:
www.poeticpower.com
or
Mail your poem to:
    Poetry Contest
    1488 North 200 West
    Logan, UT 84341

Enter an essay online at:
www.studentessaycontest.com
or
Mail your essay to:
    Essay Contest
    1488 North 200 West
    Logan, UT 84341

When is the deadline?

Poetry contest deadlines are December 4th, April 7th, and August 18th. Essay contest deadlines are October 15th, February 17th, and July 15th. You can enter each contest, however, send only one poem or essay for each contest deadline.

Are there benefits for my school?

Yes. We award $15,000 each year in grants to help with Language Arts programs. Schools qualify to apply for a grant by having a large number of entries of which over fifty percent are accepted for publication. This typically tends to be about 15 accepted entries.

Are there benefits for my teacher?

Yes. Teachers with five or more students accepted to be published receive a free anthology that includes their students' writing.

For more information please go to our website at
***www.poeticpower.com**,*
email us at editor@poeticpower.com or call 435-713-4411.

TABLE OF CONTENTS

STATES INCLUDED IN THIS EDITION:

Connecticut
Delaware
Maine
Maryland
Massachusetts
New Hampshire
New York
Pennsylvania
Rhode Island
Vermont
Virginia
Washington D.C.

Spring 2008 Poetic Achievement Honor Schools

* Teachers who had fifteen or more poets accepted to be published

The following schools are recognized as receiving a "Poetic Achievement Award." This award is given to schools who have a large number of entries of which over fifty percent are accepted for publication. With hundreds of schools entering our contest, only a small percent of these schools are honored with this award. The purpose of this award is to recognize schools with excellent Language Arts programs. This award qualifies these schools to receive a complimentary copy of this anthology. In addition, these schools are eligible to apply for a Creative Communication Language Arts Grant. Grants of two hundred and fifty dollars each are awarded to further develop writing in our schools.

Acushnet Elementary School
Acushnet, MA
Joan Akin*

Agape Christian Academy
Alexandria, VA
Linda Cason
Sharon Miser

Bensley Elementary School
Richmond, VA
Ms. Casey
Christina Frear
Maria T. MacLaughlin
Karen Struder
Ms. Swann
Mrs. Watson
Ms. Wolfe

Bradford Township Elementary
School
Clearfield, PA
Pamela L. Gabel
Mary Jo Seprish

Brookside Elementary School
Dracut, MA
Kathleen Irwin
Mary Ellen McCarthy
Sharon McGrath
Mrs. S. Ninteau

Buckley Country Day School
Roslyn, NY
Joanna Cooper
Mrs. Cross
Hillary Janik

Buckley Country Day School
Roslyn, NY (cont.)
Lynn Knox
Denise Powers
Jessica Raffaele
Stefani Rosenthal
Barbara Thomas*
Laura Uhr

Cabot Elementary School
Newton, MA
Marcie Mann
Elizabeth Stahl
Christina Thonet
Bhavna M. Vaswani*

Calvary Chapel Christian School
Farmington, NY
Morgan Gallatin
Sherry A. Jimenez*
Mrs. Leckie

Cambridge Springs Elementary
School
Cambridge Springs, PA
Donna Shorts*

Center School
Stow, MA
Carol Johnson*

Central Elementary School
Elizabeth, PA
Lois Leggett*

Chestnut Street Elementary School
Kane, PA
Robynn Boyer*

Christ the King School
Yonkers, NY
Sr. Alice Alter*

Clover Street School
Windsor, CT
Elaine Chartier
Lisa Thomas*

Dartmouth Early Learning Center
South Dartmouth, MA
Christine Hubert*

Dr Samuel C Eveleth School
Marblehead, MA
Carol Arnould*
Paula Tardiff*

Fisher Hill Elementary School
Orange, MA
Alyson DiSchino
Mrs. Gullage*

Fishing Creek Elementary School
Lewisberry, PA
Marjorie Hessler
Clair E. Richcrick*

Fox Chase School
Philadelphia, PA
David McMenimen
Brandi Wright*

General John Nixon Elementary
School
Sudbury, MA
Anderson Manuel*
Mr. Whiting

Glover Elementary School
Marblehead, MA
Brenda Perroni*

Granville Elementary School
Granville, NY
Krista Cotich
Cara Pilch

Guilford Lakes School
Guilford, CT
Louise Worrell*

Hebbville Elementary School
Baltimore, MD
Tunia Jackson
Darnell Peaker*

Heim Elementary School
Williamsville, NY
Kathy Pace*

Helen B Duffield Elementary
School
Ronkonkoma, NY
Mrs. Alway
Mrs. Kramer
Mrs. Meade
Karen Phillips
Jaclyn Zuccaro

Heron Pond Elementary School
Milford, NH
Kathy Melconian*

Houghton Elementary School
Sterling, MA
Maryanne Daley*

Jenkintown Elementary School
Jenkintown, PA
Leah Abdollahi
Doris Heise*

John Ward Elementary School
Newton Centre, MA
Sara McClellan
Naomi E. Singer
Kenneth Waldman*

Killingly Memorial School
Danielson, CT
Keri Costa*

Leicester Memorial School
Leicester, MA
Evemarie McNeil*

Lincoln Elementary School
Pittsburgh, PA
Cynthia Biery*

Lincoln Street School
Northborough, MA
Susan Grady
Catherine Simisky

Long Meadow Elementary School
Middlebury, CT
David Derouin
Dawn G. Dinallo*
Noel Siebern*
Carolyn Smith

Magnet School of Math, Science
and Design Technology
Brooklyn, NY
Ms. Graham*
Michele Kaye
Chandra A. Smith-Thomas

Mary Walter Elementary School
Bealeton, VA
Patricia Baker*

Mater Christi School
Burlington, VT
Kelly Alper
Jennifer Coulter
Sr. Joanne LaFreniere*
Mrs. Sem

Milton Terrace Primary School
Ballston Spa, NY
Kelly Morgan
Vicki Savini

Munsey Park Elementary School
Manhasset, NY
   Mrs. Kinsel
   Mrs. Levine
   Mrs. Mullowney
   Tara Pedone*
   Mrs. Puliafico
   Mrs. Reisman
   Mrs. Shapiro
   Mrs. Smith

Oakdale Elementary School
Ijamsville, MD
   Mona Clawson
   Lynne Harris

Our Lady of Hope School
Middle Village, NY
   Martha Madri*

Penn Yan Elementary School
Penn Yan, NY
   Laine Gillette
   Lisa Thompson

Penn-Kidder Campus
Albrightsville, PA
   Howard Gregory*
   Jill Klotz
   Angelina O'Rourke*
   Diane Reese*

Plainfield Catholic School
Moosup, CT
   Julie Fauxbel
   Ms. Fogarty
   Mrs. McIntosh

Pleasant View School
Providence, RI
   Deborah Castelli
   Mrs. Patricia Hillery
   Maggie Rainone

Public School 1 The Bergen School
Brooklyn, NY
   Ms. Felix
   Hedy Tessler*

Public School 105 Senator Abraham
Bernste
Bronx, NY
   Ms. Ali
   Miriam Bustos
   Kimberly Carfora
   Ms. DiPirro
   Ms. Lavergata
   Ms. Sanchez
   Ms. Vasquez
   Ms. Vera
   Mr. Weiner

Public School 148 Ruby Allen
East Elmhurst, NY
   Lois Ricupero*

Public School 152 School of
Science & Technology
Brooklyn, NY
   Mrs. Aris
   Ms. Christenson
   Ms. P. Dong
   Ms. Imperio
   Ms. Lutjen
   Mrs. McGuire
   Anna Randisi*
   Christina Romeo
   Ms. Ryba
   Ms. Scheir

Public School 2 Alfred Zimberg
Jackson Heights, NY
   Ms. Y. Castano
   Ms. Mallah
   Ms. A. Micallef
   Angela Proios
   Kristen Sliasky*

Public School 235 Lenox
Brooklyn, NY
Jennifer Moerler
Carolann Thompson

Public School 48
Staten Island, NY
Lisa Plaia*

Public School 69 Jackson Heights
Jackson Heights, NY
Michele Gilbride*
Ms. Kazeros*
Tracey Marchesini

Richland Elementary School
Gibsonia, PA
Mrs. Aiello*

Sacred Heart School
North Quincy, MA
Mrs. Gibbons
Margaret Hanna*
Patricia McGowan*
Mrs. Norris
Patricia Peck
Mr. Shea

Sacred Heart School
Groton, CT
Cathy Santangelo*

Saw Mill Road School
North Bellmore, NY
Tillie McNamara*

Seaford Central Elementary School
Seaford, DE
Laura Burke*

Sinai Academy of the Berkshires
Pittsfield, MA
Christine Kleinerman*

Somers Elementary School
Somers, CT
Jessica Kinelski
Miss Papia
Mr. Phillips

St Christopher's School
Richmond, VA
Mrs. Brown
Ms. DiLucente
Mr. Echols
Mrs. Epes
Ms. Fraine
Ms. Frischkorn
Ms. Gehring
Ms. Grinnan
Ms. Halladay
Ms. Hoge
Paula Jones
Glorietta Jones
Cabell Jones
Ms. Jones
Ms. Kirk
Mr. Morgan
Mrs. Oakley
Mrs. Prince
Ms. Sands
Ms. Vizcaino
Ann Wilson
Nancy Young

St Clement Mary Hofbauer School
Baltimore, MD
Christine Godlewski
Linda House
Janice McIntosh
Deborah Neidhardt
Wendy Parker*

St Joan of Arc School
Hershey, PA
Cynthia Miskinis*

St John Neumann Academy
Blacksburg, VA
   Mrs. Kesler
   Jenny Mishoe

St Joseph School
Gowanda, NY
   Anna Hejmanowski*

St Madeleine Sophie School
Schenectady, NY
   Deborah Flaherty-Kizer*

St Mary Magdalen School
Wilmington, DE
   Melissa Harra*
   Kristin Winchell*

St Mary's Primary School
Taunton, MA
   Erinn Grasso*
   Kristie Pelland*
   Linda M. Redmond

St Mary's School
Clinton, NY
   Irma Gualtieri*

St Rose School
Newtown, CT
   Bobbie Blizman
   Mary Jo Bokuniewicz*
   Mrs. Ferri*
   Rita Garrett*
   Judy Jewell
   Tamra Russo
   Miss Sideleau
   Jeanne Vitetta*

St Stephen's School
Grand Island, NY
   Kristy Pasko
   Daniela Schmidt*

Stony Point Elementary School
Stony Point, NY
   Maria Csernecky*

Sunrise Drive Elementary School
Sayville, NY
   Keri Athan
   Mrs. D. Morisie*

Tashua School
Trumbull, CT
   Mrs. Congdon*
   Mrs. Grosso
   Miss Nash*
   Mrs. Pope

The New York Institute for Special
Education
Bronx, NY
   Lillian M. Ludwig
   Dr. Franklin Raddock*

Thoreau Elementary School
Concord, MA
   Brad Bennett
   Margery Condon
   Nancy Dillon
   Mary Gallagher
   Tom Hourihan
   Merrie Najimy

Trinity Christian School
Fairfax, VA
   Mrs. Bode
   Constance Boltz
   Mrs. Butler
   Mrs. Datema
   Penny Gale
   Melissa Knaus*
   Miss Locke*
   Sindy Quinonez
   Kathy Rickwald*
   Jennifer Silva

Weston Intermediate School
Weston, CT
>Linda Allegretti
>Rudd Anderson
>Karen Andrade
>Mrs. Balzi
>Kellie Brown
>Gregory Cannito
>Ms. Casey
>Celeste Coulter
>Kelly Farrell
>Sharon Huynh
>Carolyn Jones
>Mrs. Knudsen
>Geri Leka
>Alison Margo
>Barbara Nardella
>Mrs. Oliver
>Kathy Pando
>Carinne Phoenix
>Renee Tomaselli
>Kendra Verdi

Willis E Thorpe School
Danvers, MA
>Ms. Burke
>Kristen D'Entremont
>Lorraine M. Errico*
>Lisa Horn
>Miss Lyons
>Kaitlyn MacDonald
>Mrs. Martin

Language Arts Grant Recipients 2007-2008

After receiving a "Poetic Achievement Award" schools are encouraged to apply for a Creative Communication Language Arts Grant. The following is a list of schools who received a two hundred and fifty dollar grant for the 2007-2008 school year.

Acadamie DaVinci, Dunedin, FL
Altamont Elementary School, Altamont, KS
Belle Valley South School, Belleville, IL
Bose Elementary School, Kenosha, WI
Brittany Hill Middle School, Blue Springs, MO
Carver Jr High School, Spartanburg, SC
Cave City Elementary School, Cave City, AR
Central Elementary School, Iron Mountain, MI
Challenger K8 School of Science and Mathematics, Spring Hill, FL
Columbus Middle School, Columbus, MT
Cypress Christian School, Houston, TX
Deer River High School, Deer River, MN
Deweyville Middle School, Deweyville, TX
Four Peaks Elementary School, Fountain Hills, AZ
Fox Chase School, Philadelphia, PA
Fox Creek High School, North Augusta, SC
Grandview Alternative School, Grandview, MO
Hillcrest Elementary School, Lawrence, KS
Holbrook School, Holden, ME
Houston Middle School, Germantown, TN
Independence High School, Elko, NV
International College Preparatory Academy, Cincinnati, OH
John Bowne High School, Flushing, NY

Language Arts Grant Winners cont.

Lorain County Joint Vocational School, Oberlin, OH
Merritt Secondary School, Merritt, BC
Midway Covenant Christian School, Powder Springs, GA
Muir Middle School, Milford, MI
Northlake Christian School, Covington, LA
Northwood Elementary School, Hilton, NY
Place Middle School, Denver, CO
Public School 124, South Ozone Park, NY
Public School 219 Kennedy King, Brooklyn, NY
Rolling Hills Elementary School, San Diego, CA
St Anthony's School, Streator, IL
St Joan Of Arc School, Library, PA
St Joseph Catholic School, York, NE
St Joseph School-Fullerton, Baltimore, MD
St Monica Elementary School, Mishawaka, IN
St Peter Celestine Catholic School, Cherry Hill, NJ
Strasburg High School, Strasburg, VA
Stratton Elementary School, Stratton, ME
Tom Thomson Public School, Burlington, ON
Tremont Elementary School, Tremont, IL
Warren Elementary School, Warren, OR
Webster Elementary School, Hazel Park, MI
West Woods Elementary School, Arvada, CO
West Woods Upper Elementary School, Farmington, CT
White Pine Middle School, Richmond, UT
Winona Elementary School, Winona, TX
Wissahickon Charter School, Philadelphia, PA
Wood County Christian School, Williamstown, WV
Wray High School, Wray, CO

Grades K-1-2-3

Note: The Top Ten poems were finalized through an online voting system. Creative Communication's judges first picked out the top poems. These poems were then posted online. The final step involved thousands of students and teachers who registered as online judges and voted for the Top Ten poems. We hope you enjoy these selections.

Top Poem Grades K-3

Shiny Beauty

Twinkling in the night,
so bright you'll see them when you go home tonight,
but there is something else shining so bright,
it's round and white, big and light,
you'll see it in the dark blue night,
when they go away the sun comes up to play,
shining its glory for half of the day.

Abigail Cadet, Grade 3
Hyannis Elementary School, MA

Top Poem Grades K-3

Life in the Clouds

I've heard of a place very high up high,
Where the night is far, and the morn is nigh.
Unicorns fly all day, there's no night,
Fly and have fun there, in the light.
The food there is so very delicious!
And the lions, well, they aren't vicious!
Hope someday that I can go there,
Wear my best dress and braided hair.
Small winged horses, with you they fly,
Every time, everywhere, God is nigh!
No hurts, no crying, no terror, no fear,
Bright flowers are blooming, there and here.
We'll run in the meadow, we'll jump in the wood.
We'll play and we'll play, as long as we could.
The place is amazing. You will never get lazy.
The animals play with you, deer and pups.
The water's refreshing, drink it from cute cups.
The sun beams upon you. You will never say "boo hoo."
Rainbows are flying, you are never crying…
That is my dreaming 'bout the life in the clouds,
And right now I'm dreaming that I was there now.

Maura Campbell, Grade 2
Mitchell Elementary School, MA

Top Poem Grades K-3

Butterflies

Butterflies are fluttering in the clear blue sky.
On sunrise they come to fly.
They make figure eights and loopty-loops all around the trees.
They float past the flowers in the warm spring breeze.
They can be tiny and delicate in the air,
or large and spotted landing anywhere.
Their beautiful wings are very colorful.
They really seem quite wonderful.
So thank you to all butterflies for being yourselves today.
I hope you magical creatures will never go away.

Alexis Chrisohoidis, Grade 2
Public School 2 Alfred Zimberg, NY

Top Poem Grades K-3

Scarlet Night

Beyond the mountains,
the grass shifts
in the breeze
and house lights dim
into the air,
of the endless
scarlet night.
The stars twinkle
like glitter
The moon is like
a huge diamond guiding
you through the night sky
The night sky is like a soft,
light blanket
covering the earth

Chenlang Gao, Grade 3
Lincoln Elementary School, PA

Top Poem Grades K-3

Amazed Fish

The fish swims in the ocean
feeling the silk blanket of water
flowing by,
discovering the beautiful sea
as a circus.

Clown Fish are the clowns
juggling
5, 6 or 7 seashells.

Dolphins are trapeze artists
balancing and flipping
on blue waves.

The Starfish is the main attraction
with his top hat,
playing every part.

And the audience claps their fins
and shouts for more.
The circus never stops.

Isabel Levin, Grade 2
Dr Samuel C Eveleth School, MA

Top Poem Grades K-3

Monarchs

The egg is as big as a pencil point. So tiny.
    How do they fit inside of there?
Crack! Crack! The egg breaks open.
    Some thing's coming out.
    It's a baby Monarch Caterpillar.
Crunch! Crunch!
    The caterpillar must eat eight milkweed leaves
    before it can turn into a chrysalis.
Big and fat!
    It climbs to a spot to hide while it forms a "J"
    and then it starts to turn into a chrysalis.
All wet and soggy! Here it comes.
    It's a Monarch Butterfly! So pretty.
    Its wings are lines of symmetry.
Flap! Flap!
    Now off they fly to Mexico!
    Somewhere warmer before the cold starts here.
The mother lays some eggs as she begins the return
    after the cold days in Mexico.
Then the cycle begins again.

Sierra Ornosky, Grade 3
Robeson Elementary School, PA

Top Poem Grades K-3

Ground Flood

Standing on the sand,
waiting for the tide
to grasp my feet
into the coldness.
The water got higher each time,
it ruined my sandcastle.
Finally, my feet got their turn.
My feet were in a large pool
of rushing sea.
Soon the water retreated,
leaving my feet to the air.

Isabelle Pascucci, Grade 3
Thoreau Elementary School, MA

Top Poem Grades K-3

Drummer

A tiny fur ball of love
Best puppy ever

Ears stick up like ice cream cones
White curly hair and stubby legs

Runs like a penguin
Barks at huge dogs
Thinks he's as big as a house

Licking monster
Sleeps at the foot of my bed

Lies on his back waiting for a scratch
Walks through the neighborhood with me

Aidan Smith, Grade 3
Meeting House Hill School, CT

Top Poem Grades K-3

Spring Time for Me

Spring is a time for fun.
A time to play out in the sun.
I would rather play in the yard.
Than stay in and work real hard.

Spring is a time for showers.
Look and see all the flowers.
I hear the thunder and see the lightning.
Sometime it can be so frightening.

Spring days can get really hot.
So go inside and find a cool spot.
Friends get together to play in the house.
Sometimes we sit quiet as a mouse.

Night time comes early in spring.
So we gather on the porch to sit and swing.
Every year spring comes and goes.
We know spring is a time to grow.

Ashley Thomas, Grade 1
Francis Scott Key Elementary/Middle Technology Magnet School, MD

Top Poem Grades K-3

Snow

Snow, snow, snow, everywhere I go.
Snowballs and snowmen all aglow.
Snow, snow, snow
it falls on friend and foes.
Mittens, fur coats and hats
keeps the cold off your back.

Snow falls on the ground
it makes no sound
It's so cold I cried,
so I had to go inside.
Sitting by the fireplace, drinking hot tea
oh what a sight to see.

Michael Watson, Grade 3
Pat-Kam School & Early Childhood Center, NY

The Dark

I was creeping
In the dark night
On a stormy night
Clouds were gray
It was raining
Thunder came
Then home at last
Michael Mello, Grade 3
Acushnet Elementary School, MA

The Sponge

Sponge it is green
and it is yellow.
It is soft and full of water
and of soap
and it washes dishes
and sponges suck water.
Kortney Whitted, Grade 2
Public School 2 Alfred Zimberg, NY

The Sky

The sky is wonderful,
The sky is blue.
Where many birds flew,
I wish I could have a
Chance to fly and jump and prance
high up in the sky.

The sky is wonderful,
The sky is blue and white.
I wish my dreams could
Take me there at night.
Victoria Douglas, Grade 3
Public School 131, NY

Train

Chug, Chug
We're like soldiers
walking down the hallway.
Not even waving or talking.
It stops at our stop
and we ran out the door for recess.
Sara Lauren DeVitto, Grade 2
Tashua School, CT

Rainbow

Rain is dripping
And dropping
I see you
Everywhere I go.
Drip drop.
What's that?
I see a
Colorful thing
A Rainbow!
So colorful
So bright
Where have you been?
Why did you leave?
So many colors
I can name them all!
Britney Chong, Grade 2
Public School 122 Mamie Fay, NY

My Love for You

It is stronger than an army
it is more beautiful than the world

Just you and me
can have that kind of love

In the scary times we'll be together

Only you and me can have
that kind of power through love

All those things will happen

If we stick together
we'll stick
through the world
Nicholas Nestro, Grade 2
Tashua School, CT

Spring

Trees are blooming now
Polliwogs are hatching in pools
Grass is turning green
Julia Lemoine, Grade 2
Guilford Lakes School, CT

June

June is blue.
It tastes like steamed crabs.
It sounds like birds chirping.
It smells like hot dogs cooking on the grill.
It looks like me blowing out candles on my birthday cake.
It makes me feel excited.

Amy Ringrose, Grade 3
St Clement Mary Hofbauer School, MD

The Gold Gifts of Spring

Spring is like a kite, floating on the weak air.
Knowing that in spring, a mighty strike of air will come
and will rise higher and higher
Until the string has reached its end, and is watching over you.
Springs orange sunset, is like a sign of wisdom and is a signal that the day is over.
The bright warm night is just beginning.
Crickets and fire flies are swarming the sky's in the golden spring sunset.
Sitting, watching, under your feet lies from the cold black rain a silver sheet of water.
Gleaming in that water is a piece of golden air flowing past me.
As I feel the wind is blowing on my face, I think I hear it whisper in my ear,
spring is near!
Spring is near, and then I wake up from my dream and I see spring looking me
in the face.
Everything silent and still wet from the midnight rain.
I run outside and receive the gift of the first day of spring.

Matthew Herlihy, Grade 3
General John Nixon Elementary School, MA

Soccer Ball

Black dots like a polka dot shirt
Round as a globe
White as clouds
As thick as a gigantic light bulb
Small as a big apple
As gentle as an ant
As heavy as an apple
When kicked as fast as a race car before the race
Colorful as a white background
Bouncy as a pogo stick
Black as pencil lead
This is what a soccer ball is to me.

Ian Ross, Grade 3
Buckley Country Day School, NY

Winter

Winter comes once a year
I know it's really cold
With cold days and nights
It brings out my frights

The days are short
The nights are long
It's about to be Christmas
Because it's winter now

Momina Butt, Grade 3
Al-Rahmah School, MD

Summer

My ice cream
drips down
to
say good bye
I will
never
see you
again.

Ryan Levy, Grade 2
Tashua School, CT

The Rolling Fat Dog

There was a really cute dog.
She was as fat as a hog.
Whenever I rolled her,
she went down the hall.
She went so far down,
that she ended up in the mall.

Priya Bommaraju, Grade 2
St Stephen's School, NY

Springtime

Sun shines.
Flowers bloom.
Birds sing.
Bees buzz.
Dogs bark.
Children play.

Carolyn O'Keefe, Grade 1
St Rose School, CT

Bees

Bees make me think of honey.
Honey makes me think of syrup.
Syrup makes me think of trees.
Trees make me think of birds.
Birds make me think of insects.
Insects make me think of bees.

Katie Duda, Grade 3
Cambridge Springs Elementary School, PA

I Am

I am special in every way
I help my mom clean every day
I help my dad cook
My aunt bought me a special book
My sister and I clean our room
I sweep the kitchen with the broom
I like to play basketball every day
Mom and Dad tell me I am special in every way

Stacie Leonard, Grade 2
St Mary's Primary School, MA

Imagine If…

Imagine if you could touch the sky
Imagine if you could do anything you want
Imagine if you were rich
Wait
I already have these things

Malcolm McCarvill, Grade 1
Buckley Country Day School, NY

I Am

I am nice.
I am funny.
I can dance.
People say that I am tall.
My mom says I'm an angel.
I am the youngest in my family.
I am also the youngest out of my cousins too.
My mom says I am good at sports.
My favorite one is soccer.
My second favorite is softball.
My mom says I am a good student.

Jenna Piatelli, Grade 2
St Mary's Primary School, MA

Sunlight

As yellow as a daisy blooming in the summer
Like a pretty white jewel shimmering in the sky
Could be as orange as a big plump pumpkin
As shiny as 100 fireflies flying in the night sky
Could be as pink as your rose cheeks after a suntan
As steaming hot after your dinner just came out of the oven
Just like the yellow sweater I gave to my cousin!

Erica D'Ancona, Grade 3
Buckley Country Day School, NY

Aqua

Aqua is the sound of the waves coming up to the golden shore.
Aqua is like the smell of a soft sweet rose in a spring garden.
Aqua is like the taste of a sweet sugary candy on Easter Sunday.
Aqua is like the feel of a soft wind blowing through a pretty sunset.

Molly Doyle, Grade 2
Long Meadow Elementary School, CT

Spring

Spring is when the sun is bright.
I love to go to the park with my daddy and brother.
I love to play video games at home.
My brother does too.
Guess what?
My dad loves to play games, too!

Darrius Thomas, Kindergarten
Agape Christian Academy, VA

Breath of Night Breathe Out...*

"By the sea, beneath the yellow and sagging moon"

Where the waves roll their way
up as the wind breathes out
The deep footprints in the sand
seem to go on forever until
the waves roll
over and they disappear

The sky fills with stars
the moon is like a crescent
roll warming, and so soft.

Gabriella Owens-Demarco, Grade 3
Lincoln Elementary School, PA
*Inspired by Walt Whitman (his line in quotes)

My Pet Penguin

I have a pet penguin
I found him at my door
He eats my dad's shrimp cocktail
And makes a mess all over the floor
He keeps his room at 2 degrees
And he has an ice floor
I guess a penguin isn't a pet
For a kid that can't even open a door.
Ted Colter, Grade 3
Our Lady of Hope School, NY

Triangle Mountain

Mountain
Big, bare, brown
Immovable triangle
Pointing at the
Deep, blue, cold sky.
Christian Dolce, Grade 1
Carlyle C Ring Elementary School, NY

The Earth

A blue and green marble
In the solar system
With land, water, air, ice
Volcanos erupting
Earthquakes shattering land
Tsunamis flooding coastal land
Tornadoes sweeping up cars
Hurricanes pouring rain
Landslides collapsing
Droughts scorching
Fires burning
But life still goes on
on our planet
Connor Flaherty, Grade 2
Tashua School, CT

Danger!

angry, wizard
spells, potions, wands
casting spells upon people
wizard
Josh Chlebowski, Grade 3
Somers Elementary School, CT

Winter's Snow

Falling down slowly
White little balls falling down
Never stops falling
Nicole Zanetti, Grade 3
Buckley Country Day School, NY

A Green Bear

I saw a
green bear
Who's as cute
as a pear.
D'Asia Wilson, Grade 1
Hebbville Elementary School, MD

Spring

S ophie loves spring
P lant a garden
R oses bloom
I love spring
N ew leaves on trees
G rowing flowers
Sophie Polatsek, Grade 1
Frenchtown Elementary School, CT

Football

Football
Fun, cool
Playing, winning, running
Equipment, field, football, coach
Bleeding, cheating, cheering
Exciting, rough
Sport
Wayne Woods, Grade 3
Brant Elementary School, NY

I Am Matthew

My name is Matthew.
My hair is brown.
My eyes are too.
Basketball is fun to play.
My mom doesn't let me
But I wish I could play WII every day.
Matthew Pruden, Grade 1
St Joan of Arc School, PA

What Is Blue

Look up in the sky you see blue! Blue is as blue paper,
And a post-it is blue. And a bird can be blue.
Even a lunch box. And blue is a color.
Look at the ocean waves it is blue.
There is a fruit called blueberries and it is blue.
Blue has a big voice. And another fruit is raspberry.
A jacket could be blue. A book is blue. A shirt can be blue.
Blue can be a blueberry pie. Blue is on the American flag.

Jake Modelevsky, Grade 2
Shady Grove Elementary School, PA

The Creature

It was hideous and slimy looking.
It appeared in the classroom a quarter after nine,
The thing gobbled the teacher,
I'm sure its teeth shine.
It ate the apple and left the core.
I threw away the core.
I calmly said,
"Want some more?"

Steven Truong, Grade 3
Public School 105 Senator Abraham Bernste, NY

Flying Higher Than Low

Bird makes music, bird sings,
Bird one day spreads her wings.
She starts off low,
Slowly ascending to the sky, away from her pretty tree.
She, bird, was in the sky, but low in the sky.
Chilly winds took advantage of the beautiful sight,
Nearly freezing bird to her bones.
She gets higher than low.
Now bird is on the go and flies south for the winter
Many days pass.
Bird comes back fully grown with a tight feather gown
The sky turns gray and misses bird.
Then, I know that she must go.
Our friendship is parted as she flies off
And the sky greets her again.
Now I miss bird and her tweets that flow
Now our friendship is known
As long, long ago.

Jediael Fraser, Grade 3
The UFT Elementary Charter School, NY

What I Like

Basketball is my favorite sport,
I play it all day
I also like to play guitar
I really rock away.
Building Legos is also fun
especially when I am done,
Video games are also fun
I play them all day long.
Daniel Macri, Grade 3
Holy Rosary School, NY

Soccer

S hooting
O pen goal
C ompetition
C ommitment
E arly in the morning to play
R acing for the ball.
Samara Rozen, Grade 2
Memorial School, NH

My Spring

Pink
Flowers
Blowing
Spring is here!
Kayla Boyce, Grade 1
Trinity Christian School, VA

The Stream

The beauty of a stream
flowing seemlessly,
steady, still. A wonder.
Rachel Jozwik, Grade 3
Saw Mill Road School, NY

Springtime Is Here!

Springtime is in the air.
Winter is no longer here.
Spring — Baseball season,
Hyacines smell good,
Spring is here.
Jeff, Grade 1
Kanner Learning Center, PA

Shining Stars

Shining stars in the night
Floating in gravity
Shining down on us
Shooting stars make our wishes come true!
Rose Marie Donnell, Grade 2
Buckley Country Day School, NY

Christmas

Christmas,
Christmas,
Christmas,
White snow,
Sweet cookies,
Tall, prickly, green trees
Sparkly, delicate, colorful ornaments
These are just a few
Beautiful reindeer
Shiny bells,
Narrow, brown, cold roof
Black, bumpy, hard coal
Squeaky boots, too!
Colorful scarves,
Hot chocolate,
Don't forget, wrapped presents
Last of all, best of all, I have a loving family!
Amanda O'Connor, Grade 3
Stony Point Elementary School, NY

Saturn

S ixth planet from the sun
A tmosphere made up of hydrogen and helium
T he lightest planet
U p to 75,000 miles across
R ings are made up of dust particles and ice
N amed after the Roman God of Agriculture
William Marcus Jones, Grade 3
Brant Elementary School, NY

March

March is my birthday
My cat's birthday is in March
I like March so much!
Katie Dunham, Grade 2
Fonda-Fultonville Elementary School, NY

All About Me
Alex
Shy, athletic, spoiled, fast
Sibling of Kodie
Lover of chocolate
Who feels happy
Who needs a Nintendo DS
Who gives money to church
Who fears bears
Who would like to see Washington DC
Resident of Uniondale
Warring

Alexandria Warring, Grade 3
Susquehanna Community Elementary School, PA

Spring
People get light from the sun.
Flowers grow.
Birds are flying high up in the sky.
It is Spring now so everyone comes out to play.
The weather gets warm.
I like to bike ride in the Spring too.
Spring is my favorite season.

Kristian Darby, Grade 2
Public School 152 School of Science & Technology, NY

Recycle
R ecycle
E nvironment
C an you use less things?
Y ou can use less electricity!
C an you recycle?
L ess trash
E arth

Lacee Hodge, Grade 3
Susquehanna Community Elementary School, PA

Summer
I smell lake water and fresh strawberry rhubarb pie.
I taste fresh watermelon and fresh strawberries,
I see birds flying through the air when I go to Diamond Cove,
I hear kids celebrating and jumping,
I touch beach sand, water, grass and mud!!!!!!

Ashley Maynes, Grade 3
Granville Elementary School, NY

Jaiden, the Angel

One blond beautiful
Angel in the sky
Looking down at me,
My best friend
Is that angel in the sky.
And when I dream of her
It's like she's down on Earth
And at night there's the brightest star
And I know it's her
Looking above me while I sleep.

Geena Ciardelli, Grade 3
Heron Pond Elementary School, NH

School

S cience
C olor
H omework
O h I like Math.
O h I like Social Studies.
L earning.

Amandalynn Mullins, Grade 2
Bensley Elementary School, VA

Tornado

So powerful
so strong
people rush,
buildings crush,
Run! Run! Run!
The tornado
is coming
to you.

Jose Lopez, Grade 3
Public School 69 Jackson Heights, NY

Cats

Cats, cats you are here.
Cats, cats you are there.
Cats, cats you are everywhere.
Cats, cats can you come to my house?
Cats, cats can you be wild?
Cats, cats can you really eat mice?

Lyla Husein, Grade 3
Public School 2 Alfred Zimberg, NY

Cheetah

C heetahs can run fast.
H unt for food.
E ndangered
E at meat.
T hey are nice.
A lmost can climb.
H ave a long tail.

Ryan Andersen, Grade 3
Penn Yan Elementary School, NY

Cats

C razy cats,
A wesome cats,
T all cats,
S cratching cats!

Tahari Barbosa, Grade 1
Milton Fuller Roberts School, MA

Sunshine in the Spring

The sunlight in the spring shines
bright in my eyes.
The breezy air flows right
through my body.
The rain jumps down
from the sky to my soul.
The flowers jump up
just so they can get
rain and grow until they
are as tall as my soul.
The puddles are as high as
my ankles.
Bikes come running past me like
wind was blowing me
away.

Devin Johnson, Grade 2
Public School 235 Lenox, NY

The Tornado and I

The tornado and I whirl
And spin, crash, burn
And smash like a spoon.
The tornado and I are just alike.

Callum Pearman, Grade 2
Buckley Country Day School, NY

Golden Yellow

Golden yellow is like the sound of Labradors barking at the top of their lungs.
Golden yellow is like the smell of peppers roasting on the grill.
Golden yellow is like the taste of a big, fat banana.
Golden yellow is like the feel of the sun beating on my back.

Sasha Nerney, Grade 2
Long Meadow Elementary School, CT

An Everything Pizza

I ordered an everything pizza,
which I probably shouldn't have done.
It came with a shoe, a window, and a hot dog bun.
It came with a boy, a desk, and an unloaded gun.
It came with a cracker, a man, and a library
book that's way overdue.
It came with a pen, a computer, and a broken
plastic vampire that keeps saying "Boo!"
It came with a net, a container, a cat.
It came with some paper, a briefcase, a little ol' rat.
It came with a leaf, a light bulb, and
a man that speaks Chinese.
And this is just simply amazing,
they forgot to put on the cheese!

Avery Hammond, Grade 3
Thoreau Elementary School, MA

Bear

I got a new puppy and his name is Bear,
He is really cute and has funny hair.
All he wants to do is play,
I love him more every day.
He likes his treats and sleeps all night,
He wants to play with our cat, but they just fight.
He chases her but always misses,
She looks at him and always hisses.
He sometimes throws his food on the floor,
But then my mom looks at him and says "No More."
He's a very good boy who always behaves,
He'll come to the beach to play in the waves.
I'll teach him to swim and play in the pool,
I wish he could come with me to my school.
I'm so glad he's my pup, in all kinds of ways,
I will love him forever, for all of my days.

Sari Leibowitz, Grade 3
A. P. Willits Elementary School, NY

Storm

Thunder shoots
Lightning down to the world
And crash
Loud like electric storms
The air thunder
Shoots rocks
And explodes
It's like little pieces
Of tiny
Little electric rock balls
Moves magically
Down the ground

Brian Silva, Grade 1
Fulton Avenue School #8, NY

Venice

City on water
wonderful experience
gondola boat ride

Ben Godley, Grade 3
Sacred Heart School, CT

Books

Books are the best!
You can find a quest
that leads to the best
secret ever.
You can feel like
you're in the book
or on a hook.
You don't know
what will be or see.
Once you read the book
you will find the big surprise.

Steven LaRussa, Grade 3
Our Lady of Hope School, NY

Daisies

orange
daisies
twirling
Spring is joyful!

Sophia Vetare, Grade 1
St Rose School, CT

The Fireworks Display

Boom, bang, crash, goes the fireworks.
The fireworks are very loud.
When they boom, bang, crash, it hurts my ears.
I hate it when they do that, ouch!
Other people don't care, but I do.
Crack, bang, boom!!!!!!!!
The fireworks are very loud, ouch!
I guess they are louder than I thought!
Wow!

Tristyn Brown, Grade 3
Mohawk Valley Christian Academy, NY

Spring

Spring makes me think of rain.
Rain makes me think of puddles.
Puddles make me think of playing.
Playing makes me think of slides.
Slides make me think of swinging.
Swinging makes me think of spring.

Matthew Morrow, Grade 3
Cambridge Springs Elementary School, PA

The Flag

In our room we have a flag
It doesn't sag
It's not in a bag
It's on the wall
Proud and tall
While we work
We can stop and look
At the flag looking down
At us on the ground.

Jose Luis Escamilla, Grade 2
Public School 1 The Bergen School, NY

Vegetables

I like vegetables, they taste nice.
I like spinach and broccoli too.
They both taste great
But I like corn the best.
Vegetables rock!
They are good for you too!

Christopher Batashoff, Grade 2
Public School 205 Alexander Graham Bell, NY

If You Lived on the Sun

If you lived on the sun
You wouldn't have to wait
For your toast to be toasted
Or your roast to be roasted
And it would be summer every day
If you lived on the sun.

Rebecca Agababian, Grade 3
Weston Intermediate School, CT

The Sun

The sun is bright yellow and orange
It looks like a giant ball
I hear the crackling sound
of its fire
Its fire makes everyone
nice
and
warm

Wyatt Cicarelli, Grade 1
St Rose School, CT

Nala

N ice and Loving,
A wesome as can be,
L azy, but very cute,
A n incredible dog!

Marina Coriale, Grade 3
Penn Yan Elementary School, NY

Drink, Drink, Drink

a clean drink
I place upon my mouth
that tastes plain
I spill some about
the floor
and it dries up
rather quickly
I acted as if
I didn't do anything
I drink up fast
and race out
of sight

Tiffany Diachynsky, Grade 3
Washington Elementary School, PA

Golf

Golf is very fun!
Golf is hard.
You can play it,
Under the sun.
My winning score.
Is on the card.

Brandon Jacobs, Grade 3
Central Elementary School, PA

Jerry the Leprechaun

Jerry the leprechaun went to town.
He saw a person with a frown.
What will I do?
I'll give him you!
The person was happy all around.

Grace Herrick, Grade 3
St Rose School, CT

Rose

R oses are blooming they are
O n the go. Their colors are
S carlet and blue — they are an
E verlasting beauty.

Theodora Christopher, Grade 3
Buckley Country Day School, NY

Blue Whale

This creature is so gentle.
You may swim with one in ease.
If you were to find them
in the Atlantic and Pacific seas.

Ali Roberts, Grade 3
Craneville School, MA

All About Spring

Colorful beautiful butterflies
fluttering in the meadow.
Bright loud birds chirping in the trees.
Pretty flowers waving in the garden.
Sweet jelly beans tasting yummy
in my tummy.
Soft bunny rabbits hopping in the park.

Abigail Russell, Grade 2
St Mary Magdalen School, DE

Gymnastics
Tumble, leap and spin!
Flips, handsprings easy for me.
Doing fly
a
ways!
Chase Davies, Grade 2
Dr Samuel C Eveleth School, MA

Romeo
R omeo is Kiara's pet
O ranges are good
M ommy loves me
E ggs are yellow inside
O val is a shape
Kiara Baxter, Kindergarten
Montessori Development Center, PA

Giraffes
Giraffes have brown spots
Giraffes move slow
Giraffes live in the zoo
Giraffes eat leaves
Giraffes are awesome
Joshua Norris, Grade 1
Richland Elementary School, PA

Kites
I fly my kite
high over the ocean.
It dips and dives,
twirling and whirling
in the bright
blue sky.

It waltzes through the air,
greeting the birds
and other kites.

It whirls and twirls once more
before I reel it in.
My day of kite flying
is over.
Alex Dalton, Grade 2
Dr Samuel C Eveleth School, MA

The Flag
The flag of all colors
showing upon us
it is on everything
even a bus

The flag up there
high in the sky
so nobody touches it
up there so high

When the British attacked
there on the sea
it showed that we won
so that we could see

So in the end the Americans had won
and they all celebrated
by eating bonbons

Now the peace in the world
is all the same
with the flag
to thank for the game
Christian Slezak, Grade 3
Buckley Country Day School, NY

What Am I?
What am I?
I am a cat.
I am funny and silly.
I jump through a hoop.
Why would I jump through a hoop?
What am I?
I am a cat.
Amanda Rossi, Grade 1
Buckley Country Day School, NY

Water
Water flows down a mountain river
Quickly peacefully
Finding its way to a pond below
Such a beautiful sight.
Hadley Anderson, Grade 1
Dartmouth Early Learning Center, MA

What Is Yellow?

Yellow is the burning sun way up high,
It is lightning flashing from the rainy sky,
A number 2 pencil used for CMTs
And the dry sand on the shore of a beach.
Yellow is people cheering for an encore at a rock concert,
And a chicken's bawking beak.
A whoopy cushion on my teacher's seat.
Yellow is the roar of a lion
And a star burning in the night,
It's a punch from a fight.
Yellow is petting sheep's wool that is soft,
Dog's fur that is long and fluffy.
It is sweet candy from the Easter Bunny
Or honey made from bees.
Yellow is chewy bubble gum
Or hot dogs made on the stove.
It's a yellow perfume or sweat dripping down my face.
Yellow is the smell of hot noodle soup,
Or sunflowers growing in a group.
Yanking! Yawning! Yelling yellow!
Would yellow let someone say "Hello?"

James Stroffolino, Grade 3
Middlebury Elementary School, CT

A Monit

This is a Monit.
A Monit lives in Michigan, Maryland, Mexico and Missouri.
A Monit eats macaroni, moist moose, and mice.
A Monit likes mechanical mouths, massive maps, miracles, and can run miles.
A Monit has moon shaped eyes, a monster shaped body and messy teeth.
My Monit made me mad because he messed up my math homework.

Marley Kocent, Grade 3
St Clement Mary Hofbauer School, MD

Spring

S unshine on my face
P retty flowers blooming all day long with a smile
R ainbows appearing from the rain
  you never know when the luck will come to you
I n the flowers bees are sucking nectar
N othing in the world is greater than spring
G iant sun all day with a smile on the sun's face

Veronica Blanco, Grade 3
Public School 2 Alfred Zimberg, NY

Spring

Spring
calls the
birds to sing
in the
warm wind
among
the trees
listening
to the
sound of
spring

Meagan Kubicko, Grade 2
Tashua School, CT

Spring

Spring is finally here
Come on now let's cheer
The daffodils are blooming
The butterflies are zooming
Spring has sprung
It has just begun
You will see the birds
Up in the sky
Among the clouds
Passing by
Spring is great
Let's celebrate!

Isabelle Trinin, Grade 3
Willits Elementary School, NY

trees

trees give us paper
rigid leaves block the sun
trees have pine scent too

Shain Mazzarella, Grade 2
Killingly Memorial School, CT

Bubble

Round, clear
It can float
Big, small, medium, tiny
POP!

Whit Licata, Grade 1
St Christopher's School, VA

Sea

I am a lovely body of water,
With salt floating in the air,
I am a sky without a sound,
There is a smell of salt in the air around me,
Creatures are living in and around me.
WHAT AM I?

Isinsu Bastepe, Grade 3
Cabot Elementary School, MA

Spring Is Finally Here

There's a sound I hear
Through my window I peer…
The birds are coming near!
Spring is finally here!

Look at the duckling
In his little yellow suit
He waddles around so cute
Spring is finally here!

Listen to the bees
Buzzing in the trees
Feel the cool breeze
Spring is finally here!

There are lots of spring showers
That bring lots of spring flowers
I could sit and watch for hours
Spring is finally here!

The bears are coming out
From their long winter sleep
It makes me want to shout
Spring is finally here!

Olivia Blackmore, Grade 3
Chestnut Street Elementary School, PA

Spring

Red and white
Baseball
Hit by a bat
Spring is here!

Nick Camarero, Grade 1
Maureen M Welch Elementary School, PA

Slave Escape

I am a slave.
I work day and night, dark or light, picking crops.
Wait! I have a plan.
I am going to break free as fast as I can.
I have to go at night not light or I will get chased, beaten.

If I don't run they will sell me.
I'm not a thing, animal or toy.
I am a Black African American and I have feelings!

Time to run so pack my things and go.
Scared and tired I run with fear and see the road is clear.
I want to be free; why won't they let me be?

I hear something. It's them!
They are going to catch me and bring me back to be a slave again!

I run with all my might trying to fight for my rights.
I hide under the quilt of night.
I see somewhere to be free — I see they have lost me.

The Slavery is over!
No more blues, slave songs!
Time for ragtime, hip-hop and rap!

Zena Hill, Grade 2
Colwyn Elementary School, PA

Indigo

Indigo is like the sound of the silence of the town when they are sleeping
Indigo is like the smell of the salty waves crashing on the sand
Indigo is like the taste of the sweetness of a soft blueberry
Indigo is like the feel of water rushing against my hand

Jackson Yancy, Grade 2
Long Meadow Elementary School, CT

Spring Is Beautiful

Spring is in the air,
Spring is here,
Spring blossoms,
Spring is spring,
No matter where you are,
ENJOY SPRING

Isaak Basis, Grade 1
Public School 105 Senator Abraham Bernste, NY

Winter

Winter,
Winter,
Winter,
Cold snow,
Reflective ice,
White, slushy, soft snow,
Pretty, sparkling, shapely snowflakes.
These are just a few.

Warm fireplace,
Snowy blizzards,
Cozy, warm, soft, snow gear,
Giant, thick, sturdy snow fort,
Cool snowmen, too.

Friendly Frosty,
Yummy Hot Cocoa,
Don't forget fun weather,
Last of all, best of all,
I like awesome WINTERS!
Rebecca Carey, Grade 3
Stony Point Elementary School, NY

Bono

My dog is handsome
his fur so brown, warm, and soft
and big sloppy tongue
Tyla Jones, Grade 3
Sacred Heart School, CT

Birds, Birds, Everywhere

Birds, Birds, Everywhere,
there are big birds, small birds.
There are robins,
eagles, and falcons,
all different kinds.
I wish I had a bird for a pet,
maybe someday I will.
Birds, Birds Everywhere
they're fun to play with,
but some might
peck you in the head.
Rocco Pellicano, Grade 3
Holy Rosary School, NY

Trees

Trees are beautiful
I hide under them
To protect myself from the sun
It's also good to climb in winter
You don't see the leaves
You only see the trunk
And they also give us oxygen.
Lesley Isaro, Grade 2
Public School 2 Alfred Zimberg, NY

Noise of the World

I sat in the street,
listening to the beat
of the walking feet.
Listening to the tone
of the phone.
It rings and rings,
And what next
The cars go zoom, zoom, zoom,
I hear my heart go boom, boom,
Shoo! says the crazy old lady to the cat.
As the cat chases the rat,
I go inside
And hear my sister cry.
My car was towed is what she said.
I parked it at the dead end.
The sounds of the world
Make my head whirl
Oh! what a town
Oh! what a sound.
Kayla Williams, Grade 2
Public School 235 Lenox, NY

Penguins

P eace loving
E xciting to watch
N ot a meat eater
G ood
U sually loud
I ce cold water where they live
N ice
S ometimes lay eggs
Ben Donohue, Grade 2
Long Meadow Elementary School, CT

The Funky Monkey
The funky monkey came out of the forest,
He attacked all the others but he did not attack me.

The funky monkey came out of the forest,
He attacked all the others but he did not attack me.

The funky monkey came out of the forest,
He attacked all the others but he did not attack —

BOOM! PUNCH! OOW!

Molly Hackman, Grade 3
Our Mother of Perpetual Help School, PA

Laugh 'Til Your Pants Fall Off
Imagine:
A clown who acts and looks like an ice-cream cone.
A Boxer dog that acts like a real boxer.

Your friend picking up two drinks,
Pouring one on themself
And one in a box of chicken nuggets.

A donkey who has an owner who is really a scarecrow.
A hot dog that sounds like a dolphin.
Try to imagine that.

Amy Hotovchin, Grade 2
Central Elementary School, PA

Blue
Blue is like the sound of the ocean crashing into the sand.
Blue is like the smell of a flower shining in the sun light.
Blue is the taste of cotton candy on a hot summer day.
Blue is like the feel of a soft baby blanket snuggled up
on my baby brother's sleeping body.

Alexandra Nowicki, Grade 2
Long Meadow Elementary School, CT

Blue
Blue is the color of sadness in the dark night
Blue is the color of tears
Blue is the color of a gum ball ready to be chewed
Blue is the color of a marker ready to be used

Melanie Fong, Grade 1
Buckley Country Day School, NY

Lacrosse

Lacrosse
Fun, active
Running, cradling, controlling
Stick, ball, goggles, parents
Scoring, passing, practicing
Guard, face-off
Sport
Shayla Scanlan, Grade 3
Brant Elementary School, NY

The Wind

When
the wind
hits my
face
the birds
and the
wind talk
to me.
The birds
go up in the
sky
they float
in the sky
like angels.
Ryan Berard, Grade 1
St Rose School, CT

Video Game Night

I play all night
But I don't fly a kite
I play a video game
It is always the same
It always ends in a fight.
Grace Wallo, Grade 1
Geneva School, PA

The Golden Crane

The golden crane
The beautiful crane
The crane is very golden
The beautiful crane
Jackson Rose, Grade 3
St Joseph School, NY

Skiing

While I was fine skiing
My brother was eating
While I had fun skiing
My brother was freezing
While I was kneeling to take off my skis
My brother was skiing.
Andrew Brennan, Grade 2
Willis E Thorpe School, MA

Mud

Mud makes me think of worms.
Worms make me think of grass.
Grass makes me think of plants.
Plants make me think of pumpkins.
Pumpkins make me think of a garden.
A garden makes me think of mud.
Mason Meszaros, Grade 3
Cambridge Springs Elementary School, PA

Bears

Bears make me think of fish.
Fish make me think of fishing.
Fishing makes me think of water.
Water makes me think of icicles.
Icicles make me think of hibernation.
Hibernation makes me think of bears.
Kylie Boylan, Grade 3
Cambridge Springs Elementary School, PA

Christmas

Christmas time I love it so.
When I grow up I only know
Wherever I'll go
I'll love it so.
Jordy Mejia, Grade 2
Public School 1 The Bergen School, NY

My Friend and I

With my friend David, I play.
With my friend David, I say hooray!
With my friend David, I have fun outside.
With my friend David, I hide.
Nathanael Wise, Grade 2
Trinity Christian School, VA

Tennis

Throw, hit, run and play
In tennis those are the actions I portray
Friday, Saturday, and Sunday I play
Sometimes on hard courts, sometimes on clay
When I play a match I like to win
It always makes me grin
On the weekends I play with my dad
And when I lose a point I tend to get mad
He always says "Zan, it's okay!"
"Tennis is only a game you play!"
I listen to my dad, and I like to take water breaks
Whenever I am thirsty or tired I like to take
A few minutes to relax and rest
Because that is when I play tennis best!

Zan Ahmed, Grade 3
Willits Elementary School, NY

Winter Is

Winter is the smell of fresh cookies.
Winter is the touch of a snowman.
Winter is seeing a snowflake fall from the sky.
Winter is the taste of yummy chocolate chip cookies.
Winter is hearing bells that bring joy.
Winter makes me happy.

Jenna Citone, Grade 1
St Teresa of Avila School, NY

Devil's Day

Halloween night!
Halloween night the scariest night of all.
Halloween is the day we celebrate the devil's day,
On that day people dress up in costumes.

Raymond Dourant, Grade 2
Walker Memorial School, ME

Ghost Under My Bed

The spooky ghost said a joke.
Knock, knock. Who's there?
No one knew about him. Only I did.
No one came in my room not even a kid.
The only one who knows about him is my fish, Dash.
He swims from the ghost and he crashed.

Arianna Clemenzi, Grade 2
Fisher Hill Elementary School, MA

The Music Assembly

I was very nervous
I thought I might faint.

I went up to the piano
everybody clapped.

Whoo! Whoo! Yea!

I sat down
I started playing
I kept thinking
I can't do this!

Suddenly, I made a mistake!
My hands were in the wrong position!
I was shaking.
I moved into the right hand position.
I started playing again
and before I knew it I was done.

I heard my sister Charlotte screaming,
"Go Caroline!"

I did it!!!
Caroline Smith, Grade 2
Buckley Country Day School, NY

Friends

Friends, friends, always sweet
Friends, friends, together is a treat
They help me when I'm sad
To me they're never bad
I always love my friends
Together till the end.
Allison Caravella, Grade 3
Somers Elementary School, CT

A Hunting Tiger

I wish I had fur.
I wish I could run really fast.
I wish I would hunt.
I wish I was a tiger.
Samuel Scarton, Grade 1
Artman Elementary School, PA

Deep Water

Deep water, silent
The sea is hushed
Skies are dark
A breeze blows
Making rippling lines
Deep water, cold and still.
Chazanna Williams, Grade 2
Dartmouth Early Learning Center, MA

A Pencil

A pencil is always
standing tall
waiting till it's needed.

When the point
is wounded dull
it needs a little rest.

When it is again sharpened
it's ready for duty.

But…down, down, down
it goes again.
Charles Morgan, Grade 2
Dr Samuel C Eveleth School, MA

Water Visions

Wind moves the pond's surface
This way and that, making ripples.
I put my foot in and
Ripples change to waves.
As fish swim deep in still water.
Rachel Seiders, Grade 2
Dartmouth Early Learning Center, MA

Spring

S is for sunflower
P is for parade
R is for roses
I is for ice cream
N is for nice weather
G is for go to the beach
Starr Morin, Kindergarten
Fisher Hill Elementary School, MA

Castle of Food
Cinnamon buns form a steaming castle,
honey makes a glistening lake,
silky mountains of chocolate mound up behind it,
there's so much I can make!
Marshmallow clouds sit above it all,
so steaming hot and gooey,
I'll be so sad if it's ever gone,
but I'm sure it'll end up in my belly!
In the lake I place bright red Swedish Fish,
and I'm sure whoever takes a bite will surely love this dish!

Alison Sivitz, Grade 3
Lincoln Elementary School, PA

I Am!
I see red.
I smell pollen.
I feel little drops of water.
I can hear little bumble bees.
I rock in the breeze.
I am!
I am!
Just a flower.
A simple little flower.

Damion White, Grade 2
The New York Institute for Special Education, NY

Chocolate
I love chocolate!
It is such a tasty treat.
Oh, all the chocolate
that I can eat.

I love chocolate —
chocolate bars,
chocolate kisses,
chocolate, chocolate
and more chocolate.

I love chocolate!
So what if I get fat,
I will still eat chocolate.
Lots and lots of it!

Adeliere Dorce, Grade 2
Public School 152 School of Science & Technology, NY

Stars

I play dot to dot
with the glistening diamonds
in the midnight sky.
Brianna Girard, Grade 2
Killingly Memorial School, CT

Spring

S wing
P ark
R un
I ce cream
N osegay
G rasshopper
Brett Palladino, Kindergarten
Willis E Thorpe School, MA

Spring

Blue
Easter egg
Rolling
Spring is here!
Tess Green, Grade 1
Trinity Christian School, VA

Dogs

When I look at a dog,
I feel like I'm in
H
  E
    A
      V
        E
          N!
They look so cute;
And they make me very
H
  A
    P
      P
        Y!
They are very soft and
they like to play too!!!
Matthew Little, Grade 2
St Mary's Primary School, MA

Spring

Spring makes me think of turkey season.
Turkey season makes me think of the woods.
The woods make me think of mud.
Mud makes me think of tracks.
Tracks make me think of animals.
Animals make me think of spring.
Jarrott Ruhl, Grade 3
Cambridge Springs Elementary School, PA

This Poem

I've written poems so many times.
I hope this poem really rhymes.
I need help from someone older.
Now this poem is getting bolder.
I am having so much fun now,
I don't know why, and I don't know how.
Some people think that this is boring.
Maybe you can hear them snoring.
This poem is now my favorite one.
I think this poem was a lot of fun!
Tia Waterhouse, Grade 3
Ellicott Road Elementary School, NY

What Is Green?

Without green this world would be a desert,
Green is sneaky like an alligator,
Green is a new recycling bin,
Green sounds like flubber,
Green is as tough as a bear,
Green is a dark pit,
Green is grass,
Green is a shining jewel on a crown,
Yellow is nothing compared to green,
Green is the best color in the world,
Green is the leaves,
Green looks like goo,
Green will rule the world,
Green tastes sour,
Green is a mountain,
Green is a green light
On a traffic light,
Green is a beast locked up in a cage.
Andrew Tuchman, Grade 2
Shady Grove Elementary School, PA

Dad

I miss you Dad —
I miss you every day
I love you every day
Where are you every day.
Kassandra Homayuni, Grade 1
Buckley Country Day School, NY

Friend from France

There once was a friend from France,
Who didn't know how to dance.
I taught,
Then we fought,
About the color of her pants.
Alyssa Lemay, Grade 1
Mater Christi School, VT

Allergies

I have allergies
In every spring.
It itches my eyes,
It ignores me,
I don't like to get allergies
In my eyes.
I can't pick up flowers!
Soobin Jeong, Grade 1
Buckley Country Day School, NY

Light Houses

Light houses flash,
With white bright light,
Sailors don't crash,
When the waves roll.

A lot of them,
In New England,
Make history,
Visitors love.

Whatever the weather,
They all stand together,
All through thick and thin,
That's why most still stand today.
Corinna Ostiguy, Grade 3
James Russell Lowell School, MA

The Sunset

Orange, yellow, purple and red
Mixed together to make the sunset
It's only 6:00 at night
But, since I'm at the beach
It only feels like 2:00
The sea is still sparkling
The sand is covering my small feet
But the sunset is still there
And when I'm here tomorrow
I'll see it again
Kayla Egan, Grade 3
Saw Mill Road School, NY

Snowboard

S now
N onstop
O n a hill
W avy ride
B lowing air
O n a ski lift
A wesome
R iding
D ay to dawn
Nolan Toohey, Grade 3
Houghton Elementary School, MA

The Wand

Twinkle, dinkle,
The pointer is lying down.
Slowly little shapes are sliding.
My heart is beating.
It's soft inside me.
I am wondering
what it feels like
to be inside the wand.
It's magical and floaty,
An extraordinary glass stick
With little blue dots
Floating in the
shiny turquoise liquid,
dissolving
every time you shake it.
Marina McKeever, Grade 2
Dr Samuel C Eveleth School, MA

The Yellow Foggy Moon
By the river beneath
the yellow and foggy moon
You go outside in your pajamas,
your feet feel
the prickly and cold grass
You swish your hand
in the warm soft river water,
next to the reflection
of the moon
Quinn Dunphy, Grade 3
Lincoln Elementary School, PA

Coco in the Fog
My dog Coco
Doesn't like the fog
She fights it
Like a stranger
Is creeping into the yard
She barks
She growls
And she keeps
Me from sleeping
Jake DeTerra, Grade 3
Acushnet Elementary School, MA

All About Me
My name is Kailey
But people call me Kail.
Sometimes in the winter
My skin is very pale.
In the summer I like to swim.
When I'm at school I like gym.
I have two brothers
And two sisters too.
When I'm at home
There's lots to do.
Kailey Kleimenhagen, Grade 1
St Joan of Arc School, PA

Under the Sea
Under the sea,
  where the octopus will be!
  where I can see,
  all the coral
  beneath the waves.

In a yellow submarine,
  you can find the unseen,
  all those little fishes,
  and a big Great White Shark!
Spencer Riding, Grade 2
St Mary's Primary School, MA

Colors
Green is the grass that grows.
Pink are the flowers that bloom.
Blue is the water that flows.
Orange is the color of my room.
Noah Giunta, Grade 1
Calvary Chapel Christian School, NY

A Beautiful Butterfly
Beautiful, small, cute
Sparkling, colorful, smooth, nice
Their wings feel very soft
Rhiannon Daniels, Grade 3
St Stephen Regional School, PA

Koala
Koala
Gray, cute
Climbing, eating, moving
Australia, explores, free, leaves
Sleeping, hanging, sitting
Black, furry
Animal
Darcy Paradiso, Grade 3
Brant Elementary School, NY

Spring
Spring is near,
Let's give a cheer.
Children play in the park.
They stay until it is dark.
The leaves on the trees turn green.
Many flowers can be seen.
Baseball season is here.
It's the best time of the year.
Amanda Hardardt, Grade 3
Our Lady of Hope School, NY

Desserts

Cookies and cakes
I love to
bake these cookies
and cakes,
I want to scream
with delight!

Maurice Lewis, Grade 2
Public School 152 School of Science & Technology, NY

Friends

F riends are fun to be with.
R ound and round and up and down at the playground we play
I gloos are what they like to build in the winter.
E mily is a great best friend.
N ever ending friendship
D o great things for each other
S ends nice letters to each other.

Kimberly Sullivan, Grade 3
Brookside Elementary School, MA

My Guinea Pigs

Fluff looks just like Moose, her mother
Peanut Butter looks like Rocky, the other
I have two babies, one is a boy
And one is a girl, she's a joy
Fluff's fur is just like Moose's — sticking up like a hat
Peanut Butter's fur is just like Rocky's — flat

Franco Abbatessa, Grade 2
Willis E Thorpe School, MA

If I Were a Blue and Gold Macaw

If I were a Blue and Gold Macaw,
I would show off my blue and gold feathers
To every animal in the Amazon rainforest.
I'd fly high up in the canopy and see the view
Overlooking green trees and colorful animals.
I'd squawk to my friends and listen for their replies
While munching on nuts, seeds, fruits, and berries.
Below me, the animals carry on
Beside me, a wasp and a bee buzz by
Above me, the emergents grow tall
This rainforest home is special and perfect.

Christine Yu, Grade 2
Heim Elementary School, NY

Statue of Liberty

The Statue of Liberty
is a huge pencil
planted
in the ground
a gift from France
to New York
with its crown
lighting up
every day.

Shane H. Carley, Grade 2
Tashua School, CT

Outer Space

It's never ending
long, mysterious beyond
different than earth

Vincent Gocon, Grade 3
Sacred Heart School, CT

Spring

Buttercups sprouting
Singing birds everywhere
Eggs are hatching now

Gavin Popkin, Grade 2
Guilford Lakes School, CT

Whistling Wind

Oh, wind
Oh, wind
Whistle to me
Whistle! Whistle! Whistle!
Tell me your secret
how you whistle
Whistle! Whistle! Whistle!
Oh, wind
Oh wind
whisper to me
Whisper! Whisper! Whisper!
Tell me your secret
how you whisper!
Whisper! Whisper! Whisper!
Whistle! Whisper!

Jackson Lobo, Grade 2
Tashua School, CT

Butterflies

Butterflies, butterflies
fluttering through the sky.

One day I saw a beautiful butterfly sit down
on a leaf and it laid two tiny eggs.
Out popped those caterpillars.
They were very hungry as you can see.
I was standing there right next to them,
then one climbed right onto me.

I laughed as its small body climbed up me.
The next day I came outside and what did I see?
A tiny chrysalis!
I turned around, and then looked back.
Out popped a butterfly, orange and black.

Butterflies, butterflies
fluttering through the sky.

Samantha Talecki, Grade 2
Hopewell Elementary School, PA

Fantasy Water

I was nearly touching the sea sand.
I elevated down and my feet scraped the sand.
I saw fire coral and seaweed
Fantasy water is beautiful
I noticed that behind the seaweed
I saw a mermaid house
I saw sea fairies, mermen and mermaids
I heard my mother calling me
So I said "good bye fantasy water
I will come back."

Ronnie Nemec, Grade 2
Pomperaug Elementary School, CT

Flower

F locks of birds are here
L eaves are growing
O range flowers are blooming
W ater is flowing in streams
E aster arrives
R ain falls down

Austin Labesky, Grade 3
Chestnut Street Elementary School, PA

Little Brother

I have a little brother, and he follows me around.
He tries to be funny when he makes a weird sound.
His favorite season is summer, but I prefer fall.
He likes baseball, but I like basketball.
He is always screaming and shouting when he doesn't get his way.
So I have to watch out for what I do and say.
Sometimes he gives me happiness sometimes he gives me fear.
But this would be a boring house if my little brother wasn't here.
Now I know we have our differences as you can see,
But I love my little brother and he loves me.

Laura Jans, Grade 3
Our Lady of Hope School, NY

Red

Red is a juicy apple. Red is as hot as a chili pepper.
It is as liquid as fruit punch. It's as sugary as a watermelon.
It looks like a heart as lovable as could be.
It's red as a speeding fire truck.
As hexogoney as a stop sign.
It's as hard as a brick.
It's red as a cherry so good and sweet.
Red sounds like an ambulance rushing down the street.
It sounds like a fire alarm beeping for mercy.
Red feels mad like if somebody hated your picture.
It's embarrassing "blush" like if somebody showed a
Picture of you when you were a baby.
Red smells like smoke burning. It's burning hot.
It sometimes bursts what am I. I'm a volcano.

Maclane DeMarco, Grade 2
Shady Grove Elementary School, PA

My Backpack

My backpack is so heavy
I don't know what to do
My mother says that maybe
I put inside my shoe.
Sometimes I feel I'm falling
From all the books inside
If only I could slide
And not carry the books
It would be so great
If I didn't have this heavy weight on my back so straight!

Maritza Romero, Grade 3
Public School 1 The Bergen School, NY

Butterfly

B utterflies are flying everywhere.
U nrolling its tongue on a flower.
T ired from flying that you rest.
T ired from all that flying.
E ggs laid on a leaf.
R est Butterfly on a leaf.
F ly away Butterfly a turtle is coming.
L anding on a flower.
Y ellow as a yellow Butterfly.

Peter Nekos, Grade 2
Primrose School, NY

Icicles

Icicles hanging from the roof
Frozen crystals
Reaching their points
Trying to touch the ground.
Sun appears,
Drip, drop, drip.

Oona Clarke, Grade 1
Dartmouth Early Learning Center, MA

He Loves Basketball

There once was a boy from Montreal
Who loved to play basketball
For a team he tried out
But if he made it, I doubt
For you see he's just three feet tall!

Danika Chicklis, Grade 3
Houghton Elementary School, MA

Yo-Yo

Who can make a yo-yo?
Dun-can.
How few can ride the yo-yo?
None can.
What can cut the string of a yo-yo?
Scissors can.
What was used as a weapon of war?
Yo-yo was.
Who can write more about the yo-yo?
You can.

Nathan Bartlett, Grade 3
Craneville School, MA

Rainbow

R ain
A nice look
I like them
N ot snow
B ut not in winter
O range, red, purple, blue
W et

Anna Cutler, Grade 3
Heron Pond Elementary School, NH

The World

The lands of the
world are as green
as a tennis ball

God says
this is mine
and I will make it so kind
and the sea is for
the animals in the sea
but most of all
The world says God bless you all
And a mother
or a brother
may help you.

William Pelisson, Grade 1
St Rose School, CT

Untitled

As you close your eyes,
you see nothing,
but everything,

you float,
gliding as an angel,
soaring through the air,
landing smoothly as a leaf,

as you do this,
you express your mind,

in poetry

Jake Duggan, Grade 3
Thoreau Elementary School, MA

Lost

I watch a TV show its name is *Lost*,
They're stuck on an island without any frost.
There is Jack and Kate, the rescue boat is very late.
Locke and Boone found a hatch, in there is a guy and his clothes do not match.
I have some advice, it's really cool and just for you.

Olivia Tureby, Grade 3
St Madeleine Sophie School, NY

The Delicious Gingerbread Man!

I make you want to eat me when you see how sweet I am!
I feel sad when you drop me, I feel happy when you put goodies on me.
I would like to change my shape to a heart.

Jahaira Dixon, Grade 2
Bensley Elementary School, VA

If I Were in Charge of the World*

If I were in charge of the world,
I'd cancel smoking and also bombs.
If I were in charge of the world,
There'd be food for everyone
And Wiis for everyone.
If I were in charge of the world,
You wouldn't have vegetables.
You wouldn't have to stop playing outside.
Or stop playing Wii.
You wouldn't even have to take a shower.
If I were in charge of the world,
You wouldn't have to write what I am writing.
And a person who sometimes forgot to turn off the TV,
And sometimes forgot to wash the dishes,
Would still be allowed to be in charge of the world.

Justin Jasper, Grade 2
St Christopher's School, VA
Patterned after "If I Were in Charge of the World" by Judith Viorst

Summer Birthday

Summer Birthday, Summer Birthday.
Here comes my birthday!
I get to have it on the beach.
I get to have cake, pizza, ice cream, plus presents
    and swimming and fun games.
I love my birthday and I hope this day never ends!

Daniel Kagan, Grade 2
Dr Samuel C Eveleth School, MA

Lightning from Heaven
When we look
Outside closely
You
Could see
Lightning
Bones
It
Is like razor blades
Falling from the sky.
GOD
And everybody
Up in
Heaven
Make
The lightning and
Thunder because
They're bowling in heaven.
Kyle Madden, Grade 1
Fulton Avenue School #8, NY

Stars
Shining in the night
They are a wonderful sight
So beautiful and bright
They give off heat and light
Shining in the night
Kelly Finke, Grade 3
Memorial School, NH

Winter Snow
This is my snowball.
Wheeeeeeeee, it goes!
It is as fast as lightning.
Boom! It hit the window.
Splat! The snowball is smush.
Brody Sercu, Grade 2
St Joseph School, NY

Presents
Fun birthday parties
chocolate cake with sprinkles
friends playing outside
Anna Singleton, Grade 3
Sacred Heart School, CT

My Kitten
I love all my toys but most of all
I love my kitten who is very small.
She has cute little eyes and a button nose
And is so cuddly from her head to her toes.
Her fur is pink and not like the rest
And that is why I like her the best.
Taylor Foley, Grade 3
Public School 2 Alfred Zimberg, NY

The Creamy Goodness of Ice Cream
Chocolate, strawberry, vanilla-bean;
Ice cream, ice cream is the queen.
Chocolate-chip, or cookie dough;
All of our ice cream is running low!
Cherry Farm — all ice cream places —
We've got to go to 'em, so tie your laces.
Mouthwatering ice cream has been sold.
Wanna know why? 'Cuz ice cream's gold!
So go sit down; don't hog it all…
Maybe give your friends a call.
Now your friends are on their way,
What a way to spend the day!
Cup, cone, soft-serve or low-fat,
It's best when shared — even with your cat!
So, if you're hungry or dying of thirst,
Go get some ice cream; ice cream comes first!
Teagan Elizabeth Gilliss, Grade 2
Willis E Thorpe School, MA

Spring
Red
Robins
Flying in the sky
Spring is here!
Isaac Webster, Grade 1
Maureen M Welch Elementary School, PA

The Flute
How I wish I played the flute
I'd go toot, toot
I'd put on my suit
I'd look very cute.
Jimmy Jimenez, Grade 2
Public School 1 The Bergen School, NY

Ticks
Ticks, ticks, they suck your blood,
They are like mosquitoes except…ticks jump and mosquitoes fly.
If you go to the train tracks, the ticks will be in the woods.
They can't jump really high and they live in trees.

Mason Rosenfeld, Grade 1
Joseph Greenberg School, PA

Firework Explosion
Bang! Kaboom! Crack!
There were colors in the sky,
While the fireworks fly.
The firework factory and sign went crackle, crack!

Tyler Eicholtz, Grade 3
New Freedom Christian School, PA

What Can I Do When I Go Swimming
I can swim with my brother.
I can race swimming with my brother and my cousin.
We can jump in the pool.
We can sit in the hot tub.

Lorez Simms, Grade 2
Bensley Elementary School, VA

Friends
Friends are helpful
Friends are fun
We all have a great time
Playing in the sun
Friends are there for you
They always care for you
Friends, friends, friends are so much fun
When we fight we talk it out
Having fun is what it's all about
Whenever I'm sad or feeling blue
My friends always know what to do
Friends, friends, friends are so much fun!
Friends can be tall
Friends can be short
But they always give you a lot of support
When you're bored or lonely or don't know what to do
True friends will always comfort you
Friends, friends, friends are so much fun!

Allyson Newman, Grade 3
Willits Elementary School, NY

The First Real Spring Morning

I hear footsteps outside and inside
Outside the footsteps are playing
Inside they are getting lunch boxes
    ready for school.
Going to school in the morning,
    I touch monkey bars
    and the jungle gym
The metal feels cold and damp
The spring sun will warm the metal
On the first real spring morning.

Summer Karl, Grade 3
Lincoln Elementary School, PA

Months

January, February, March
That's when it's cold.
April, May, June and July
That's the time to play outside.
August, September
Leaves fall from the sky.
October, November, December
That's candy and Christmas time!

Elijah Ward, Grade 2
Cabot Elementary School, MA

Spring

Pretty butterflies flying in the meadow.
Beautiful birds chirping everywhere.
Yellow flowers growing in my garden.
Delicious fruit sprouting in the ground.
Fast rivers flowing by the hills.

Gina DiCicco, Grade 2
St Mary Magdalen School, DE

A Beautiful Thing

Very pretty, very loud, very creative…
Fireworks!
Looks good at nighttime,
not so much at daytime.
Could burn down something
so be careful!
Fireworks!

Emily Wyrick, Grade 2
Pomperaug Elementary School, CT

Puppies Are Great!

P ets
U nder the bed
P erfect
P ick them up
I ntelligent
E xciting
S leepy

Delaney Palovitz, Grade 2
Highland Elementary School, PA

Laundry Basket

Everything is raining down on me:
muddy socks,
grass-streaked pants,
shirts covered with coffee stains,
sweaty gym shorts,
stinky diapers, eww!
Why can't those people
just carry those things?
How lazy do they really
have to be?
I hate that lint
and all the dust
(They make me sneeze).
When I get to the laundry machine
it's such a relief.
Now I can be left alone…
for now.

Katie Metro, Grade 3
Thoreau Elementary School, MA

Dreams

Real in your head
Unreal in life
Running
Swimming
Summer
You wake up
Feeling the cold
Wrapping in blankets
Dreaded
Winter

Emily Scherneck, Grade 3
Robeson Elementary School, PA

A Christmas Tree

I am a Christmas tree.
I stand in the middle of my room.
I feel sad when you put too many hot lights on me.
I feel happy when you decorate me with things.
I would like to be decorated with flashing lights.
I would tell my owner I like the way he decorates me.

Tyrese Taylor, Grade 2
Bensley Elementary School, VA

In My Dream

In my dream I am a princess.
In my dream I dance in my new sparkly shoes on a starry night.
In my dream I sleep in a dazzling bed
In my dream I wake up on a sunny day of sunshine.
In my dream I run in a castle
In my dream I thank Allah for every single thing I have.
And for being a princess.

Aminata Sall, Grade 3
Al-Rahmah School, MD

When Spring Comes

When Spring comes, it leaves behind old winter.
Spring will bring up new baby yellow Buttercup flowers, with new baby bumble bees on its way.
When Spring comes, the sun will be calling, "Will you be my little sunshine,"
When Spring comes, bears will teach their cubs how to get fresh golden yummy honey.
When Spring comes, the grass will become as green as a brand new carpet.
When Spring comes, children's minds will be filled with mystical creatures as they read their green covered books.
When Spring comes, kids will be hunting for green Easter eggs all around screaming when each finds one.
When Spring comes, rain showers will have every shade of blue.
When Spring comes, blue birds will come back chirping their beautiful song as they lay their tiny blue eggs.
When Spring comes, you can sprinkle water on flowers and wait for them to grow.
When Spring comes, there will be pink roses in a garden.
When Spring comes, pink Easter bunnies will hop around placing pink Easter eggs in every corner
When Spring comes, a beautiful rainbow will appear after a rain shower.
When Spring comes, birds will chirp and people will find love.
When Spring comes, there will be sunsets with pink right in the middle.

Alexandra Neeser, Grade 3
General John Nixon Elementary School, MA

Stars
Shining at nighttime
Spreading all over the sky
making night sparkle
Edyta Wolk, Grade 3
Sacred Heart School, CT

Nature
Hiking in the woods
Gnats following us around
Biting our soft skin
Christion Swan, Grade 2
Guilford Lakes School, CT

Spring
S un
P ickle
R abbit
I ce cream
N osegay
G rass
Madison Kelley, Kindergarten
Willis E Thorpe School, MA

My Spring
Happy
People
Picking flowers
Spring is here!
Anna Figueroa, Grade 1
Trinity Christian School, VA

Snow
Snow, white and fluffy
Soft and shiny in the sun
darker in the moon
Valerie Corrado, Grade 3
Saw Mill Road School, NY

Spring
It's soccer season
Sun is shining in my face
Frogs hop near the pond
Matthew Barrett, Grade 2
Guilford Lakes School, CT

Spring Fever
Light green frogs hopping near the pond.
Red and blue birds chirping in the trees.
Pretty flowers swaying with the breeze.
Fresh fruit being picked on the trees.
Newly grown grass growing in the front yard.
Josh Mottola, Grade 2
St Mary Magdalen School, DE

Spring
White bunnies hopping in the grass.
Black and yellow bees buzzing in the fresh air.
Beautiful roses blooming in the meadow.
Delicious apples growing on a tree.
Green grass reaching to the sky.
Ashton Marini, Grade 2
St Mary Magdalen School, DE

Spring/Seasons
Spring
Sunny, warmer
Playing, swinging, growing
I really love spring.
Seasons
Madyson Whippo, Grade 3
Chestnut Street Elementary School, PA

Wish Upon a Star
I shine all night my light is bright.
When the sun comes out I really want to shout.
I have to shine to be glad.
If I don't I'll be mad.
The stars could come out night and day.
I hope they never go away.
Mariah Jackson, Grade 2
Bensley Elementary School, VA

Spring Things
Pretty birds soaring in the sky.
Yellow and black bees in the park.
Colorful flowers blowing on the ground.
Delicious vegetables being eaten in the house.
Green grass growing on the yard.
Bryce Wallace, Grade 2
St Mary Magdalen School, DE

Dad

D ad is my best friend
A nd he's really fun
D ad plays with me
Lucas Bermudez, Grade 2
Milton Fuller Roberts School, MA

Winter

I am freezing
And it is snowing
I can ski
But sometimes I fall on my knees!
I play in the snow
Even if I'm cold
Emma Murray, Grade 2
Willis E Thorpe School, MA

Maine

I see sea shells and boogie boards,
I hear the ocean waves,
I taste the buttery lobster,
I smell the ocean's salty water,
I feel the water when I go swimming.
Chaisleigh Cosey, Grade 3
Granville Elementary School, NY

Soccer

S occer is the best sport
O ur coach is my dad
C oach helps us with soccer
C an you score a goal
E at apple before you play
R ed is our team color
Dorian McMenamin, Kindergarten
Montessori Development Center, PA

Spring

S howers are coming
P lay outside with everybody
R un in the sun
I n the spring, fields with flowers
N o more winter
G o share spring
Maddie McGee, Grade 1
Frenchtown Elementary School, CT

Dream

D octor, dancer
R eader
E xplorer
A uthor
M ountain climber
Kayla Barlow, Grade 2
Bensley Elementary School, VA

Families

My family sweet as peach
how we help each other as a team
sometimes we fight
sometimes we are happy
we came together and make a family.
Carolina Jeronimo, Grade 3
Public School 148 Ruby Allen, NY

Walk My Dog

"Walk my dog!" I said to my mom.
My mom won't walk my dog.
I said, "Why won't you walk my dog?"
One day my dog was walking around
and around in circles.
He was soooooo dizzy.
I was very very tired.
Marina Skouros, Grade 2
Public School 2 Alfred Zimberg, NY

Easter

Easter is so fun
We go see some bunnies
We go egg hunting
Chocolate marshmallow sweet eggs
Easter presents everywhere
Kimberly Morales, Grade 3
Penn-Kidder Campus, PA

Secrets of the Forest

Listen to the forest
Hear its whisper
Learn its secrets
Feel the connection
Marcos Felipe, Grade 2
Dartmouth Early Learning Center, MA

A Talking Tree

Somehow I can talk.
I like to tell jokes a lot.
My jokes are funny.
Sydney Paces, Grade 2
Fisher Hill Elementary School, MA

Frog

F rogs can jump high
R ain is good for tree frogs
O ut of the canopy came the tree frog
G reen is a nice skin color
Ethan Chong, Kindergarten
Montessori Development Center, PA

My Dogs

My dogs are loving,
Caring too.
They love me
And I love them too.
One is fat,
One is skinny
And one is in-between.
They love on me,
When I get home,
I care for them too.
Toby, Collen, and Lilly are
The best dogs ever!
Katy Walters, Grade 2
Public School 122 Mamie Fay, NY

Hockey Star

I wish I had a hockey rink.
I wish I could play hockey.
I wish I would be a captain.
I wish I was a star.
David Greenburg, Grade 1
Artman Elementary School, PA

Lizards

Australia, plains, grass
Beautiful, fast, slimy, soft,
Run, jump, sit, climb, move.
Daniel Germain, Grade 2
Long Meadow Elementary School, CT

Starfish

A golden star in the sea
In the sea way down
At the bottom of the sea
At the bottom of the sea

Lighting the sea up
At the bottom of the sea
At the bottom of the sea
And that is a starfish
Caitlin Schleimer, Grade 1
Buckley Country Day School, NY

Jaguar

Climbs really fast.
He belongs to the cat family
Lives in the jungle or rainforest
Likes to eat meat (like us)
He has sharp claws
And sharp teeth
So he can kill predators.
He can blend in
So his prey
Can't find them.
Jeffrey Moore, Kindergarten
St Christopher's School, VA

Calmly, Gently…

The fish are gliding
gently through the water,
a school moving calmly
and jumping up,
saying Hi to the kites
that are twirling
like ballerinas
under the cotton clouds.
Olivia Schauer, Grade 2
Dr Samuel C Eveleth School, MA

Water Music

Drip drop drip drop plop!
Waterfalls spilling over rocks.
The air sweet as Maine.
Charlotte Hadley, Grade 3
Dartmouth Early Learning Center, MA

What Am I?

I'm messy or I'm clean, I don't dress up for Halloween.
The kids shove their stuff in me. I'M SO MESSY!
Next year I get a new kid, who cares for me so truly much,
papers in folders, pencils in tool kits, crayons on the side
I feel like I'm new, man!
I look beautiful, better than ever.
I don't want a new kid ever!

Liana Glennon, Grade 3
Cabot Elementary School, MA

A Flipbo

This is a Flipbo.
A Flipbo lives with frogs in floppy flowers in Florida.
A Flipbo likes to eat fruit, fries, Fritos, and fish.
A Flipbo likes fun rides, football, Frisbee, and fishing.
A Flipbo fell five feet from Farmer Fred's fence
    and flew to France to get french fries.
My Flipbo tickled my feet and fingers with his fuzzy fur.

Jason Young, Grade 3
St Clement Mary Hofbauer School, MD

I Am Justin Touhey

I am smart and respectful
I wonder why some men have long hair
I hear God saying always tell the truth
I see in the future that I will fight for freedom
I want a dog that loves me
I am smart and respectful

I pretend that I am rich
I feel that my great grandma is watching me
I touch the hot sun
I worry about people with cancer
I cry when people in my family die
I am smart and respectful

I understand that a war is happening in the world
I say God really loves us
I dream that I am a movie star
I try to get good grades on my tests
I hope I get a dog for a present
I am smart and respectful

Justin Touhey, Grade 3
Stony Point Elementary School, NY

Yikes

The dentist tells me to open wide
So he can take a look inside
My teeth are shiny and white
I brush my teeth day and night
He pulls out the drill
I start to shout
I need to run before I pass out
It's not funny I'm scared to death
I hope he doesn't smell
My Doritos breath.

Jacob Shipe, Grade 2
Mary Walter Elementary School, VA

Leaves

Leaves might be yellow,
Or red or green or orange.
Some are pointy,
Some are round
And in the fall,
They all end up on the ground
There are different kinds of leaves,
There are maple
And there is oak
And picking them off the ground
Is a lot of work.
Some might be wrinkly and droopy
Some are blooming and happy.
So make a collection of leaves,
And see how wonderful they are.

Leeor Harel, Grade 2
Francis J Kane Elementary School, MA

Cat

I am a Cat
My whiskers are as white as snow
My claws can scratch my back
My fur sheds in the spring
I am a cat
My teeth kill my prey
My tail swishes very fast
My mouth makes a noise like a mouse
I am a cat

James Vaughen, Grade 3
St Christopher's School, VA

Spring

Spring is when you see the grass,
I never want it to pass.

Spring is when you smell the fresh air,
You can feel it rush through your hair.

Spring is when you see new trees,
You also see brand new leaves.

Also in Spring you can ride your bike,
You can also take a hike.

Spring is one of my favorite seasons,
Those are my many reasons.

Elyssa Synor, Grade 3
Ellicott Road Elementary School, NY

The Box

I seem
to see a box and inside
is a fox

Rajae Garriques, Grade 1
Hebbville Elementary School, MD

Birds

Chirp, chirp, flap.
They flap their wings
as quick as the wind.

Fly south when New York is very cold.
Stay in New York when it's hot.

Flap, flap
Birds are peaceful.

Chirp, flap.

Swish, swish
goes the birds in the air.
Black, white in the air.

Fly! Fly! Fly!

Olivia Lynch-Burgdorf, Grade 2
Buckley Country Day School, NY

The House
It creaks like footsteps and gives off light like a giant lantern.
The sinks are like mini waterfalls.
The wood, so smooth, is like a tree still standing.
The metal is as hard as a steel crate used for traps.
I feel glad when I enter.

Spencer Seward, Grade 3
St Christopher's School, VA

Oh It's Spring
Oh, it's spring
Oh it's spring
Hear me sing
birds fly by.
It's the blue sky!

Nicholas Hernandez, Grade 1
Public School 105 Senator Abraham Bernste, NY

My Basketball
M y very special basketball
Y ou helped me out a lot

B ut sometimes you stress me but I'm still going to like you
A s you get older every day
S aying words as you bounce
K eep going on you're still the best ball
E ven when I throw you out I'll never forget you
T hinking of you makes me happy
B ecause you rock!
A t the championships I wish you were there but I remembered you
L ead me to victory
L ead me through BASKETBALL!

Jonathan Kim, Grade 3
Willits Elementary School, NY

Zakazie
There was a girl named Zakazie.
She was lazy and not so very nice.
She would not listen to helpful warnings.
She once got in trouble for doing things she shouldn't have.
She was very foolish.
The mouse and frog tried to warn her.
But she just ignored them.

Joelle Michetti, Grade 2
Sacandaga School, NY

I Have a Dozen Dragons

I have a dozen dragons
I   them   the
  bought   at   mall.

I   closet.
  keep them in my

It's fortunate

they're
       small.

Their horns   and silver
        are red

Their   gold
    scales are green and

All of them
      are beautiful

And   of   are
   all   them   bold.

Tenzing D. Sherpa, Grade 3
Public School 69 Jackson Heights, NY

School

S tudents hear the bell
C hildren get in line
H ave to pass in homework
O pen up the school door
O pen up your backpack
L unch will be soon.

Isabella Garcia, Grade 1
Milton Fuller Roberts School, MA

Cats

Cats are all colors
Cats can walk, cats can run
Cats live in homes
Cats eat cat food
Cats are cute and playful

Kayla Grumski, Grade 1
Richland Elementary School, PA

Frost

The sun glazed the frost
that had crept in
with strong winds.

The frost was bitter and gleaming
with mist rising
in the morning.

Jacob Phillips, Grade 3
Somers Elementary School, CT

My Big Red Helicopter

My name is Roger
I would love to fly a helicopter.
So big and so wide.
Right by my side
Red is my favorite color.

So bright and light
With power ranger designs
cause there can be no other
from blue to green
and the rest of the team.
Looking mighty as ever.

The gangs all here,
so now its time to try it for a spin.
I'll tell the truth
I will not lie.
This is the most greatest
ride I'd ever taken in my life
Good bye for now
I'll see you soon.

Roger Samuels, Grade 2
Great Oaks Elementary School, NY

Summer

S unflowers are beautiful
U nder the deep blue sky
M other nature is awesome
M ore sunny days
E ating ice cream
R ainbows leading to gold

Paulo Pereira, Grade 3
Edgartown Elementary School, MA

If I Was a Lion...

If I was a lion, I would outrun zebras.
If I was a lion, I would have a long tail.
If I had a lion, I would run away with fear...ROAR!

Luke Anderson, Grade 2
Dr Samuel C Eveleth School, MA

Baby Animals

Baby animals make me think of my dog Cowboy.
My dog Cowboy makes me think of love.
Love makes me think of my family.
My family makes me think of fun.
Fun makes me think of friends.
Friends make me think of playing.
Playing makes me think of baby animals.

Joshua Slayton, Grade 3
Cambridge Springs Elementary School, PA

Trees

Trees stand up high.
With branches and leaves that are green in the
seasons Spring and Summer.
Old in Fall and Winter.
They stand up proud and almost anywhere you go you see
Trees.
Trees are amazing plants.

Hunter Gajewski, Grade 3
Robeson Elementary School, PA

Special Days

Special days can be long or short it depends on the day and how you feel.
Special days can be sad, glad, or great!
It's your day that you can make!
Special days are telling jokes and laughing with your pals.
Special days can be with your favorite guys and gals.
Special days can be spent with relatives, friends, anyone you'd like.
Every day can be special if...you're having fun
Special days can be with your family...and your loved ones.
Special days can be at the beach, or at a park,
Special days can be playing in the snow.
When you have special days you want to go, go, go!
I treasure all my special days
I enjoy my special days in so many ways.

Sarah Rockitter, Grade 3
Willits Elementary School, NY

The Bomb

The bomb was scary.
The bomb was very deadly
to the Japanese.
Charlie Valone, Grade 3
St Joseph School, NY

Spring Days

Beautiful birds chirping
down the road.
Cute fluffy chipmunks
jumping in the trees.
Well cooked hot dogs
boiling on the stove.
Sweet tasting lemonade
sitting on the bench
on the sunny day.
Soft energetic dogs
running in the front yard.
Glennamarie Rivers, Grade 2
St Mary Magdalen School, DE

Virginia Beach

It's a city
people on every side
street shops are there too.
Meghan Babb, Grade 3
Sacred Heart School, CT

Dolphin

A big fun dolphin
a flippy, flappy dolphin,
chasing in the wake.
Walker Leake, Grade 2
St Christopher's School, VA

Summer

Summer's here
School is out
Time to play
Go on vacation
Invite friends
The only rule is to have fun
Daniel Houser, Grade 3
Trinity Christian School, VA

I Am Spider Man

I am spider man.
I wonder if I quit being a hero.
I see a whole crowd cheering for me.
I want people to be safe.
I am a hero.
I pretend I am just a regular person.
I believe I will help people be safe.
I touch the person that needs help
I feel I will be a good hero
I worry about the dying
I cry if someone in this city dies
I am spider man

I understand with great power comes…
Great Responsibility
Jacob Dutcher, Grade 3
Robeson Elementary School, PA

Sick

When you're home sick and have nothing to do,
Why don't you grab some stew?
Grab a pillow, and plop yourself down,
Be sure to stay in your comfy nightgown.
Watch a movie or fall asleep,
Perhaps you should watch Little Bo Peep.
But…it's not as good as it sounds…
'Cause I got that bug that's going around!
Jenna Topping, Grade 3
Craneville School, MA

Spring

White
Baseball
Running fast
Spring is here!
Ryan Strobel, Grade 1
Maureen M Welch Elementary School, PA

Eagles

Eagles finding food
gliding high above the ground
and laying some eggs.
Thayne Morgan, Grade 3
Bradford Township Elementary School, PA

A Shadow Is a Shadow

Shadows are dark and black.
This shadow is mine.
When I write it writes with me.
When I pick up my leg my shadow does the same.
My shadow will always be with me.

Katia Acierno, Grade 2
Public School 2 Alfred Zimberg, NY

If I Were…

If I were white, I'd be a board that gets written on with a marker.
If I were yellow, I'd be a banana from the store.
If I were red, I'd be an apple in the tree.
If I were pink, I'd be a flower waiting for my water.
If I were blue, I'd be the sky so big.
If I were orange, I'd be an orange round and juicy.
If I were brown, I'd be a log that gets cut.

Julia Conner, Grade 1
St Clement Mary Hofbauer School, MD

Mac and Cheese

One day I asked my Mom for some mac and cheese,
She would not give it to me until I said please.
I threw a fit and hid her car keys.
I snuck six boxes of mac and cheese,
So from now on whenever I want mac and cheese,
I always say please.
PS: my Mom never found those Ford car keys.

Maura Fleming, Grade 3
Rossmoyne Elementary School, PA

Birds!

Birds are flying south and north.
Twigs, sticks, and leaves are what nests are made of…
Bluebirds, robins, blue jays, and cardinals, too.
Bird food, Bird feeders, and bird shirts.
But also don't forget your binoculars.
Soaring, flying, and pecking.
Screaming, "Get off of me predators!"
Worms…bugs…that's what birds eat.
Baby eggs, big eggs, blue eggs,
or just plain old eggs.
Birds are great!!!

Taylor Knorr, Grade 3
Robeson Elementary School, PA

Dark Colors

I can see the dark colors,
in the dark black rain
I can feel the wind touching
the leaves
I can almost touch the sky like I was
so so high
I can think of the wonderful things
that have passed
I can hear the church bell ringing.

Kenan Z. Rustamov, Grade 3
Lincoln Elementary School, PA

Turtles/Dolphins

Turtles
Cute, green
Walking, playing, laying eggs
Hard, kind, fun, blue
Sleeping, swimming, eating
Wet, friendly
Dolphins

Lauren McNeill, Grade 3
Sunrise Drive Elementary School, NY

Imagine If

Imagine if —
Imagine if I could reach the snow
Imagine if I could reach heaven
Imagine if I could reach my Nana
Imagine if I could reach my heart
Imagine if I could reach Pluto
Imagine if I could reach the rooftops
of Buckley Country Day School
Imagine if I could reach love.

Caroline Thomson, Grade 1
Buckley Country Day School, NY

Cocoa

Cocoa
Sweet, rich, creamy
Boiling, making, pouring
We want more hot cocoa
Chocolate drink

Gunnar Hasselquist, Grade 3
Houghton Elementary School, MA

Sand

It's very dirty
We have fun playing in it
I love the warm sand

Jacob Martin, Grade 2
Bensley Elementary School, VA

The Beach

Almost there...
We can smell the fresh sea air
through the car window.

Let's watch the big fish
Pop Up one by one.
Look down from the dock
and watch the little school of fish
swerve from one side to another.
It is amazing how they can move
at the same time, like ballerinas.

We fly our kites by the shore
with the sand between our toes,
clutching the string in our hands.
We watch our kites gliding
in the periwinkle sky.

After a good day at the beach
watching the sunset
is the best way to end.

Eliza Howells, Grade 2
Dr Samuel C Eveleth School, MA

When You Try to Fly a Kite...

Kites are flying rapidly
when there is a fast air current,
but
when there is not
and
you try to fly a kite
it dives
down,
down,
down.

Mason Quintero, Grade 2
Dr Samuel C Eveleth School, MA

Beach Fun

I go with my family to the beach when it's hot,
We make sure to go early to get a good spot.
We set up chairs facing the sun,
As we get started on our day of fun.
I play with my shovel and pail in the sand,
I think it's easier to just use my hand.
I jump and play and swim on a wave,
Sometimes the lifeguard says to behave.
I swim with the fish that live in the ocean,
After I'm done, I put on more lotion.
My mom packs us drinks and good food to eat,
The blanket gets messy from the sand on my feet.
Before we pack up and leave for the day,
We take all our trash and throw it away.
We stayed at the beach and had fun for hours,
When it's all done we walk to the showers.
We go in our car and my dad drives us home,
And that's where I started writing this poem.

Cassi Leibowitz, Grade 3
A. P. Willits Elementary School, NY

I Am Jessica Minker

I am cheerful and beautiful
I wonder what will happen in the future
I hear the heart beat of my cat Katrina who died
I see people cheering for me on a fashion runway
I want to be famous
I am cheerful and beautiful

I pretend to be a famous singer, spit balling words into a microphone
I feel my floor quake when I am angry
I touch my warm, silk lined blanket on sad occasions
I worry that World War III will happen
I cry when I think of Katrina, my Aunt Theresa, and my Great Grandpa Max
I am cheerful and beautiful

I understand that you don't always get what you want
I say reach for the stars
I dream raccoons will take over the world
I try to be myself no matter what
I hope I am alive for a solar eclipse
I am cheerful and beautiful

Jessica Minker, Grade 3
Stony Point Elementary School, NY

My Friend

I love God.
He takes good care of me.
He gives me my food.
I love Him because
He wakes me up every day.
God is my friend.

Dylan Washington Laster,
Kindergarten
Agape Christian Academy, VA

Blue

Blue is bright
Blue is water
Blue is a window
Blue is a lunch box

Blue tastes like a carrot
Blue smells like a blueberry
Blue sounds like the wind
Blue feels like the clouds
Blue looks like water
Blue makes me feel good
Blue is bright as the sun

Andres Schnelle, Grade 1
St Rose School, CT

The Wonders of Fall

Fall is here,
No don't fear
Yellow, green, brown.
The leaves are falling down
Lazy loving leaves,
Fall in autumn.

Max Sharin, Grade 3
Center School, MA

Ice Cream Cone

ice cream
sweet, vanilla
dripping, freezing, crunching
makes me cold
cone

Thomas Luciano, Grade 1
St Rose School, CT

Dad

When I see my dad
My eyes light up,
I watch his sky-colored eyes
Gaze around the room,
His smiles are as big as
A watermelon,
His combed gray hair
Sticks up in front,
I can hear his change
Jingling-jinga-linga-ling,
We go play hockey
SMACK!
My dad scored!
At the end of the day
I realize our friendship is like a line that
Never ends

Ryan Labonte, Grade 3
Acushnet Elementary School, MA

Spring

S parkling streams
P uppies are happy
R unning and playing
I n spring it is fun
N othing is frozen
G o outside and play

Joseph Newton, Grade 3
Chestnut Street Elementary School, PA

Kent Gardens

K ind teachers and people.
E lementary schools are awesome.
N ice materials and things.
T albert rocks!

G rass and playground.
A great school.
R ecess!
D ifferent people
E veryone is kind
N eat writings
S aturday and Sunday we don't have school

Emma Kucharek, Grade 2
Kent Gardens Elementary School, VA

Winter

Winter is so cold
We need to wear
coats, jackets, and gloves
The sky turns dark
before the rain and snow comes
We can throw snowballs
and make a snowman
winter is so fun!

Gurtej Gill, Grade 2
Public School 2 Alfred Zimberg, NY

Trees

When the seasons pass by
The trees start to die
And the leaves start to cry
Because the trees start to die
Because their roots are so dry
And the leaves start to cry
Because their seeds start to fly.
We need trees so we can stay alive
Without trees the world will die!

Aidan Burke, Grade 1
Glover Elementary School, MA

My Spring

Birds flying high in the sky.
Flowers grow very high.
Fish swim in the glimmering stream.
Bears eat near the stream.
Spring is the best of all
In the spring you can play baseball.
Jesus gives us the best time of all!

Ransom Fox, Grade 1
Trinity Christian School, VA

Sister

S weet
I ntelligent
S miley
T reats me like a role model
E xtra weird
R eminding me always of love

Cailyn Chisholm, Grade 3
Heron Pond Elementary School, NH

The Cat

There was a cat
who was fat
who looked like
a fat rat

Janae Graham, Grade 1
Hebbville Elementary School, MD

My School

I love my school
I love my friends
They are sweet and kind
I even love my teachers
and my principals

Stephanie Giraldo, Grade 2
Public School 2 Alfred Zimberg, NY

Soccer

Soccer, soccer
make a goal

Soccer, soccer
run around

Soccer, soccer
pass the ball

Soccer, soccer
kick a ball

Soccer, soccer
is really fun

Pablo Rosales, Grade 3
Public School 69 Jackson Heights, NY

The Pet Shop

At the pet shop
There are wee hamsters
Towering dogs, tiny mice
Enormous snakes
Teeny weeny microscopic gerbils
TOWERING TURTLES
And half size geckos!

Anthony Lyon, Grade 2
Milton Terrace Primary School, NY

Ashley

A shley is my twin sister.
S he looks exactly like me.
H ave fun together.
L oves me.
E xcellent sister.
Y oung like me.

Lindsay Smith, Grade 3
Penn Yan Elementary School, NY

Ballet

Ballet is my favorite of them all,
Spinning,
Leaping,
Posing,
Trust me,
You won't bump into the…
Wall!

Kristin Gonzales, Grade 3
Acushnet Elementary School, MA

Soccer

Soccer is fun
You can play soccer in the sun
When you play soccer you use your feet
When you play soccer in the sun
You will have a lot of fun
You might need water
After a while you might get hotter
When you play soccer it will be fun

Mark Palma, Grade 3
Our Lady of Hope School, NY

Acrostics

A fun style of poetry
C razy words across the page
R eady to be read
O ften descriptive
S lowly expressing feeling
T imeless poems
I nteresting phrases
C olorful pictures that they paint
S ome poetry never gets old

Sarah Moore, Grade 3
Leicester Memorial School, MA

Lollipops

L ick
O utstanding
L ick
L ick
I ndigo
P retty
O range
P urple
S pectacular

Caroline Kaiser, Grade 2
Highland Elementary School, PA

The Wind and the Tree

The wind is blowing.
The fast wind snapped a branch off.
Finally it's calm.

Ricky Elliott, Grade 3
St Stephen Regional School, PA

April Picture

I smell the rain curl up
to my nose. By that
I can tell
that it is April
The weather is nice,
I can picture
the last day of school
June 10 just two
months away
The sun sits in my
eyes like eggs
over easy

Donnie Bell, Grade 3
Lincoln Elementary School, PA

Harbor

H orizon
A round the world
R eleasing
B oats
O cean's water
R egatta

Austin Martel, Grade 3
Heron Pond Elementary School, NH

If I Were a Star

If I were a star,
I will be in the sky,
If I were a star,
I will be shiny,
If I were a star,
I will be yellow,
And everyone,
Will make a wish on me!

Sameen Khan, Grade 1
Public School 105 Senator Abraham Bernste, NY

Litter

I do not understand why people litter.
I do not understand why people don't pick it up when they see it.
I do not understand why they don't throw it in the trash.
But most of all,
I do not understand why people are lazy and don't throw it away.
I do understand why I don't litter…
Because it's bad for the environment and the animals.

Kaitlyn Poplaski, Grade 3
Craneville School, MA

My Friend

S hy
H appy
A n artist
N ice
T alented
E xciting
L arge.

Giovanni Thompson, Grade 2
Public School 152 School of Science & Technology, NY

Bubble Gum

I blow my bubble up so high,
I blow my bubble up in the sky.
I blow it so high
until it is night.
So look at the height of me,
I will never get down
until I hear the morning
SOUNDS!

Danielle Allen, Grade 2
Public School 152 School of Science & Technology, NY

The Rat
Once there was a rat
Who wanted a hat.
He fell on a rug
And lost his coffee mug.
He was very sad,
So he went and told his dad.
Kyle Moore, Grade 2
Trinity Christian School, VA

I Am Just a Kid
I am a good person.
I am a smart person.

I am a fancy kid.
I am a caring kid.
I am good to my family.

I am a good helper.
I am a big sister.
I am always happy.

I am a gabber.
I am a shopper.

I am a small kid.
I am just a kid.
Amelia Correia, Grade 2
St Mary's Primary School, MA

Dad
Dad can cook.
Dad can love.
Dad can work.
Dad can be sick.
Dad can be fun.
Mark Mulhern, Grade 2
St Mary's Primary School, MA

Tigers
Tigers run fast
Hunting small prey
Roar 2 miles away
Sean Moore, Grade 1
Walker Memorial School, ME

Rain
I love the rain. I sit by my window pane.
I watch it fall. Until it's done.
and then I go and have some fun.
"Drip! Drop! Drip! Drop!"
Jarely Zarate, Grade 2
Public School 1 The Bergen School, NY

My Friend Sophie
With my friend Sophie, I'm at the beach.
With my friend Sophie, I'm eating a peach.
With my friend Sophie, I write.
With my friend Sophie, I fly a kite.
Catherine Howard, Grade 2
Trinity Christian School, VA

What's Up?
My dad says what's up when he's down
My mom says we got a new pup
He thinks up is down and down is up
So you must remember what up means!
Arielis Vazquez, Grade 2
Buckley Country Day School, NY

Puppies
P layful rascals
U nder and over obstacles
P oor obedience skills
P erforming tricks
I s very active
E very puppy is cute
S mells scents from far away
Leana Radzik and Allison Virzi, Grade 3
Leicester Memorial School, MA

Me
I like Star Wars and Star Wars light sabers.
My favorite thing to do is play
with my friends Colin and Connor.
I love to play with them.
They are not mean to me.
That is why they are my friends.
Now you know a lot about me.
Robert Furtado, Grade 1
Hyman Fine Elementary School, MA

Aquamarine
Aquamarine is like the sound of the shiny ocean waves
making their way up to the sand.
Aquamarine is like the smell of sweet lollipops.
Aquamarine is the taste of round Lifesavers falling into your mouth on a kayak.
Aquamarine is the feeling of wet nail polish resting on your fingernail.
Isabella Pasqualucci, Grade 2
Long Meadow Elementary School, CT

A Pretty Color
Pink is the color of a pig that is ready to jump in the mud
Pink is the color of a sunset going down
Pink is the color of a heart that loves you
Pink is the color of the people who love you
Sirena Winakor, Grade 1
Buckley Country Day School, NY

Halloween
Halloween night,
Scary, exciting, scaring, haunting
This holiday is fun!
Darkness!
Omair Naeem, Grade 1
Public School 105 Senator Abraham Bernste, NY

Friends, Friends
Friends, friends,
Friends are nice,
Friends, friends,
Friends are kind,
Friends, friends,
Friends, are helpful;
I love friends!
Mishelys Rodriquez, Grade 1
Public School 105 Senator Abraham Bernste, NY

My Hero
My hero is my dad.
Yes, he is a soldier.
He protects our country,
Every night I pray that he will be safe.
Right now he is in Afghanistan.
Only our love will bring him home.
Aaron Wetherington, Grade 3
Public School 105 Senator Abraham Bernste, NY

Fishing

Fishing is fun,
when you go fishing you could
catch a big fish,
you could also catch small fish,
the most important thing is the rod.
The rod is so strong that it
does not break if you catch a
really big fish.
The string is also important because
if you have a strong rod but no string
how would you catch fish?
The best thing about fishing is that
you could get together with your
friends and family.
When you catch a fish you could
bake it and eat it,
that's why fishing is so fun!
Damian Ostaszewski, Grade 3
Holy Rosary School, NY

Yellow

Yellow is the color of the sun
That shines in the morning light,
The arch of McDonalds,
The stars of the Chinese flag.
Yellow is the color of a bulldozer
And a star that is glowing in the night.
It is also the color of some rulers,
The color of a crayon or a
Colored pencil or marker.
Yellow is my favorite color!
Anna Boloyan, Grade 2
Cabot Elementary School, MA

Twilight

Twilight comes at the end of each day,
It's when the day meets the night.
The sky turns yellow, pink, and orange
and all seems too quiet
It is a beautiful time.
It is a wonderful time.
TWILIGHT
Andrew Fish, Grade 3
Center School, MA

Summer

Summer is hot
Summer is fun
You can go to the beach
and eat lots of pizza and ice cream
Summer is fun you can go to the park
to play, run and race.
Sarah Aly, Grade 2
Public School 2 Alfred Zimberg, NY

I Am

I am
special to my mom and dad
and my whole family

I am
very good at soccer,
the best one on my team

I am
really nice and kind and
good to my mom and dad all the time

I am
funny and sweet and loving
and will always love my family
Noah Slivka, Grade 2
St Mary's Primary School, MA

The Sky

Sky is blue and white
The windy day
Wind is blowing the flags
The lonely sky no one to play with
Justin Son, Grade 2
Tashua School, CT

Spring

Green leaves blowing on a branch.
Colorful chicks chirping in a tree.
Pretty flowers growing everywhere.
Wonderful fruit hanging on a tree.
Painted eggs sitting on the ground.
Rita Offutt, Grade 2
St Mary Magdalen School, DE

Seals

S ilky wet seals
E very seal knows they need their water
A lso, the seals need their air and go up on dry land
L unch usually happens during the day
S eals enjoy the best of it

Austin Smith, Grade 3
Edgartown Elementary School, MA

Violence

Blood is red
Guns are black
When you shoot someone
They can't come back
Stop the violence
Cause it is wack
Why is there violence?
Violence is all over the world
North America, South America, Asia, and Africa
Why don't we just stop the violence and have a peaceful and calm world.
Why would you take out your anger by using violence?
It's just wrong
You can solve problems with conversations
You don't have to use violence
I take my anger out by counting to ten
There are all sorts of ways you can do it
We have to stop the violence
Think about it??
It is a shame

Mark Palmer, Grade 3
Anna B Pratt School, PA

Basketball

My favorite sport is basketball.
It's so hot.
I like the way you dribble up
And down the court. Fast.

Court fast.
Court fast.
I bob. Fake.
Court fast.
We win!

Earl Holloway, Grade 3
The New York Institute for Special Education, NY

Jump Rope
jump rope
long, colorful
swish, tap, thump
friends jumping
recess
Kristen Cirone, Grade 1
St Rose School, CT

Spring Is Here
When it is spring...
flowers bloom,
I play outside,
it gets warmer,
and birds build their nests.
Amanda Fedele, Grade 3
Our Lady of Hope School, NY

Spring
S urf
P ear
R ain
I nchworm
N est
G rass
JR Cravotta, Kindergarten
Willis E Thorpe School, MA

Bible
It spreads through the world
everlasting Holy Word
written as Gospels
Shenandoah Terry, Grade 3
Sacred Heart School, CT

Cats
Cats
Soft, furry
Purring, meowing, hissing
Cute, friendly, playful, cuddly
Running, chasing, eating
Brown, black
Felines
Madison Stevens, Grade 3
Brant Elementary School, NY

Snow
When you look at snow,
it glitters like a diamond.
When you tilt your head and look at it,
it looks like a blanket of snow.
It makes me melt when I see it.
For you may never see
such a sight like this again,
when snow falls
it seems like tunes in my ear.
Snow is a magical sight.
Sandra Knepp, Grade 3
Bradford Township Elementary School, PA

I Am
I am not shy
I wonder if I could fly
I hear music all the time
I see monkeys who love to climb
I want cancer to have a cure
I pretend that Felicia has no more
I feel scared when she starts to cry
I touch birds wings and say fly
I worry that Felicia will never come home
I cry when people make fun of me or my poem
I am a writer, dancer, and more
I understand people when they feel sore
I say I can do it when I'm feeling sad
I dream Felicia has no more cancer and
I am glad
I hope the world will never end
I am a kid who doesn't blend
Because I'm unique
Rosalie Connell, Grade 3
Davis Elementary School, PA

Horses
Horses, horses, what a treat.
Oats are what they like to eat.
Always there, when you need them.
They like when you regularly feed them.
They love you and you love them too
Yay for horses, Whoo hoo!!
Ashley Wagnblas, Grade 3
St Rose School, CT

Dad

D ad makes lots of money
A nd I would like another toy, but
D on't work too hard at night.

Gail Guay, Grade 2
Public School 152 School of Science & Technology, NY

I Would Rather Be

There's lots of things that I would be
And lots of things that I wouldn't be like:

I would rather be a girl than a boy;
I would rather be a book than a paper;
I would rather be a dolphin than a shark;
I would rather be Cleopatra than Marie-Antoinette;
I would rather be wearing pink than black;
I would rather be clean than smelly;
I would rather be a horse than a bunny;
I would rather be a queen than a king;
I would rather be a pegasus than a unicorn;
I would rather be rich than poor;
I would rather be a gown than a skirt;
I would rather be famous than unknown;
I would rather do fencing than running;
I would rather do charity than selling;
I would rather be charming than pretty;
I would rather be flaming than glimmering;
I would rather be myself than someone else.

Salome Tkebuchava, Grade 3
Memorial-Spaulding Elementary School, MA

Skyscraper

As I pass by a skyscraper,
I wonder,
How high does this building go?
And at the top what's up there?
As I gaze upon the soaring structure,
I barely notice the cars passing by
Vroom, Zoom, Vroom
I watch the skyscraper till the sun hides beyond the hill.
Then I walk home happily, full of questions, but happily.
I go to bed,
Wondering when or what questions will be answered.

Jinie Eom, Grade 3
Oak Park Elementary School, PA

Red Rocks!

Red is a rock.
Red tastes like an apple.
Red smells like steam.
Red sounds like a bubbling pan.
Red feels like a house on fire.
Red looks like a pepper.
Red makes me warm.

Luke Sansonetti, Grade 1
St Rose School, CT

1, 2, 3, 3, 2, 1

"1, 2, 3
1, 2, 3
1, 2, 3"
Someone said.
I didn't understand
But I replied
"3, 2, 1"

Simon Blank, Grade 3
Alexander Robertson School, NY

Planets

Stars shining, soaring
Solar System, Pluto, Moon
Mars swirling, glowing

Robbie Moore, Grade 2
Long Meadow Elementary School, CT

Springtime

We have fun today
And flowers grow
Anna grows flowers
The sky is blue.
I have fun
Trees grow
And kids have fun
We have fun in the sun
The sun is hot and warm
And it is cool!
I like it; it is so warm
People can go swimming
And the sun is wearing sunglasses!

Rebecca Ryan, Grade 2
St Madeleine Sophie School, NY

Steve the Cat

He's orange and the only male,
and lays in the litter box.

If I don't pet him,
he nibbles on my fingers.

Sometimes at night,
he nibbles on my toes.

Last night I watched a movie,
and Steve watched it with me.

Riley Bloomer, Grade 1
St John Neumann Academy, VA

My Cat's Nose

My cat has
A little pink nose
She twitches it
And crinkles it
While my mom is cooking
Meow!

Cynthia Robert, Grade 3
Acushnet Elementary School, MA

Penguins

The penguins are black
They go in a sack
They like a hot pot
Feathers are furry
The others worry
I like penguin's feet
Because they are neat

Elijah Holmes, Grade 3
Bensley Elementary School, VA

School

S cience
C rafts
H op in gym
O wn work
O pen books
L unch

Emma McConnell, Grade 2
Bensley Elementary School, VA

Lollipops

They are sometimes sticky, but very good.
I lick them until they are gone.
I love the taste of the sugar inside of them.
I love the taste of the flavor of strawberry, blueberry,
watermelon, cherry, and all the other flavors.
I LOVE Lollipops!

Jasmine Variam, Grade 2
Dr Samuel C Eveleth School, MA

Spring

In spring birds sing happily.
In spring flowers are calling to butterflies "dance with me."
In spring the Earth smiles telling the sky "today is my birthday."
Come one, come on every day we celebrate…happy, happy birthday.

Youssef Naimallah, Grade 2
Public School 2 Alfred Zimberg, NY

Baby Animals

Spring is all around
Baby animals make all kinds of sound
Baby birds chirping
Baby bears growling

It's a rainy spring day
The baby animals want to play
They roll in mud throughout the day
The rain washes it all away

Baby animals go inside
Because mothers say go hide
The baby animals ask why
Because it's too rainy today

Baby animals beg to go out and play
But their mothers still say it's time for little ones to lay
So close they huddle
And dream of splashing in puddles

As they dream
Their mothers beam
And their fathers watch
While they sleep

Nicholas Grube, Grade 3
Chestnut Street Elementary School, PA

Terror
There was a big war.
America bombed Japan.
People died from it.
Joshua Rebmann, Grade 3
St Joseph School, NY

Spring
Yellow
tulips
blooming
Spring is here!
Scott Clark, Grade 1
Trinity Christian School, VA

The Frog
With a frog,
I go to the log.
With a monkey,
We dance all funky.
William Lee, Grade 2
Trinity Christian School, VA

Pencil
Pencil
you help me
write poems
you help me
erase letters
all the time
you look like
a blue and gold
tornado
crossing over the paper
writing the words
creating my poem.
Gino Baldelli, Grade 2
Tashua School, CT

Hermit Crab Shadow
A tree hermit crab
Climbing up a giant tree
When the shadows glide
Hope Niemczyk, Grade 3
West Branch School, PA

Honeybee
Resting in its hive
waiting for a busy day
to get some honey.
Paige Luzier, Grade 3
Bradford Township Elementary School, PA

If I Were a Yanomamo Child
If I were a Yanomamo child
I would help my mom make dinner.
I might start by grating bitter manioc
After that perhaps I would play
With other Yanomamo children
And later I would go to the Amazon River
To watch my father and brother go fishing.
Sarah Swihart, Grade 2
Heim Elementary School, NY

Spring
I like the showers.
They bring the flowers.
Can you see
The new buds on the tree?

Bees fly from their hive.
Look, I see five!
They start to make honey.
It's yummy in my tummy.

I like to see the sun.
I like having fun.
It's starting to warm, not freeze.
I can even wear short sleeves.

The flowers poke out.
I want to shout…
"Hello, spring.
Come do your thing."

Spring is here.
Let's give a cheer!
I like the showers.
They bring the flowers.
Trey Wennerstrom, Grade 3
Chestnut Street Elementary School, PA

Wind

Wind blowing all day,
Leaves falling to the big ground
and it continues.
Michael Stutts, Grade 3
Saw Mill Road School, NY

Cats

Meowing soft cats.
They are very, very cute.
Lots of cats like to play.
Conrad McDonald, Grade 2
Long Meadow Elementary School, CT

Smoking

When you're smoking.
You're probably choking.
I know people that start.
I don't think they are very smart.
If you are smoking, you should stop,
Before you get real sick and drop.
Michael Hickey, Grade 2
Public School 2 Alfred Zimberg, NY

Today

Door
swishing open,

chair gliding
back,

pencil folk dances
across the
paper

sheet smacked
in the inbox

work done for
the day

tomorrow soon
to come
Ori Lazarovich, Grade 3
Sinai Academy of the Berkshires, MA

Spring

S urf
P ool
R ain
I nchworm
N est
G rass
Dillon McDermott, Kindergarten
Willis E Thorpe School, MA

Summer

S unshine tickles my nose
U p come the flowers
M aybe I can catch fireflies
M oths in the moonlight
E arthworms wiggling in the dirt
R ainbows after showers
Olivia Wharton, Grade 1
St John Neumann Academy, VA

Tuft

When I cut my cat's tufty
I felt so very guilty,

I thought he needed a hair cut,
My poor little kitty,

Word got out,

And my mom found out.
I was in big trouble,
I felt so sick.

I never want to be guilty again!
Jessica Cooper-Vastola, Grade 3
Buckley Country Day School, NY

Springtime

Springtime!
We play outside.
The sky is blue today.
Green, it is cool, I really like it!
Springtime!
Augustine Vielkind, Grade 2
St Madeleine Sophie School, NY

Winter

W e love to play in the snow.
I t is cold outside.
N ever stick your tongue on metal.
T he snow is cold.
E at icicles because it is good!
R ide on a snowmobile!

Matthias Caryofilles, Grade 3
Granville Elementary School, NY

4 Leaf Clover

I like you
4 Leaf Clover
Because
You give people
Good luck.

Danny Nunez, Grade 2
Public School 122 Mamie Fay, NY

The Floor

The floor looks like a monster
growling for some food…
When it is dirty!!!
When the floor is clean…
it looks like a ballet dancer
leaping and twirling on stage!
But…
when the floor is clean
and a little dirty…
it looks like
a ballet dancer
leaping and twirling
with a monster.

Isabella Castineyra, Grade 1
Glover Elementary School, MA

Mrs. Sandee

Mrs. Sandee
You are so pretty
You have long and blonde hair.
You have a nice smile.
She treats me right and I treat her nice.
She helps me and I help her.

Bianca, Grade 3
Kanner Learning Center, PA

At Springtime

In my nice front yard
The birds sing and flowers bloom
Every day in spring.

Anthony Butler, Grade 3
St John Neumann Academy, VA

My Pillow

My pillow feels like a
Big, fluffy marshmallow.
It's very soft and mushy
And warm and squishy.
It's as light as a feather
And as warm as a sweater.
It's like my dog's hairy belly
Except not so smelly.
It's as jiggly as jelly
And like Santa's big belly.
I love my big
Marshmallow Jell-O pillow
A lot!

Eric Slocum, Grade 2
Milton Terrace Primary School, NY

Thunderstorm

Wind whistling,
Trees falling,
Lightning crackling,
Dogs howling,
Rain falling,
Babies crying,
Thunder booming,
Getting closer,
House rattling,
Power down,
Shaking with fear,
Screaming,
Closer,
Closer,
BOOM! It's here! It's here!
AHHHHH! Run! Call 911!
Help! Police! What? It's done? Ok.
Yay!

Deanna Burguiere, Grade 3
Meeting House Hill School, CT

My Day at School
I wake up so happy,
and get dressed so snappy.
I eat my breakfast meal,
so my brain power I will feel.
I get on the bus,
without making a fuss.
In school I learn science, math, and reading.
There is also book time and work I'm completing.
There is time for fun out in the yard,
I play, I skip, I jump real hard.
School is the place I love to be,
My teachers are so good to me!
I'm so lucky to go to school,
A place where I can rule!

Arielle Lipsky, Grade 1
Bnot Shulamith of Long Island, NY

Things That Make Me Happy
Things that make me happy
Is like smiling bright shining teeth
Things that make me happy is my mommy and daddy
Grandpa and Grandma
Things that make me happy is my friends
Things that make me happy is everyone

Chelsea Chetram, Grade 1
Buckley Country Day School, NY

Spring
Spring feels hot.
It is sunny.
We wear sunglasses during the sunny weather.
It rains during the spring.
We wear raincoats and umbrellas during the rain.
Spring is a beautiful season.

Jovan Hayes, Kindergarten
Agape Christian Academy, VA

Blue
Blue is like the sound of the waves reaching the sand.
Blue is like the smell of amazing blueberries.
Blue is like the taste of a sweet lollipop.
Blue is like the feel of splashing water against my face.

Sean Melanson, Grade 2
Long Meadow Elementary School, CT

Giraffe
Big large, spotted neck
Rare long legged animal
I like its black tongue
Seth Rockwell, Grade 3
Sacred Heart School, CT

Horse
Horse is
Soft
Horse is
Bursting
Out
Horse can run
Super fast.
Sera King, Grade 1
Fulton Avenue School #8, NY

Eraser
Tiny white eraser.
An active mouse.
Devours bad errors.
Munch! Chew! Gobble!
Especially E.
Especially W.
Jessica Parillo, Grade 2
Tashua School, CT

Spring
Leaves coming back to life
Getting warmer
The cold is going away
Yeah!
Sarah Griffin, Grade 3
Center School, MA

Red
Red is like a red berry
Red is like an apple
Red is like a book
Red is like the world
Red is like a red box
I like red!
Caterina Folchi, Grade 1
St Rose School, CT

Easter/Holiday
Easter
Chocolatey, funny
Decorating, hiding, eating
We are eating candy
Holiday
Madison Selan, Grade 3
Chestnut Street Elementary School, PA

Joe the Leprechaun
There once was a leprechaun named Joe.
He liked to dance on a rainbow.
He liked to hunt for gold.
But he always found mold.
He always puts on a big show.
Madeline Meier, Grade 3
St Rose School, CT

I Can't Write a Poem
I can't write anything.
It's not my job!
I can't think!
I'm crying!
My dad said "Write it or you're grounded!"
My mom said "Get it done!"
She made me cry.
I'm so sad cause I have to work!
I need to stop! Call the police!
Help me! Help me!
It's too hard! My head's on fire.
Call the emergency people!
Call the fire department.
Please! Help me now!
Sabryna Renaud, Grade 3
Plainfield Catholic School, CT

Softball
Softball is fun!
You can throw, pitch, and run.
You can also be catcher, or batter.
You can get hit in the eye.
You can bust yourself in the thigh.
It takes a lot of energy to play softball!
Katlyn Smith, Grade 3
Seaford Central Elementary School, DE

Cold
When I am cold I like to play
In the snow a lot all day.
I sled and skate and put bait to fish
In frozen lakes.
And when it's not snowing I like going
To bed and thinking about stuff in my head.
That's why I like when cold is here.
Thank you for listening to my poem with your ears.

Connor Ames, Grade 3
Trinity Christian School, VA

I Am Lauren Foote
I am loving and helpful
I wonder if we will ever have peace
I hear my uncle's voice at night
I see my mom being a good teacher
I want there to be world peace
I am loving and helpful

I pretend I am a teacher
I feel my mom's hand touching me when I am sick
I touch my dad and mom's heart when I am sad
I worry whether I will live for a long time
I cry when someone in my family is sick
I am loving and helpful

I understand that nothing is easy
I say I believe in God
I dream about being a teacher
I try to do every thing right in school
I hope people will live for a long time
I am loving and helpful

Lauren Foote, Grade 3
Stony Point Elementary School, NY

Dominique's Sneak Peak
I am in first grade and my name is Dominique.
You can see that I am tall and I like to speak.
St. Joan of Arc is my elementary school.
And I have lots of friends who are really cool.
Basketball and claw machines are what I really like.
But I'm also happy just riding my bike.

Dominique Preate, Grade 1
St Joan of Arc School, PA

Untitled

Soft water
    big heart,
Powerful sun
    gentle heat,
Quiet moon
    strong mountains.
Splendid day.

Willie Page, Grade 3
Thoreau Elementary School, MA

Tigers

Tigers
Are so, so cute
They are aggressive
Tigers live in the rain forest
Tigers

Alexxis Gibbs, Grade 2
St Madeleine Sophie School, NY

Spring

Dark green frogs jumping in the pond.
Colorful birds chirping in their nest.
Pretty flowers growing everywhere.
Red shiny apples hanging on a branch.
Yellow chicks hatching from their nest.

Cameron Miles, Grade 2
St Mary Magdalen School, DE

Beautiful Flowers

Flowers are blooming
So beautiful as can be
Bright pink, white, and green

Sarah Antanavage, Grade 3
St Stephen Regional School, PA

Spring

S pring is here
P laying outside
R un around
I play with my friend
N ot do homework
G oing outside to play with my family

Cesar Bueno, Grade 3
Edgartown Elementary School, MA

Spring

Warming up outside.
Kites are blowing in the wind.
Freshness fills the air.
Birds fly north to make their nests.
The hot sun melting the snow.

Kevin Stone, Grade 2
Wells Central School, NY

Maggie

I have a dog named Maggie
She's not a dog that's shaggy
She's pretty good for a puggle
With her I like to hug and snuggle.
I like to play with her
and pet her soft fur
She sits in the car in the back seat
After we give her tasty treats
She likes to sit on my lap
Where she takes a long nap
We like to call her Maggie-May
She likes to play with my friend Renee.
When I left her for a week
I couldn't help but weep!

Natalie Rogers, Grade 3
Fannie E Proctor School, MA

Sponge

I rub the dishes
I rub the toilet
I rub the sink
I rub the sponge anywhere.

Michelle Zyla, Grade 2
Public School 2 Alfred Zimberg, NY

Fluffy Cloud in the Sky

Cat, cat
You look so sweet
You're soft
You look like
A fluffy cloud in the sky
You look as sweet, as sweet
As a butterfly.

Noreen Abouelnaga, Grade 2
Public School 122 Mamie Fay, NY

The Very Funny Puppies
They chew on the chair they're a very funny pair.
When they are bad I am sad.
They tried to catch a frog in a log.
Their friends Marly and Carly came to help.
They played hide and go seek
and they couldn't find Scout so they began to yelp.
She was in a log next to a frog.

Nicole Finn, Grade 2
St Stephen's School, NY

Sparkling Red
Sparkling red is like the sound of Clifford running to the beach with his big strong legs.
Sparkling red is like the smell of Koolaid on a hot day.
Sparkling red is like the taste of a cherry lollipop being licked.
Sparkling red is like the feel of me hugging my soft blanket.

Megan Gould, Grade 2
Long Meadow Elementary School, CT

If I Were...
If I were red, I'd be a little flower in the garden.
If I were white, I'd be a dog just like my new puppy.
If I were yellow, I'd be the sun so pretty in the sky.
If I were green, I'd be the grass so soft that I could play in it.
If I were blue, I'd be the sky so big and bright.

Jillian Toomey, Grade 1
St Clement Mary Hofbauer School, MD

Red Is Like Love
Red is like love
And it always will be.
Red is the color of your heart so you should love your heart.
And love is thankful for who you are.

Petros Efstratoudakis, Grade 3
Cabot Elementary School, MA

A Slark
This is a Slark.
A Slark lives in slippery, sliding seas in South America.
A Slark sloppily eats strawberries, and seven spicy shrimp in a day.
A Slark likes to bathe in sticky slime with bath salt in a square tub.
A Slark put on a small starry slip coat that wasn't his size and slobbered on it.
My Slark splattered seaweed on my bedspread and slept on it.

Evan Sigler, Grade 3
St Clement Mary Hofbauer School, MD

I Am Joshua

Joshua is my name.
And I like to play games.
My favorite number is eight.
And my parents are great.
My heart is pure.
And that's one thing I'm sure.

Joshua Po, Grade 1
St Joan of Arc School, PA

Friends

Friends are nice
Friends are sweet
Won't you be my friend
You are my best friend
To each other
Letters we will send
Friends

Erin Peterseim, Grade 2
Klein Elementary School, PA

The Ball

I kicked the ball
It twirled and so did I
It hit the ground
It rolled in the grass
It went into the post

Zachary Florin, Grade 2
Walker Memorial School, ME

Spring Time

When spring comes,
I see a flower
in the ground.

The flower is
nice and bright
when the sun hits.

I see apple
trees all over
the park.
I love this season!

Jayde Botelho, Grade 3
Westall School, MA

Family

I love my mom
I love my dad
I'm always good
I'm never bad
they make me happy
and never sad
I'm always glad

Iliana Roman, Grade 1
Public School 1 The Bergen School, NY

Summer

I see skateboarders doing kick flips,
I hear wheels going across half pipes,
I taste BBQ in the summer,
I smell sweat when I'm at the skate park,
I feel grip tape running on my fingers.

Chayse Manell, Grade 3
Granville Elementary School, NY

Friendship

Friendship happens when people
Are nice to one another
And are thoughtful to you.

Friendship happens when people
Wish you happiness.
They would even share with you.
Friends can be far away or nearby.
Friends can be younger or older than you,
But friends are the ones you can
Count on wherever you are!
In happy times and sad times
Friendship

Linda Liu, Grade 3
Public School 131, NY

The Earth

The Earth is bright
it has land filled with people and animals
and lots of trees too
The water is blue
with fish and whales and sharks too!

Kevin Mendez, Grade 2
Public School 2 Alfred Zimberg, NY

The Tan Seashell

That big tan seashell
Just sitting there
Like a moon sailing through the sky
Listening through it hear tropical beaches
that never seem to end

Just looking at that big tan shell
You see the sand and feel it too
You might just see a hammock swinging there.
Just barely out of reach
You grasp it gently
it disappears

Suddenly you seem to remember that big tan seashell
Just sitting there.

Annie O'Donovan, Grade 2
Cabot Elementary School, MA

Winter Is

Winter is the smell of hot cocoa.
Winter is touching wet snow.
Winter is birds flying south.
Winter is the taste of snow falling on my tongue.
Winter is the sound of happy people playing in the snow.
Winter makes me feel happy.

April White, Grade 1
St Teresa of Avila School, NY

What Does Swimming Mean to Me?

Fun
Hard work
Fast
Playing
Toys to swim with
Changing clothes
Teachers
Friends
Sports
Swim trunks
Water splashing
Running water
Boys and girls

Ricardo Montanez, Grade 2
Magnet School of Math, Science and Design Technology, NY

Ice Cream

I love ice cream,
It's so good.
I wish it would never go away,
Ice cream Ice cream Ice cream.
It's so good,
When you eat it,
and say it.
Yum Yum Yum,
It's so good.

Sara Sequeira, Grade 3
Westall School, MA

Creek

The time of the afternoon sun glow
glazing down on the lake
When the night moves on
the mist grows the fire,
the fire crisps
the marshmallow moon
making a never-ending treat

Cam Potter, Grade 3
Lincoln Elementary School, PA

Easter

Easter is so fun
Eggs, money, in my basket
Flowers everywhere
Bunnies hopping here and there
Bunnies are so cuddly.

Samantha Alonso, Grade 3
Penn-Kidder Campus, PA

Dear Dog

Dear Dog,

I heard that you broke your leg
And I feel sad.
Do you want me to come over
And play dominoes?

Yours truly,
Cat

Eddie Collado, Grade 1
Glover Elementary School, MA

Leprechaun Fred

There was a leprechaun named Fred
Who wouldn't even get out of bed
He went to sleep
Until the alarm went beep
And jumped up and hit his head.

Maria Ringes, Grade 3
St Rose School, CT

Parties

Parties are lots of fun
They have lots of balloons
It can have many presents
There could be decorations everywhere
Maybe there could be games to play
It also has cakes and candles to blow
Parties are always very fun.

Ariana Perez, Grade 3
Public School 69 Jackson Heights, NY

Krill

Ah!
Swim away!
It's getting closer!
GULP
Man down,
Swim faster!!
Hurry!
It's going to eat us!
Swim fast — GULP
Too late

Patrick Jennings, Grade 3
Thoreau Elementary School, MA

Mr. Grass Frog

The grass frog is very small
Sitting atop a stone wall,

He calls to all his friends,
"Stay inside when winter begins."

When winter is done,
He calls, "C'mon, let's have fun!"

Katie Flynn, Grade 3
St John Neumann Academy, VA

Daphnie

Daphnie
Nice, friendly, active, neat
Lover of brother, mom, and dad
Who feels happy, sad, glad
Who needs family, friends, and food
Who gives money to the poor
Who fears ghosts, people saying "boo," and scary things.
Who would like to fly to Disney World
Resident of Newton
Lin

Daphnie Lin, Grade 3
Cabot Elementary School, MA

Math and Writing

Math, math, math —
all I do is math.
So much fun,
sometimes hard,
sometimes easy.

Writing, writing, writing —
I love writing,
so, so much fun.
Talk about yourself
and never stop.
It is the best thing to do.

Jamilia Desir, Grade 2
Public School 152 School of Science & Technology, NY

The Bragger and the Onlooker

The sky lights up in the morning light,
And the ocean looks on with envy.

The sky fills up the universe, spreading for miles,
And the ocean looks on with envy.

The sky shouts down, bragging about all it has,
And the ocean looks on with envy.

The ocean looks up, spilling with anger,
With a never ending feeling of envy,
Realizing some things can never change.

Noah Cohen-Harding, Grade 3
General John Nixon Elementary School, MA

Hot Chocolate

Warm and steaming

Marshmallows on top
Great in winter

You take a sip
It can't be more delicious
As it is now

But it can get better
You drink it in front of a fire
Devin Coughlin, Grade 2
Cabot Elementary School, MA

Coco the Leprechaun

Coco does have many feet.
But she does not wear cleats.
She does have a hat.
But she's not fat.
Maybe she has a good beat.
Justin Maurina, Grade 3
St Rose School, CT

Cheetahs Mountains

C ool
H ides in trees
E xcellent camouflage
E ats meat
T errific animals
A cheetah has spots
H unts for food
S peedy fast

M ountains are purple
O n land
U p high climbing
N o sand
T hey are terrific
A lways cold
I never saw one before
N ever hot
S now on the top
Nicole Zarzeczny, Grade 2
Klein Elementary School, PA

Raindrops

A
raindrop
is as quick as a
tiger. A raindrop
is slow when it falls
on window glass. A raindrop
is cold when it falls on your face.
A raindrop is as soft as a pillow. A
raindrop is wet. A raindrop falls from
the sky. A raindrop is thin. A raindrop
is t h i c k. A raindrop is sweet when
it falls in your mouth A raindrop
shines in the light A raindrop
makes its way to the ground!
I love raindrops!
Lila Mullins, Grade 3
Jenkintown Elementary School, PA

Spring

S unshine is here
P lants are growing
R ain is making the flowers bloom
I see a bunny who likes the signs of spring
N uts are falling
G rowing flowers all around
Cami D'Addario, Grade 1
Frenchtown Elementary School, CT

Spring

The growing grass is hair covering the ground.
Pollen is a feather tickling my nose.
I feel the cool air that is a strong fan.
Flowers are bright collages by a clever artist.
Jack MacDonald, Grade 3
Cornerstone Academy, MA

Friends

I love to play
with my friends
in the park
in the day
and in the dark.
Jennifer Perez, Grade 1
Public School 1 The Bergen School, NY

Tennis Ball

Ouch!
Says the tennis ball
when it hits the racket.

Bounce!
Says the tennis ball
when it hits the ground.

But it hurts the most
when the racket hits an ace serve!
Katelyn Walker, Grade 2
Buckley Country Day School, NY

Dumb Fred

There once was a person named Fred
He always lays in his bed
He tried to do a trick
Got knocked out with a brick
So there he was in his bed, dead
Micheal Crabtree, Grade 3
Houghton Elementary School, MA

Lacrosse

L ax
A wesome sport
C radle with a stick
R un really fast
O ut of control
S pecial sport
S lide in the mud
E xciting to play
Brenna Voigt, Grade 3
Penn Yan Elementary School, NY

Black Is a Color

Black is night.
Black tastes like blackberries.
Black smells like licorice.
Black sounds like a cat purring.
Black feels like a spider.
Black looks like nothing.
Black makes me feel wonderful!
Charles Asetta, Grade 1
St Rose School, CT

What the Fish See

In the water
the fish look up

seeing
birds gliding
across the sea,

seeing
kites flying
in every direction,

seeing
their world
surrounded by water.

Then
smoothly, slowly
they swim away.
Emma Johnson, Grade 2
Dr Samuel C Eveleth School, MA

Ice Cream Is Sweet

Ice cream is nice like ice
if I was ice cream
I would be chocolate with spice.
I would throw the cherry away
and shake the whipped cream.
Ice cream is sweet
just like sweets,
I like sweets
but ice cream is my favorite.
I always like my ice cream.
John Malczewski, Grade 3
Holy Rosary School, NY

Joshua

J oshua
O rganized
S ophisticated
H yper
U niversal name
A ctive
Joshua DeCambre, Grade 3
Alexander Robertson School, NY

Baseball

Screaming fans are banshees,
when a baseball is a soaring bird.
An out makes the other team
melt from disappointment.
A grand slam makes the team who hit it
explode with happiness.

Hunter Platzman, Grade 3
Cornerstone Academy, MA

Thunderstorms

I hear crashes,
I see flashes,
Everywhere around me,
I get so scared,
When nobody is with me.

Sky turns gray,
It starts to rain,
Drip, drops fall from
The window pane.

In the dark, alone,
Nobody at home.
I was so frightened,
I started to read.

Catherin Canales, Grade 3
James Russell Lowell School, MA

Spring

Flowers bloom on spring days.
It rains a lot during spring.
Baby birds are born.

Jahaira Soriano, Grade 2
Bensley Elementary School, VA

Bunny

Hop hop to it bunny
Go go to it bunny
B-U-N-N-Y B-U-N-N-Y
Get some eggs
Get some candy
Get some for all of us

Makayla Machado, Grade 2
Milton Fuller Roberts School, MA

Good Animals Gone Bad

Polar bear, penguin, raccoon, turtle
Chimpanzee, panda, shark, squirrel
Cougar, gorilla, dragonfly
All of them use wi-fi!

Meerkat, lion, iguana, bird
Seagull, guinea pig, lizard
Hermit crab, sea horse, whale,
Guess which one broke the scale!

Tiger, owl, catfish, eagle
Bush baby, bobcat, bunny, beagle
Monkey, chicken, jaguar, mosquito
Going to eat a big burrito!

Pigs, bees, fish, snakes
All of them like chocolate cakes!
Pitbull, cat, coyote, crab
Went for a drive in a cab!

Ms. Kim Yetter's 2nd Grade Class
Henry Clay Elementary School, VA

Ice Cream

Blueberry and mint
Peach, cookie dough, coffee bean
Lemon, orange, grape

Heather Haddon, Grade 3
Sacred Heart School, CT

Strawberries

S trawberries are yummy
T hat fresh smell
R ed and ripe
A t the market
W ith a juicy taste
B erries are growing
E very strawberry is a different size
R eady to eat
R eally sweet
I t is the best
E very strawberry is delicious
S trawberries are fruit.

Vincent Leung, Grade 3
Sacred Heart School, MA

A Crabit

This is a Crabit.
A Crabit lives in a crazy, creepy, crowded country near California.
A Crabit can eat chicken, candy, cabbage, chips, and creamy cakes.
A Crabit likes cool cars, chitchatting, cats, and candles.
A Crabit wore colored costumes, children's clothes,
    chomping teeth, and a camouflage shirt.
My Crabit called camping confusing and clearly caused a commotion.

Luca Greco, Grade 3
St Clement Mary Hofbauer School, MD

If I Were a Flower

If I were a flower,
I'd have a stem
If I were a flower,
I'd be very beautiful,
If I were a flower,
I'd be a present
For a friend!

Katarina Bojovic, Grade 1
Public School 105 Senator Abraham Bernste, NY

Gymnastics

There is floor and there are bars.
There is a mat stack and beam.
Floor is to flip and beam is to balance.
Mat stack is to handstand and bars is to pull over.
Gymnastics is for everybody.
We all work hard for meets and mocks.
That's not all we have fun too.
We all work as a team so we can win
Because first places makes everybody scream.

Rocely Urizar, Grade 3
Pleasant View School, RI

Because I Love Spring

In the springtime flowers bloom and bees buzz.
When it rains I look out the window and I hear drip drip.
I stay inside. It clears up.
I go outside again. We have a barbecue.
I smell hot dogs and hamburgers.
I heard the birds go tweet tweet.
That is why I love the spring!

Madyline Jagielski, Grade 3
Concord Elementary School, PA

Skeleton

S kull
K nee
E ye socket
L eg bone
E lbow
T oe
O ne
N eck

Devon Salzler, Grade 2
St Joseph School, NY

Funny Bunnies

Funny bunnies are very
Cute and funny too,
They hop around everywhere
Like hopping kangaroos.

Patricia Kizito, Grade 2
Cabot Elementary School, MA

The Hamster

A hamster is furry
and cute
They can be small like
a speck of dust
When he looks at me
I know he loves me

Joshua Hanson, Grade 1
St Rose School, CT

Lightning

Lightning
Bolts
Hitting the ground
Ziggy zag lights in the sky
Lightning is fast

Jack Candiotti, Grade 1
Fulton Avenue School #8, NY

Cupcakes

Cupcakes are yummy!
So many toppings to choose.
They are oven fresh.

Brendan Skewis, Grade 2
St Rose School, CT

Almost in College

I am almost in college,
and I am happy too
I just can't wait for all that knowledge
I don't know what to do.
I will get a car
It will be a Viper
It will take me far
and keep me safe from a Sniper.
I know that it is true
I just want a Viper
and I want one brand new.
I want to feel the wind
blowing through my hair
Whistling around me and
I won't have a care.

Trevet Williams, Grade 3
Seaford Central Elementary School, DE

The Sea Creature

Sea creatures are blue, red, purple and green
Sea creatures move fast
Sea creatures live in the ocean
Sea creatures eat little sea creatures
Sea creatures are scary

Michael Zappa, Grade 1
Richland Elementary School, PA

My Dear Cat

Once I bought a little cat
Who was eating fish and bread
My cat plays and runs and jumps
He also makes a mess all times.

I named him Stripey he is black and gray
I teach him how to eat and play
He also waits for us at the doors
He misses me, sometimes he snores.

O love my dog and help my cat
My dream to be a greatest vet
I wish to have another pet
I am confused…What tell me dad?

Elizabeth Shoykhet, Grade 2
Our Lady-Grace Elementary School, NY

The Bunny

There was a bunny in my yard.
It stayed there every day.
Then something happened one day.
There was something strange.
The flowers changed.
The bunny ate the flowers.
I wanted to keep the bunny,
But my grandpa said "No!"
I said, "It might be cold,"
But he had to let it go.
I really wanted that bunny.
It could keep me company.

Jessica Tran, Grade 3
Public School 105 Senator Abraham Bernste, NY

Gateway

I am the gateway to learning.
I am the doorway to friends.
I am an opportunity.
An opportunity, waiting to be taken.

To people that hate school, I am dreadful.
To people that love school, I am one of their best friends.
To teachers, I am the beginning of work.

I am the passageway to fun.
I am the transporter to teachers.
I grab children and take them to a whole new world.
I am
The classroom door.

Kiran Butte, Grade 3
General John Nixon Elementary School, MA

A Liefin

This is a Liefin.
A Liefin lives on leafy lilacs and lilies in Louisiana.
A Liefin leisurely eats large lemons and lettuce.
A Liefin likes lots of laughter, lavender, and lava.
A Liefin needed a lawyer when he broke the law
    while weeding the lawn and laughing very hard.
My Liefin got into my pool and ripped the liner
    while licking a lime-flavored lollipop.

Sarah Single, Grade 3
St Clement Mary Hofbauer School, MD

Blue Birds
Baby birds chirping.
Their beautiful blue color.
They are very cute.
Abby Schroding, Grade 3
St Stephen Regional School, PA

Football
Football
Zoom zoom zoom
Trying to get the ball
Got the ball!
You got to be kidding
Someone stole the ball
Now he got a goal
Come on!
Marc Anthony Scaccia, Grade 2
Tashua School, CT

What Is Purple?
I taste jellybeans.
I smell popsicles.
I color with a purple crayon.
I touch grapes.
I see an umbrella.
I see a violet.
I see a sunset.
I see an octopus.
I have a purple shirt.
A purple sky is a sunset.
I feel purple in summer.
I feel a purple rug.
I eat grapes.
Music makes me think of purple!
Anna Dobkowski, Grade 1
St Madeleine Sophie School, NY

Dolphins
Woosh, splash dolphins
Jump through the Florida Ocean.
How beautiful the
Shimmery water is flying
In the air.
Elisabeth Summer Ellison, Grade 3
Somers Elementary School, CT

The Wish
I wish I had a mansion.
I wish I could fly.
I wish I would dance all day.
I wish I was 11.
Morgan Huey, Grade 1
Artman Elementary School, PA

My Clock
My clock goes
tickty tock
the hand goes around and around
ding, ding
it's midnight
the clock struck 12
well got to go to bed
that's what the clock said
bye, bye zzzzzzzzzzzzzzz
Emily Fernandez, Grade 3
Public School 148 Ruby Allen, NY

Frosty
F rosty is still a puppy
R ough though
O ff track all the time
S illy a lot
T akes his toys to his secret layer
Y aps a lot
Alex Gurba, Grade 3
Penn Yan Elementary School, NY

Lines
Lines zigzag
All around
Twirling, swirling
Lines across a blank sheet of snow.
Laura Voltmann, Grade 3
Carlyle C Ring Elementary School, NY

Dolphins
Dolphins go splish splash
Dolphins are cute, very cute
Dolphins love people
Megan Murphy, Grade 3
Somers Elementary School, CT

The Shark
It has razor sharp teeth that can kill anything.
The smooth long body is waiting for prey to come by.
Sharp teeth are moving to eat a clown fish.
The sharp teeth move up and down chewing on the clown fish.
I feel worried when I am around a shark.

Scott Gullquist, Grade 3
St Christopher's School, VA

Spring Is Good
Spring is good.
Spring is good because winter is gone.
Spring smells good,
Spring rain and blossoms on trees make me smile.
In spring I can play outside,
Basketball, soccer and football.

Donnell, Grade 1
Kanner Learning Center, PA

Winter Is
Winter is the smell of chocolate cookies baking.
Winter is playing in the cold, fluffy snow.
Winter is seeing people with hats, scarves, and mittens.
Winter is tasting hot cocoa and soup.
Winter is hearing the children playing on the hills of white, cold snow.
Winter makes me happy.

John Nocus, Grade 1
St Teresa of Avila School, NY

Brown
Brown is the color of chestnut.
Pintos grazing in the meadow.
It is fudge popsicles in the summer.
Cozy by the fireplace winter times and sledding in the snow.
Hot brownie just out of the oven and a group of newborn kittens.

Maya Manaktala, Grade 3
Cabot Elementary School, MA

Summer
Summer is fun you can play sports outside
like baseball and basketball and soccer in the park
Hockey and tennis and swimming too!
Summer is fun you can eat so much ice cream.

Adrian Polanco, Grade 2
Public School 2 Alfred Zimberg, NY

Plants

Plants
Nutritious, healthy
Eating, drinking, standing
Tall, beautiful, ugly, different
Falling, planting, growing
Weak, strong
Vegetation
Julia Niedziela, Grade 3
Brant Elementary School, NY

Cars

Speeding across the highway
bright lights flashing in the night
vehicles pass by
Daniel Clark, Grade 3
Sacred Heart School, CT

The Stars

The stars are high
Up in the sky
They are bright
What a beautiful sight.
Lilly Gallatin, Grade 2
Calvary Chapel Christian School, NY

Spring

S is for sun.
P is for poppy.
R is for rain.
I is for ice cream.
N is for nice weather.
G is for grass.
Lela Festa, Kindergarten
Fisher Hill Elementary School, MA

Spring

S is for sun
P is for playing tag
R is for rose
I is for ice cream
N is for nice weather
G is for going outside
Caden King, Kindergarten
Fisher Hill Elementary School, MA

The Soccer Game

I like to play sports.
Even if I'm short.
I got the last goal.
Inside the big hole.

I was so happy.
I went to pappy.
I got a present.
I am so pleasant.
Jadon Madeo, Grade 3
Bensley Elementary School, VA

A Sick Dragon

A dragon who developed strep throat.
He wore a very fluffy coat.
He burned his coat and ran away.
People said he was a stray.
So he took a trip on a boat.
Dylan Carey, Grade 2
Oakdale Elementary School, MD

Books Everywhere!

I always see books here,
then way over there.

Books, books here and there,
I always see them everywhere!

One book is really fat,
that it looks like a fat cat.

The other book was tall and thin
all about people's skin.
Anthony Fallah, Grade 3
Holy Rosary School, NY

Belize

Belize
Warm, sunny
Swimming, sun bathing, sailing
Best place to be
Paradise
Kyle Cruz, Grade 2
Buckley Country Day School, NY

Dogs

Dogs are cute and fuzzy like a teddy bear.
They make me smile every day when they play in the hay.
When I come near them I make their day they say.
I love them so much all in a bunch.
They are cool in the pool.
They bark all day because whenever I lay
they get all mad so they pounce in the hay.

Skyla Owens, Grade 2
Shady Grove Elementary School, PA

Kent Gardens

K ids that listen to their teachers
E lementary that our teachers work, day-in day-out.
N ew days that we have to learn about the world.
T albert, the teacher she rocks!

G ardens, that we are seeds of
A rt we all love.
R ound of applause.
D octor Strats she's our P.E. teacher
E xcellent kids and teachers that work side by side.
N ice people helping us to learn.
S ounds that are every where calling us to learn.

Sheilan Pouri, Grade 2
Kent Gardens Elementary School, VA

My Horse Teddy

Teddy is always there waiting
waiting as proud as a peacock
waiting for me to come
as he runs up to me as quick as lightning but still keeping safe safer than a house
but I still know he is as delicate as a flower but still as wise as an owl
as I watch him run as free as a bird I can tell he is happy and I am too

Sarah Noyes, Grade 3
General John Nixon Elementary School, MA

Love

Oh, dear,
Oh, dear,
what can I say?
Just take my hand
and we will go away.

Julian Ledesma, Grade 2
Public School 152 School of Science & Technology, NY

Baseball

I am a baseball
My white cover is the shiniest
When I get hit I soar over the fence
My red stripes give people grip
I am a baseball
When I get caught I am trapped
When I get thrown I soar into gloves
My core is as hard as a rock

Thomas Jackson, Grade 3
St Christopher's School, VA

Horses

galloping, clip-clop-clopping
through town
at parades
or festivals
it sounds like
music
to my ears
snapping hooves on the tar

Haley Furtado, Grade 3
Acushnet Elementary School, MA

Silver

I look into my silver mirror
and I see me
Someone is driving a silver car
Stars look silver at night sometimes
I can hear my silver radio
I like to hear the song called
"If Cupid Had a Heart"
You can buy some apples
with a shiny silver nickel

Ann Nguyen, Grade 1
Willis E Thorpe School, MA

The Moon

The moon is bright
near the stars at night
The moon is so bright
you can go camping
and watch the moonlight.

Santiago Barrera, Grade 2
Public School 2 Alfred Zimberg, NY

Cake

Cake is good.
Take a cake.
Yellow cake or chocolate cake.
Blue frosting or green icing.
Sweet, sweet maple cake.
I love to bake!

Ilona Ludanyi, Grade 2
St Rose School, CT

Spring Has Sprung

Spring has sprung
Oh yes, it has begun
Everybody is playing
And having some fun
So come on let's go

The sun is shining
While I play
The flowers are blooming
So let's all smell
The beauty of spring
Hurray!

Noorshifa Arssath, Grade 3
Public School 69 Jackson Heights, NY

Sunset

Golden rays with red and orange,
Peel across the sky,
All of peace and quiet,
See a starry night.

Anna Moffat, Grade 3
Center School, MA

Lion

Lion, lion
You run so much faster than me.
Lion, lion
You are warm and furry.
You eat meat,
Take a bath,
Drink water...
Just like me.

Tyrone Greene, Grade 2
Public School 122 Mamie Fay, NY

Spring

Spring smells good!
Hyacines, Morning Glories, Gardenias and Tulips.
Spring is pretty.
Daffodils, Crocuses, Daisies, Cherry Blossoms, and Roses are pretty.
It makes me feel good.
The weather feels good, it makes me comfortable.
I like to hear the birds singing.
I like to see baby bunnies.
Thank you, Spring!

Ashley, Grade 1
Kanner Learning Center, PA

The Strangest Moment

I go down the mountain waterfall and look in the river and see
Someone's reflection but it can't be me
It's definitely someone else, I start to say "No"
But the reflection tells me "Please don't go"
I don't know how but I think I've turned into this person inside
Then I thought I've got nowhere to hide
I looked at her and I was sad
I learned in those moments to be the person you want to be
And then your reflection you'll be happy to see

Savannah McClendon, Grade 3
Orenda Elementary School, NY

Birds

Birds fly and tweet and they wake up in the morning. There are different
birds. There are birds that are scared and birds that are not scared. There are
baby birds, big birds. There are lots of birds in this world. Birds can fly high in
the sky. There are hummingbirds, macaws and fish hawks. Some birds swim in
the water. There are brown birds, white birds, ducks, whistling ducks.

Sammy Touati, Grade 2
Public School 2 Alfred Zimberg, NY

If I Were...

If I were yellow, I'd be a banana from the store.
If I were red, I'd be a heart pumping blood.
If I were people, I'd be sprinkles on my ice cream.
If I were gray, I'd be a race car speeding on a track.
If I were orange, I'd be a ribbon in my hair.
If I were brown, I'd be a piece of wood on the ground.
If I were colorful, I'd be a rainbow in the sky after it rains.

Bailey Mullen, Grade 1
St Clement Mary Hofbauer School, MD

Flowers
Blooming everywhere
colors all around me now
sprouting joyfully
Jarod Kosman, Grade 3
Sacred Heart School, CT

Spring
S unflower
P igs
R ose
I nchworm
N est
G rasshopper
Gavin Nolan, Kindergarten
Willis E Thorpe School, MA

Addi
My sister, Addi
Falls in the house.
After a long nap
She gets up and giggles
She has not hurt herself.
Grayson Walsh, Grade 2
St Christopher's School, VA

Winter
Snow is great
I can't wait!
We'll build snowmen
We won't go in until ten.
Sledding we will go
It's fun you know!
Angelique Volper, Grade 3
Penn-Kidder Campus, PA

Winter Bloom
The snow is white
The light makes it so bright!
The snow is white
Let's have a fight!
We are going skating
But now I am stuck waiting!
Trinity Zapata, Grade 3
Penn-Kidder Campus, PA

Winter Woes
Winter in which thin, white, snow is spread,
Just like butter on bread,
The trees are bare and leafless,
Everything looks dull and dead.

Frosty are the leaves that lie,
On the snow covered ground,
Little flakes fall from the sky,
And land on earth without a sound.

Every thing covered white,
Oh what a sad sight,
Specks of white coming from a great height,
Engulfing me in a desire to take the next
international flight.

But if I wait, the birds will come,
Out with them, will come the joyous sun,
Time to laugh and have some fun,
Soon winter will be finally done.

Sorrow and joy will come and go,
Like spring and winter will always flow,
But if I stand firm and tolerate,
Joy and peace will be my mate.
Nimai Agarwal, Grade 3
The Learning Community, MD

Beach
Waves bashing and crashing into me.
Surfers riding the water.
Dolphins jumping with joy.
Kids riding boogie boards.
Parents relaxing on the hot soft sandy beach.
Darren Sipf, Grade 3
Robeson Elementary School, PA

Who's Right Jack
Once I saw a man named Jack
Who had a tan all over his back.
I told Jack I came back from Mr. Funkin.
He told me I looked like a pumpkin.
Sam Grigsby, Grade 2
Trinity Christian School, VA

Spring

S un shining
P opsicles melting
R aining hard on rooftops
I ce cream being eaten from the D.Q.
N oses smelling flowers
G etting to hear birds chirp.
Caroline Moffet, Grade 3
Edgartown Elementary School, MA

The Star

Shining bright on a starry night
Floating higher than a plane
We wish on the highest height
We hope we get a wish every night
That's a star alight
The star is so very bright
Sydney Hay, Grade 2
Buckley Country Day School, NY

Zipping Electricity

Zipping,
zapping
electricity,
around and around
it goes.

Down
down
down
to the ground.
It travels deeply
through the ground!
Adam Lebowitz, Grade 2
Dr Samuel C Eveleth School, MA

Spring

S is for sunshine
P is for plants
R is for run
I is for ice cream
N is for no snow
G is for grass
Sam Tucker, Kindergarten
Fisher Hill Elementary School, MA

Rose

A beautiful garden.
Sharp thorns can prick you.
A pretty rose.
Asia Hilliard, Grade 2
Bensley Elementary School, VA

Wild Wonders

galloping across a wide
stormy beach,
soaring through the tide pools,
crashing against the waves,
making rain of their own,
water flying through their
glistening manes,
splashing, a storm of
their own
Olivia Ross, Grade 3
Thoreau Elementary School, MA

How to Find a Poem

I keep on trying
trying
trying
trying to find the secrets
of the world

Hidden under the bramberry bush
or in the lilacs
and the design and craft

And so much depends
depends
depends
on everything,
everything around us,
everything with us
trying
trying to tell how important
we are and
I keep on trying
trying
to learn the hidden secret place
Ari Oser Miller, Grade 3
Slingerlands Elementary School, NY

Dinosaur

D estructive and very naughty.
I ncredible creatures.
N ot very nice.
O dd monsters.
S uper strong things
A ngry animals.
U nusual species
R ough animals

Dylan Czymmek, Grade 3
Penn Yan Elementary School, NY

Sky Pie

I spy a pie in the sky
Why?
I don't know why
It's found in the clouds,
Could it be round?
Wow!
I wonder how?

Lindsay Wright, Grade 3
Heron Pond Elementary School, NH

Baseball

B ases are loaded
A aron, our best batter is up to bat
S everal people are cheering
E verybody screaming
B est batter hit the ball!
A Homerun!
L osing team lost
L ine up and we all shake hands.

Brayden Armpriester, Grade 3
Robeson Elementary School, PA

My Car

Zooming!
Stopping!
Going!
Running down the highway.
R-r-r-t…Stop!
Keep on going.
Almost there.

Natalie Smith, Grade 1
Hyman Fine Elementary School, MA

Leprechauns

Silly, tiny
Golfing, working, playing
Always making a shoe
The wee ones.

Nolan Frisbie, Grade 2
Long Meadow Elementary School, CT

My Dad

Dad is cool.
He helps me with school.
He works all day.
Then he comes home to play.

Jacob Gohring, Grade 1
Hyman Fine Elementary School, MA

The Pretty Dog

I like that
pretty dog.
It looks like
a pink and red hog.

Akira Williams, Grade 1
Hebbville Elementary School, MD

Winter

Crunch crunch
as I step
into the diamonds
of winter

I look up
in the indigo sky
and see the
winter birds
fly by

and I see
the clouds that
look like cotton candy

I wish
winter would
never end

Meryl Phair, Grade 3
Sinai Academy of the Berkshires, MA

Flowers

Flowers make me happy
Even on the days that I'm feeling grumpy

Some are small and some are big
Some flowers smell good some smell nasty
Some are cute like a Pansy
Flowers grow everywhere even the park
Flowers have different names
You can use them in games
Flowers are pretty and different size petals.
Everyone love flowers even if you listen to heavy metal.

Britney Boothe, Grade 2
Great Oaks Elementary School, NY

Letter to March*
Dear March:

I am having a good time in school.
How are you doing?
You are nice and cold to warm my heart.
How glad I am to see you.
And your winds are lovely and soft to blow me away.
Your whispers make me giggle and laugh.
Oh March, oh March.
I have met all your friends, like September and October.
I have so much to tell you in my days.
How are you feeling?
How's Mrs. March and Mr. March?
My days are wonderful.
Winter is cold and so are you.
You wash away the snow.
I'm very, very fine.

Love, Luca

Luca Swinford, Grade 2
Roger E Wellington School, MA
*In the style of Emily Dickinson

Butterflies

Butterfly, butterfly flying through trees feeling the breeze.
Isn't it so swell to be a butterfly and to be free outdoors?
A butterfly is special because it's a butterfly and its own self.

Evita Burgjia, Grade 2
Public School 2 Alfred Zimberg, NY

Strawberry Lollipop
The strawberry lollipop flavor
swirls in my mouth
and it gets ready to explode
into a...
rainbow of flavor!
Christina Vlamis, Grade 2
Tashua School, CT

A Catching Moment
The sound of fans cheering,
screaming, yelling fans.
The sound of breathing,
nervous breathing.
The tall batter,
the pitcher,
small and far away.
The feel of the mask,
loose on my face.
The glove,
warm and wet.
The taste of sweat.
The smell of leather,
Rawlings leather.
The smell of sunflower seeds.
Andrew Theve, Grade 3
Fannie E Proctor School, MA

Bakery
The cashier
asks me
what I
want
I say
unbelievable
goodies
Tyler Blose, Grade 2
Tashua School, CT

Me
I like pink roses.
I love to sing in the rain.
I like to jump rope.
Teah Renzi, Grade 2
St Rose School, CT

Aggression
Aggression is as red as blood.
It sounds like the fires of war.
Aggression tastes like stale bread.
And smells like smelly old gym socks.
It looks like a bloody battlefield.
Aggression makes you feel ready for an attack.
William Horne, Grade 3
St Christopher's School, VA

Going to High School
Going to high school will be a big change.
At first it could seem a little strange.
I hope it's not extremely hard.
So I get good grades on my report card.
Dimitri Kombogiorgas, Grade 3
Public School 2 Alfred Zimberg, NY

School
I'm in second grade
I like gym, art and music
School is my favorite
Dillon Guiberson, Grade 2
Fonda-Fultonville Elementary School, NY

A Beautiful Day
On a beautiful day like today;
I can't wait to go outside
With my sisters and play.

We jump, skip and run everywhere;
Until my mom tells us "Come over here."

We have lots of fun;
All day in the wonderful sun,
I wish I could always be young.

Later we'll all sit down to eat;
When we are done,
My mom gives us a treat.

When it is dark, it's time for bed;
I can't wait for the next day ahead.
Lenny Isaacson, Grade 3
Our Lady of Hope School, NY

Conch Shell

I can hear the ocean in that tiny conch shell
there must be an ocean there with sharks and whales
and dolphins everywhere
fish starfish and octopuses too
crabs and lobsters that try to pinch you
seals sea lions and sea anemones
are all in that tiny shell
I wish I could just go inside and see the ocean in that
tiny conch shell

Isabel Larkin Isselbacher, Grade 2
Cabot Elementary School, MA

Rain Drop

I am a wet, sparkly, cold rain drop,
as I fall through the sky I go plip, plop, plip, plop.
As I splash on the ground making big puddles for little kids to play in,
because of these raindrops all of the children will wear a grin.

Lauren Proulx, Grade 3
Calvary Road Christian School, VA

Deep Forest

Ribbons of pine trees
cover this land
roots with soggy wet soil rise up —
a liquid so strong
and with a tree-like smell
Nature peeks around everywhere
with the plumpest tree trunks
and the most moist air anyone could dream of.
When you're in the deep forest it looks like
your trapped in brick walls and just through the bushy
tree tops you can see the smallest light glow.

Meghan Hurley, Grade 3
Lincoln Elementary School, PA

A Bumblebee

Oh I wish I were a bumblebee,
Stinging people some two or three.
I'm black and yellow on the outside
But a pure little mean fellow on the inside.
I have a bottom with a stinger
You better not touch me with your finger.

Hamzah Naeem, Grade 3
Public School 105 Senator Abraham Bernste, NY

Flower

Flower, Flower
you're beautiful
you're smelly
you're pretty
like a butterfly's
wings, stand in
the sun
morning to
night
don't even
take
don't even
wake
don't even go
to the
lake

Tasnim Hyder, Grade 3
Public School 69 Jackson Heights, NY

The Game of Life

Night time
When the world
Shuts down
Like a video game
Not a sound can be heard
Except a cricket a mile away

In the light
Quite the opposite
The game is on
Ready to play
The lovely game of
Life

Tanner Reed, Grade 3
Acushnet Elementary School, MA

Fall

I love fall.
In the fall, I like to play ball.
When I play ball, my sister will fall.
When she falls she will call.
I'll help her even though she's tall.

Rose Bailey, Grade 2
Willis E Thorpe School, MA

Crazy Dog

People say this dog is nice,
It's not

When you walk past his yard,
He barks

He doesn't care who it is,
He just barks

This dog chased me down the street
This dog is as fierce as a lion
This dog thinks he's a guard dog

This dog is crazy!

Reed Oettinger, Grade 3
Meeting House Hill School, CT

Leprechauns

Happy, small,
Tricking, dancing, singing,
Happy, little, wee ones
Little people

Danielle Schloss, Grade 2
Long Meadow Elementary School, CT

The Fish

I met two
funny fish their names are
Bliss and Miss

Kiersyn Fisher, Grade 1
Hebbville Elementary School, MD

Elephants

E xcellent
L ovely
E ndangered
P hysical
H igh
A wesome
N omads
T usks
S pecies

Lindsay Garbacik, Grade 2
Highland Elementary School, PA

What Am I? Fun, But More
I need to be sharpened after I'm used.
I need to be waxed after I'm used.
They jostle me, they carry me,
What's more they always slam the door on me.
I wear a leash, sometimes it's long, sometimes it's short.
Sometimes it's white, sometimes it's black.
I come in all colors and sizes.
I'm tall and I'm small.
Used by the young, used by the old.
They have fun when they're using me.
Ouch! They always step on me.
What could I be?

CJ Thacker, Grade 3
Cabot Elementary School, MA

Summer Time
Summer is a lot of fun.
I love to jump and run.
My favorite snack is a honey bun.
Among the beautiful flowers the bumble bees hum.
I love the hot, long, sunny days.
My friends and I love to play, play, play.
Some things I do keep me cool
Is go to the beach or swim in the pool.
I also eat icies or ice cream to keep me cool.
Every summer I go to the Great Oaks summer school
Where learning is fun and that is cool, cool, cool!

Lauren Harris, Grade 2
Great Oaks Elementary School, NY

All About Me
Slone
Fast, lover, sad, artistic
Sibling of Selena, Cody, AJ, Shaun, William and Billy
Love of whole family
Who feels loved
Who needs a hug
Who gives a present
Who fears wild animals
Who would like to see New York City
Susquehanna PA
Sissy

Slone Chandler, Grade 3
Susquehanna Community Elementary School, PA

Our Times

I'm glad
I live
In our times
Where it is
Not full of distractions.
For if I lived in
Prehistoric times
When I went to school
There would be
interruptions.
So I'm glad
I live
In our times
Where I
Am safe!

Thurston Moore, Grade 2
St Christopher's School, VA

Bunnies

Bunnies
Are funny,
Silly and soft
They can run far
Without having to stop!

Max Huntington, Grade 2
Cabot Elementary School, MA

Maps

Maps,
Google, Yahoo
Driving, printing, searching
Maps make me happy
Streets

Jesse Corey, Grade 2
Cabot Elementary School, MA

Pillows

So soft and fuzzy.
Just like a stuffed animal.
I doze on it every night.
Guess what I don't have
A PILLOW!

Hannah Cohen, Grade 2
Tashua School, CT

Cocoa

C ocoa is my favorite food.
O ver the top with marshmallows or,
C overed with whipped cream if you like.
O ver all the states cocoa is good
A little pinch of cinnamon makes it nice.

Aisha Foster, Grade 3
Sacred Heart School, MA

My Poppop

My Poppop was living not too long ago.
But he died at 10:15 at night in September.
I was sad when he died.
My Mom, Dad, and I were sobbing.
I was sad…

Nathaniel Stoddard, Grade 3
Robeson Elementary School, PA

What Is Spring

S uper cool days
P retty flowers blooming
R unning in the cool wind
I ce cream man coming down the road
N ice green grass
G oing to baseball games

Jenna Scudero, Grade 3
Helen B Duffield Elementary School, NY

Xena My Dog

I have a dog named Xena.
She knows a dog named Leena.
Xena and Leena moved to Argentina.
Then they had some Leena and Xena lemonade.
Leena and Xena are the nicest dogs I know.

Alex Sipinick, Grade 2
Public School 205 Alexander Graham Bell, NY

Frogs

Frogs are green like the grass of a backyard.
Frogs hipitty hop a lot through the sky.
It doesn't make a frog stop.
If you have a pet tell them to stop hopping a lot.
Also set them free for a new life.

Nicole Mendoza, Grade 3
Public School 2 Alfred Zimberg, NY

Scarlet

Scarlet is a ripe, autumn apple dangling from a branch.
Scarlet sounds like a cardinal's sweet song.
Scarlet looks like shiny cherries in a dessert bowl.
Scarlet feels like a ladybug tickling my arm.
Scarlet smells like a tulip scenting the spring air.

Lily Berkin, Grade 3
Weston Intermediate School, CT

Spring Is Coming

Spring, spring it is fun.
You can do anything in spring like swim or ride on a bike,
or even have a picnic with your mom.

Brendon Fridman, Grade 1
Joseph Greenberg School, PA

My Mom*

My mom my mom my mom.
I love my mom I hug my mom,
I kiss my mom I cuddle with my mom,
I sing with my mom and dance with my mom.
I watch TV with my mom and I play with my mom.
I tell stories with my mom and I build things with my mom,
I do puzzles with my mom and I swim with mom,
I type with my mom and laugh with my mom.
I go to the beach with my mom.
I go to the park with my mom.
I go to vacations with my mom.
I eat with my mom,
I draw with my mom,
I plant with my mom,
I jump with my mom.
As you can see I love my mom so very much
I love my mom

Anjali Bisaria, Grade 2
William B Ward Elementary School, NY
*Dedicated to my mom

The Season

Spring is a time of year when birds make their nest.
Summer is a day you can go to the beach.
Fall is a time when the leaves fall off the trees.
Winter is a time of year when you can sled.

Gabriella Kovalski, Grade 1
Hyman Fine Elementary School, MA

I Love My Family

I love my mommy.
She is nice and she is kind.
And I love my daddy. He is nice.
And I love Ily.
And I love Cajun.

Hannah Fleenor, Grade 1
St John Neumann Academy, VA

Loose Tooth

Wibble tooth
Wobble tooth
Pulling teeth
Slamming doors
Ahhhh!
The tooth is
Running away!
Running, jumping!
Help! Get my
Tooth!

Nick Sierzenga, Grade 2
Milton Terrace Primary School, NY

Rain*

Pitter patter pitter patter
helps plants grow
makes puddles on the street very neat
the sun a spark between dark and dark
colors like rainbows
very peaceful
as you can see
a rainbow for
you and me

Li Huan Shandross, Grade 2
Cabot Elementary School, MA
*Inspired by John Updike's "January"

Ben's Life

There once was a fox named Ben,
Whose family lived in a den,
His family died.
And he married a bride,
So the family expanded again!

Henry Hu, Grade 3
Middlebury Elementary School, CT

Clarabelle

Clarabelle is a cat,
she likes to chase rats.

She is so kind,
she's also mine.

She likes to play,
once a day.

She sleeps in my bed,
and is always near my head.

Alexa Casacci, Grade 3
Ellicott Road Elementary School, NY

Spring

S pring is here!
P lants are growing
R ain comes down
I like to see raindrops fall
N o more winter
G reen leaves grow

Savir Madan, Grade 1
Frenchtown Elementary School, CT

Salamander's Search

Stream
Water
Moving quickly
Over the rocks.

Salamander
Slimy
Crawling fast
To the stream.

Alex Vaught, Grade 1
St John Neumann Academy, VA

Rockets

Rockets are like pencils
Except humans can't lift them
They lift themselves
Rockets draw orbits

Evan Rubinstein, Grade 1
Buckley Country Day School, NY

Spring

Springtime is finally here.
Best season of the year,
The birds are singing.
People are walking, jogging, and laughing.

Erik Reyes, Grade 3
Public School 105 Senator Abraham Bernste, NY

Spring Is Here!

Leaves, leaves everywhere,
Down, up, all around. Zip zap to the ground.
Colors in the air, even in your hair. 1 2 3 spring is here.

Samara Reisbord, Grade 1
Joseph Greenberg School, PA

A Dream

As a baby I was as red as a fiery red tomato
Lying there in my jail like crib carefree as a Great Blue Heron.
As I sat there on those long, long days resembling a comfortable and happy pony.
Just lying there still, while a dream was hatching.
As my life went on it was starting to get harder
But my dream went on.
As a 3rd grader my dream grows stronger soon it is as strong as a bull.
For now I know about facts and reality.
One day it is a dream no more it is a thought, a hope, a possibility.
In my future the thought will grow stronger
Just like it did when I was a baby.
That's how I know I will be President.

Ryan Ewing, Grade 3
General John Nixon Elementary School, MA

Birds

Winter's the time when birds fly south
Because there's no food to fill their mouths.
Spring's the time for birds to sing.
Mallard hen's ducklings are out,
And mama hummingbird's little babies are fluttering all about.
Summer's another happy season for birds,
They have all the food they need, both insects and worms.
Fall's another time when there's not food for all,
And birds fly south both big and small.
So now the birds have flown away, the end.
Or should I say, another year begins.

Soledad Green, Grade 3
Trinity Christian School, VA

The Storm

Lightning strikes! Little sharp
Bullets so pointy when
It gets sharp and pointy
It's like a needle on the end.
Then it starts to strike
Pshshsh!
BOOM!
here comes the
Thunder
Bowling balls
Tumbling down out of
The clouds
BOOM BOOM BOOM
The lightning is back
BxtBaBoom Zap tiny bullets
coming down to earth
Bzzt
Pshshsh!
The clouds are
Crying so hard
Pshpshshm!

Noah Eisel, Grade 1
Fulton Avenue School #8, NY

Money Bunny

My funny bunny
Has lots of money
She is very rich and funny!
I like to play with her
She is so funny!
I said "ha, ha, ha,
I love my funny bunny."

Victoria Zelaya, Grade 1
Park Avenue School, NY

Summer

Hot, sunny
Jogging, swimming, tanning
Pool, beach, sun, camp
Snowing, raining, sledding
Cold, enjoyable
Winter

William Howells, Grade 3
St Christopher's School, VA

A Book

A book looks as creative as a lovely paragraph
A book sounds as great as a cute little puppy
A book smells as clean as a washing machine
A book tastes as sweet as a birthday cake
A book feels as smooth as a piece of ice
A book is my favorite thing

Kristen Eichele, Grade 3
Sunrise Drive Elementary School, NY

Baseball

B atting a baseball out of the park
A iming the ball toward the catcher's mitt
S imple to get a single
E dgar Renteria is a baseball player
B arry Bonds is too
A lex Rodriguez is my favorite
L opez is a player on the Red Sox
L oving the game of baseball

Noah Ng, Grade 3
Center School, MA

I Am

I am special,
So are you.
I am nice, I am sweet,
I am like a big treat.
I am honest, I am respectful,
I have good self-discipline.
I am very responsible,
I take care of my little sister Molly and
my dog too.
I am a good daughter and good at helping,
I am perfect just the way I am.

Maggie Cox, Grade 2
St Mary's Primary School, MA

Little Miss Red

My favorite color is red.
I dress in red from my toes to my head!
I even sleep in a red car bed!
It is often said,
"I'm little Miss Red!"

Jocelyn Wazolek, Grade 1
Christ the King School, NY

Spring
Spring is here
Shout and yell
Flowers blooming as wonderful
As can be
Good days in spring
Mackenzie Wyllie, Grade 3
Somers Elementary School, CT

Fall Is…
Fall is orange, red, yellow, and brown.
It tastes like sweet, juicy apples.
It smells like rotting leaves.
Fall reminds me of a full moon
And sounds like crows.
Fall feels like squishy pumpkin pulp.
Joshua Solomon, Grade 2
Curtisville Primary Center, PA

Spring
S weet fresh air
P rize of joy everywhere
R ipe fresh fruit
I n the spring kids play for fun
N othing better than lemonade
G ood smiles of joy
Ashley Nguyen, Grade 3
Heron Pond Elementary School, NH

Baseball
Hitting a homerun.
Sitting in seats like a fan.
It is so much fun.
Andy Clough, Grade 2
Dr Samuel C Eveleth School, MA

Spring
S pring signs are here
P lant your flowers
R ain is coming
I n spring, it is warm
N ot a lot of snow
G rowing plants
Karissa Delli Carpini, Grade 1
Frenchtown Elementary School, CT

The Butterfly
Up in the tree
I see it move
It flies away
It dances in the sky
It flutters up
It flutters down
The beautiful butterfly.
Eleana Tsiamtsiouris, Grade 2
Buckley Country Day School, NY

My Dog
Charlie
Black, smart
Runs a lot
He has a brother
Chihuahua
Nicholas Kapon, Grade 3
Alexander Robertson School, NY

Star Dazzle
Hello, my name is Myah,
And I do not like papaya.
I can sing like Sharpay,
And I like to do ballet.
Whenever I get the chance,
My feet just LOVE to dance!
Someday I might be in a show,
Just keep watching you never know!
Myah Koepfer, Grade 1
St Joan of Arc School, PA

The Beach
The beach is as pretty as a flower
So, I could be there for hours
And then,
I saw a whale in the sea
And now I'm as happy as can be
The day was nice
The day was fun
But now it's time to be in the sun
I looked up at the sky
And it was as blue as the sea.
Cana Courtney, Grade 3
Edgartown Elementary School, MA

Poems

Poems come, poems go
Poems hide, poems don't
But all the rest is not better
Then poems we read in a book
Kyle Horning, Grade 3
Washington Elementary School, PA

The Googley Wooden Puppet

That googley wooden puppet —
looks like somebody
wiped his mind, he looks
so dusty —
      like he's been
in the attic —
        for years
Jack Vasu, Grade 2
Cabot Elementary School, MA

The Sun Is Away

The sun is away
For a great summer day
For now there is rain
Which is a big pain
I miss you sun
Rain be done
The sun is away
For a great summer day

Rain is in store
It's coming some more
I will say it again
And then, and then…
WAIT
It stopped!
Julia Schreder, Grade 3
Weston Intermediate School, CT

Summer

Summertime
It's summertime
I play ball with Ryan Eddy.
The waterslide is really cool!
John Schickedanz, Grade 2
St Madeleine Sophie School, NY

Dear God

Dear God,
I want peace in the world.
At home, in bed, I say 'hello'
to you in my mind.
I like it to be quiet when I'm in bed.
In school, in the library,
it is peaceful in the corner
reading books with the music on.
No one talks.
Loud and noisy is not peaceful.
No fights at school either.
I like peace because it is always quiet.
Ben Brennan, Grade 1
Glover Elementary School, MA

Kite Thoughts

Seeing kites outside
The gentle breeze carries them
What a lovely sight
Grace Zhou, Grade 2
Guilford Lakes School, CT

Subway

Driving
In the tunnels
Dark and deep
When the train
Stops
The man
Opens the doors
Then he says
The next stop is
Time Square 42 street
When the train starts
It moves
Slow
Faster and faster
Faster faster faster
Makes too much noise
Then it slowly
Goes to the last stop
On the train.
Freddy Reyes, Grade 2
Public School 122 Mamie Fay, NY

The Win

T he coaches teach you the moves. You push harder and harder trying to get it
just right for the win.
H itting the mat again and again, sometimes on top sometimes on bottom.
Working hard for the win.
E xercising and getting yourself in the very best shape, knowing that it will help
you get the win.

W hen the job is done you just might have won
I know how hard it is because I've been there and I can say that
N othing beats the win. Well, the wins are good, but it's really all about having fun!

Cole Cutright, Grade 2
Thomas Jefferson Elementary School, VA

I Am Kylie Priest

I am smart and cheerful
I wonder if the wars will ever stop
I hear the ocean waves crashing on the beach in Hawaii
I see the soft golden sand and palm trees of the beach
I want all people in my family to be healthy
I am smart and cheerful

I pretend my dog can speak
I feel one day all wars will stop
I touch God's hand above
I worry someone bad is watching me
I cry when I think of my family members that have died
I am smart and cheerful

I understand that I can think for my own self
I say if you don't believe in yourself, you're wrong
I dream that one day all of my dreams will come true
I try to achieve at everything I do
I hope I will achieve success in the future
I am smart and cheerful

Kylie Priest, Grade 3
Stony Point Elementary School, NY

Dark Blue

Dark blue is like the sound of a river quickly going past me.
Dark blue is like the smell of a fresh new shirt from the store.
Dark blue is like the taste of a fresh Lifesaver from a bag with all different colors.
Dark blue is like the feel of a smooth piece of paper.

Michael Savoyski, Grade 2
Long Meadow Elementary School, CT

Wind

Wind is whistling
Swirling
Wind is spinning
around around
Wind is moving
Swoosh, swoosh
Wind is fading away
in the distance
So long wind.

Lianne Iassogna, Grade 2
Tashua School, CT

My Mouse

I have a mouse,
She lives in my house
She will play
For one day
She ripped my blouse.

Danielle Demming, Grade 1
Geneva School, PA

Golf

Bam!
Here I come
Zoom!
So close
Bam!
Here I come
Oh yeah!
Hole in one!

Valerie Eigenrauch, Grade 2
Tashua School, CT

Igneous Rocks

Igneous rocks
Are made from fire.
They come from volcanos
Across the world.
Some are
Basalt,
Pitchstone,
And Granite.

Alston Hackney, Grade 2
St Christopher's School, VA

Bears

Bears are nocturnal
Live in caves when winter comes
They mate in the spring.

Brittany Graham, Grade 3
Bradford Township Elementary School, PA

Frogs and Flies

Frogs,
slimy, slippery,
jumping, slurping, eating,
A fly flew by —
buzzing, pesting, biting,
the frog flicks out his tongue,
lunchtime!

Joshua Houser, Grade 3
Our Mother of Perpetual Help School, PA

The Seasons

Today we are in spring
It is such a wonderful thing
It is when the flowers spring
And that's why they call it spring.

Now it is summer
We have no school
The sun comes out
And we can play in the pool
I wish these three months were every day.

Now it is fall
It is one of my favorite times of the year
But sometimes I have fear
Of the winds outside.

Now it is winter
We can build a snowman
And then when we go inside
We can make a fire.
I love all the seasons
From spring to winter
But the season that I love the most
Has to be winter, brrrrr!!!

Tora Crank, Grade 3
Trinity Christian School, VA

Red
Red is like my
big sweet apple.
Red is like my
boat.
Red is like
my rose.

Ashley Haynes, Grade 2
Public School 152 School of Science & Technology, NY

Phrases Heard
Wake up!
Get out of bed!
And don't forget to eat your bread!

Brush your teeth, and fix your hair.
Is that really what you'd like to wear?

Have you practiced the piano?
I really am hoping so.

Let's march out the door.
The bus always comes at 8:34.

Welcome Home!
Unpack your bag and grab a seat.
Would you like a pineapple treat?

Go over your reading, check your math.
I can't remember your last bath.

I love you my Clare, could you please get all snug?
I really want to give you a great big hug.

Good Night!

Clare Meehan, Grade 3
East Farms School, CT

I Ate a Ton of Sugar
I ate a ton of sugar.
It was very, very sweet.
It made me so round.
Now I can't see my feet.

Kiara McGill, Grade 3
Public School 105 Senator Abraham Bernste, NY

Martial Arts Are Cool
My Martial Arts are cool
I could do a back flip
10 times in
one minute
and I
also know
how to
do back
jump flip
Martial Arts are cool
Varun R. Chennamdhava, Grade 3
Public School 69 Jackson Heights, NY

Conductor
If I were a conductor
I'd like cool trains.
Trains that go underground
Trains that go fast and
Trains that you can drink cocoa on.
Charlie Whitlock, Grade 1
St Christopher's School, VA

Heartbroken
Heartbroken
is red like the color of a
broken heart and also like
a hard brick wall.
It makes me feel upset like
I'm in the red hole in Jupiter.
Ava Roche, Grade 3
Somers Elementary School, CT

Twins Are Not Fun
Twins are not fun.
Because I have one myself.
All she does is boast and complain.
I hate my twin.
Oh no, she ripped, she ripped!
In a weird way, I'm sad.
I miss my twin.
I'm sorry twin. I ripped you.
I guess I'll just draw another one!
Helena Sabo, Grade 2
St Rose School, CT

My Mom
With my mom, I snuggle
With my mom, I "huggle."
With my mom, I play dodge ball.
With my mom, I play softball.
Annabelle Patton, Grade 2
Trinity Christian School, VA

Spring
S pring is awesome
P lant the flowers
R ain is falling
I love spring
N ew flowers growing
G rowing roses
Mackenzie Neary, Grade 1
Frenchtown Elementary School, CT

When School Is Out
I see my hyper puppy running all day,
I hear birds every day in the trees,
I taste chocolate, soda, and cookies,
I smell fresh air floating in my house,
I feel the new green grass in my yard.
Bailey Winch, Grade 3
Granville Elementary School, NY

Dear Seed
Dear Seed,

I heard that you got planted yesterday
So can I come and see you tomorrow?
If you can't we can do it the next day.

Your friend,
Flower
Ben Gansenberg, Grade 1
Glover Elementary School, MA

March
On a cold March day.
Rain comes down fast and furious.
Thunder rumbles loud.
Jeremy Fisher, Grade 2
St Rose School, CT

School
School,
I like school.
It is fun
and it helps me learn.
School makes me smile.
It is nice to get to another grade.
School,
I like school.

Kalli Roye, Grade 2
Public School 152 School of Science & Technology, NY

Fireworks!
Fireworks are flashy.
They light up the sky with all the different colors.
I love to see them fly on Fourth of July.
I like to watch the fireworks in the nighttime sky.

Kirsten Pettinelli, Grade 2
Dr Samuel C Eveleth School, MA

Imagine That…
Imagine that you are a bird soaring in the sky.
Imagine that you are a star glittering in the moonlight.
Imagine that you are a flower in a meadow.
Imagine that you are a leaf moving in the wind.
Imagine that you are a tree growing in a field.
Imagine that you are a deer walking with pride.
Imagine that you are a rabbit hopping with pleasure.
Imagine that you are a rock sitting in the woods.
Imagine that you are a bush showing off its beauty.
Imagine that you are a fence protecting a treasure.
Imagine that you are a plant growing in a pot.
Imagine that…

Claire Covino, Grade 3
Weston Intermediate School, CT

Spring Is Almost Here
Spring is the loveliest time of the year.
The flowers start blooming and the gray skies turn blue.
We get a sign that school is almost over.
Everybody should love spring.
With all the beautiful colors like on the Easter eggs.
Yummy! Easter chocolate!

Mercedes Mueller, Grade 3
Concord Elementary School, PA

My Friend

J okes
O ut of control
E nergy
Y ikes
Ryan Pronko, Grade 2
Klein Elementary School, PA

The Beautiful Trees

The beautiful trees
look at the leaves in the wind
They dance in the breeze
Julia Losciale, Grade 3
Saw Mill Road School, NY

What Is

What is blue?
The sky is blue.
Watching over me and you.

What is bitter?
Lemon is bitter.
But sugar makes it better.

What is loud?
Thunder is loud.
Making us go underground.

What is bumpy?
The road is bumpy.
Making everyone slumpy.
Juwairiya Muneem, Grade 3
Al-Rahmah School, MD

Guess Who?

Guess who has eyes that shine,
lashes to be adored,
a personality so fine,
and hates to be bored.
Guess who is a pal,
and likes to play,
you guessed, it's Al,
and he likes to pray.
Alec Kulina, Grade 1
St Joan of Arc School, PA

The Komodo Dragon

This dragon lives in Komodo Island.
They live in rain forests in the tropics.
A weird thing is that people live with them
The legend said, komodo dragon will save them
From cheetahs, wolves to earthquakes.

The big dragon is the world's biggest lizard.
Great swimmers, spend a lot of time on trees.
Komodo dragon eats a sheep to dine.
They have good eyesight, not as good as mine.
Juan Morales, Grade 3
James Russell Lowell School, MA

Spring

Beautiful butterflies fluttering in the meadow.
Colorful birds swirling in the sky.
Pretty flowers blooming in the field.
Perfect vegetables growing in the garden.
Fluffy bunnies hopping in the park.
Anna Gallo, Grade 2
St Mary Magdalen School, DE

If I Were in Charge of the World*

If I were in charge of the world,
I'd cancel school and also work.
If I were in charge of the world,
There'd be free ice cream and free toys.
If I were in charge of the world,
You wouldn't have homework.
You wouldn't have to take showers.
You wouldn't eat healthy foods
Or seltzer water.
You wouldn't even have manners.
If I were in charge of the world,
You would have two birthdays
And a person who sometimes forgot
To put his shoes away
And sometimes forgot to read a book
Would still be allowed to be
In charge of the world.
William Rodriguez, Grade 2
St Christopher's School, VA
*Patterned after "If I Were in Charge of the
World" by Judith Viorst

The Easter Bunny

E veryone loves him.
A t Easter he comes to play.
He **S** prings all around the world.
T agging all the Easter baskets.
E ggs are colored and put in trails.
R ed cherry on cakes and other delights.

B eautiful eggs are found outside.
A lot of g **U** ests in the house.
N ot much food left.
N o more eggs to find.
Y awn, good night sleep tight.

Kate Suba, Grade 3
St Rose School, CT

My Life

My life is better than a hot summer's day.
Sometimes it's better when I'm away.
My family is not that big,
but they are big to me.
They love me unconditionally.
When we go away together, we have a good time;
caring, sharing, and being kind.
I wish the world could see how we are, so they could be just like us, near and far.
I'm glad my life has been real good so far.
There are so many people that can't understand the meanings of love; kindness
and to be hand in hand.
I pray every day for the world to see,
how happy I am with my life and me.
Smart, strong, and willing to be, the one who will try to make the world just like me!

Matthew Davis, Grade 3
Powells Lane School, NY

Mom

I can see my mother.
I can smell her beautiful hair.
I can touch the beautiful flowers in her garden.
I hear our dog barking in the backyard.
I can taste the candy we made together.
I love you mom.
You bring me joy.

Jonathan Edouard, Grade 2
The New York Institute for Special Education, NY

Families

No matter the weather
Families are together

A family is sweet and very, very neat
No matter what you eat
You cannot beat the treat
Of being with your family

A family is important
We need them every day
We love them in our own special way

No matter the weather
Families are together
Mrs. Sandra Lynne's Class, Grade 2
Henry Clay Elementary School, VA

Blue

Blue is the color of a bird.
The color of the sky too.
Blue is the color of the ocean.
The color of a blue shirt and pants.
Michaela Teixeira, Grade 1
Hyman Fine Elementary School, MA

My Friend

With my friend Trin, I play.
With my friend Trin, I pray.
With my friend Trin, I go on ferries.
With my friend Trin, I pick berries.
Ariana Porter, Grade 2
Trinity Christian School, VA

Fall

Hay rides on sunny days with my family
finding our way out of the corn maze.
Picking pumpkins big and orange
Colorful leaves remind me of fall.
Rainbow
I like jumping in leaves
I like fall weekends
I like fall!
Julie Bilcheck, Grade 2
Long Meadow Elementary School, CT

My Dog Reggie

Reggie is my big old dog.
He eats more than a hog.

He chews and chews,
And steals my shoes.
He bites our kitty's belly
Because it feels like jelly.

When he goes to the vet
It puts us in debt.
He likes to go to school
Especially TCS carpool.

He shreds and he sheds.
And he sleeps on the beds.
His breath does smell
But I think he's swell.

I love him to death
But I don't smell his breath.
He's my big Golden Retriever...
Reggie!
Adam Brabec, Grade 3
Trinity Christian School, VA

Sick

S o dead; can't move.
I 'm feeling queasy,
C alling Mom from school.
K ills people sometimes.
Seth Andrews, Grade 2
Memorial School, NH

Whispers

a whisper,
a gentle voice,
a key to all secrets,
a rustling leaf
a caressing breeze
a soft wind,
a tingle to an ear,
the song of whispers.
Sam Seckler, Grade 3
Sinai Academy of the Berkshires, MA

If I Were a Monkey

If I were a monkey I would swing from vine to vine.
Then for a snack I would eat bananas YUMMY! I love bananas.
Then I swing in a tree and scream AHHHHHHHHA!
I would like to be a Monkey someday but clearly that will not happen.

Catherine, Grade 2
Heim Elementary School, NY

Winter Is

Winter smells like mommy's hot chocolate.
Winter feels frosty and cold.
Winter is white like glue on the ground.
Winter sounds like the wind blowing snow around.
Winter tastes like Christmas cookies, yummy and good.
Winter makes me feel happy!

Adam Pesnel, Grade 1
St Teresa of Avila School, NY

Spring

Spring has come
By a beat of a drum,
The sun shines bright.

The birds sing their cheery song
In the morning light.

Flowers will bloom and tress will grow,
So the sun melts all of the snow.

Ice melts from rivers and lakes,
As animals scurry to find their mates.

Soccer is finally available outside,
And it's the kind of weather for pony rides.

The gentle breeze rubs against lots of faces,
It's a great season to visit places.

Out in the sky shines a pink ray,
Which means there will be another great spring day.

Out of spring, summer, winter, and fall,
Spring is the best season of all.

Susy Liu, Grade 3
Fannie E Proctor School, MA

Spring
Happy Easter
Oh yes it's here,
Time for joy
And time for cheer.
Fabiana Gagliardo, Grade 3
Our Lady of Hope School, NY

If I Were a Parrot
If I were a parrot
I would mimic myself
Over and over and over
And over and over.
Nicholas Farley, Grade 2
Heim Elementary School, NY

If I Were a Tree Frog
If I were a tree frog
And I lived in the rainforest
I would hop around
Up in the trees
And when I got tired
I would rest on a leaf.
Grace Glauber, Grade 2
Heim Elementary School, NY

My Spring
Peach
Buds
Poking through the end of
branches
Spring is here!
Natalie Wood, Grade 1
Trinity Christian School, VA

Springtime
I like to smell the flowers
for all the hours.
I like to hear the birds sing,
it makes me think of spring.
I like to see the sun,
it makes me want to run.
All day long I have fun.
Julianna Asaro, Grade 3
Our Lady of Hope School, NY

My Best Friend Yume
With my friend Yume, I sing.
With my friend Yume, I swing.
With my friend Yume, I play.
With my friend Yume, I have a great day!
Kylee Toland, Grade 2
Trinity Christian School, VA

Going Shopping with My Cousin and Mom
First we can try out earrings and finger rings.
We can buy shoes and make-up.
A nice bracelet and stuff so I make a necklace.
Then when we get home we can play with them.
Judy Vazquez, Grade 2
Bensley Elementary School, VA

Science
Science,
Science,
Science,
I
L
O
V
E
Science!

In school we're learning about matter,
There are three stages of matter
Here they are,
Solid Woo!
Liquid Woo!
Gas Woo Hoo!
Lorna Li, Grade 2
St Mary's Primary School, MA

Soccer
S occer is a fun sport
O n the grass we run
C atching the ball is the goalie's job
C heering crowds watch the game
E ach player is shooting at the other's goal
R ound balls whistle through the grass
Kyle Hooker, Grade 3
Heron Pond Elementary School, NH

Sprinkling Rain

Rain falling in air
Trying to make flowers grow
Never ending falls
Megan Fong, Grade 3
Buckley Country Day School, NY

Dogs

Dogs
Cute and cuddly
I wish I could get a Collie
Or even a Dalmatian,
A German Shepherd
Or Yellow Lab would be nice
I just love them all
I wish I could get at least one
Little dog
Elena Avradopoulos, Grade 3
Lincoln Street School, MA

My Favorite Tree

My favorite tree
Cut into three.
I sit there nice and peacefully.
I named her Lindsey.
But one night
My favorite tree
One part fell
Down.
Now Lindsey is two.
But who cares.
I still like my tree
The way she is.
Allison Dickinson, Grade 2
Milton Terrace Primary School, NY

Sky Dancer

Hello, my name is Olivia Paige,
And I am six years of age.
I am a ballerina girl,
And I like to dance and twirl.
Sometimes I leap very high,
And I wish that I could touch the sky.
Olivia Alviani, Grade 1
St Joan of Arc School, PA

I Wish I Was Not Me

I'm passed around most of the time
I have no certain side
Sometimes I'm up in the air
And when I hit the floor I make a bang
And bounce with a hand all over me
Why do people fight over me?
Oh I wish I was not me…
Elinor Graham, Grade 3
Cabot Elementary School, MA

Pluto

P eople ran to the park
L ions eat meat
U mbrella keeps you dry
T omatoes are red
O ranges are juicy
Demitri Sukharev, Kindergarten
Montessori Development Center, PA

Firefighters

The job is harmful.
They risk their lives to save ours.
I want to be one.
Michael Paige, Grade 3
Sacred Heart School, CT

Spring

S pring is here
P lant a flower
R ain falls
I see flowers
N o more snow
G rowing flowers
Nicholas Bonaventura, Grade 1
Frenchtown Elementary School, CT

Feelings

Feelings come in all different ways like
Silly
Happy
And *Proud*.
They all make you feel good.
Erika Kershaw, Grade 3
Oak Park Elementary School, PA

Clouds

Clouds flow through the skies,
looking like marshmallows and
      fluffy cotton balls.
Sierra Cassano, Grade 2
Killingly Memorial School, CT

Life

life is a whirlpool
life is a train
that picks up passengers on its way
life is a river
and we are the fish
Life!
Abby Yamartino, Grade 3
Thoreau Elementary School, MA

The Sky

The sky is blue
it can be filled with clouds
or it can be clear and sunny
it can be dark and gray
The sky is always changing.
Valery Cardenas, Grade 2
Public School 2 Alfred Zimberg, NY

Barbie

My favorite doll is Barbie,
And her name is Katrina.
I dress her up,
And she has tea from her cup!
Together we play puppets,
And tell each other our secrets!
Christa Chan, Grade 1
Christ the King School, NY

Summertime!

I play.
I play with Emma.
I swim at the pool.
Summer is fun!
Summer is not here anymore.
I'm sad.
Sophia Ryan, Grade 2
St Madeleine Sophie School, NY

Mean People

People who are mean
Always yell at you
Even when you do nothing.
Mean people often
Don't have souls or feelings.
Mean people are always yelling.
Won't they shut up!
Mean people are
As mean as stray cats.
I don't like mean people.
Peter Antonaros, Grade 2
Public School 122 Mamie Fay, NY

All About Aidan

A wesome
I nteresting
D etail oriented
A merican
N eptune, King
      of the Seas lover
Aidan Patrick Pacifico, Grade 2
St Madeleine Sophie School, NY

Play

P lay with my sister Janie
L ike to go to the Park
A nd go on the swing
Y es, we love to play together
Anna Dalessio, Kindergarten
Montessori Development Center, PA

New Life

The spring is here! The spring is here!
Butterflies fly here and there!
Caterpillars are cocooning.
Birds are singing, flowers blooming.
Wind chimes ring, bees buzz, deer run.
Grass is growing in the sun.
Fireflies glowing, bunnies hopping.
Soon after, the rain stops dropping,
There will be tasty strawberries,
And very merry mulberries!
Keefe Jackson, Grade 3
Seton Catholic School, NY

Winter Is

Winter is the smell of chocolate chip cookies coming out of mommy's oven.
Winter is the sound of children making snowmen in the park.
Winter looks like a white mattress on the ground.
Winter feels like gentle snowflakes hitting my face.
Winter tastes cold like ice cream. Chocolate is my favorite.
Winter makes me happy!

Casey Su-Morrill, Grade 1
St Teresa of Avila School, NY

The Future

I look at the future like a door with a higher meaning.
We think the future is written in stone, but, it's only the beginning.
In the time given to you from teen to adult, it's not easy,
But it's your life do the best you can.
Make your life your own, and make your future bright.

Michael, Grade 2
Kanner Learning Center, PA

All About Spring

Cute little bunnies hopping in the meadow.
Shiny gold and black bees buzzing in the garden.
Beautiful water flowing in the rivers.
Sweet flowers blooming in the garden.
Little animals sleeping inside a log.

Nicholas Gallagher, Grade 2
St Mary Magdalen School, DE

Spring

Spring is fun
you go out in the sun.
Run around crazy
and don't act lazy.

Matthew Mobley, Grade 1
Francis Scott Key Elementary/Middle Technology Magnet School, MD

My Recital

One dark night I had too much fun.
Me and my friends were almost done with dance.
I want to do it again some day.
Me and my friends hope
it will be as special as last time!
We know it will be.

Lily Nagy, Grade 2
Pomperaug Elementary School, CT

My Spring
Gold
Puppy
Running into my arms
Spring is here!
Carolyn Roan, Grade 1
Trinity Christian School, VA

My Spring
Green Silver
Grass,
Growing so fast.
Spring is here!
Carissa Burnat, Grade 1
Trinity Christian School, VA

Football
Football,
Movement, exercise
Tackling, running, passing
Block, pass, stop, score
Chasing, kicking, tripping
Injury, play
Painful
Michael Hill, Grade 3
Brant Elementary School, NY

Spring
S urf
P ear
R ainbow
I nchworm
N ature
G arden
Ezra Lombardi, Kindergarten
Willis E Thorpe School, MA

Red
Red looks like apples.
Red sounds like volcanoes.
Red smells like apple pie.
Red tastes like pizza.
Red feels like fire.
Hunter Jenkins, Grade 1
St Christopher's School, VA

I Love My Sister
I love my sister when she drools.
She doesn't know any good or bad rules.
When a hard homework is due
I always leave it for her to chew.
Paul Zwolak, Grade 3
Our Lady of Hope School, NY

Snow
The snow is coming down
Nobody has a frown.
They all run in the snow
And yell "Go Go Go."

They make a snow man
And have no fun.
I love the snow.
Do you?
Chioma Madu, Grade 3
Pat-Kam School & Early Childhood Center, NY

My Dog Bob
Bob the dog is eating too much.
He is getting too fat.
He likes to play catch and Frisbee.
He likes to take a bath.
He likes to play with his toys.
He likes to chase cats.
He likes to run so much with me.
He likes to do tricks. He also copies me.
He scratches me.
He likes to play with me all the time.
He likes to jump. He, also, likes to roll over.
Bob is my dog.
Andy Lika, Grade 2
Public School 205 Alexander Graham Bell, NY

Spring
I see blooming flowers and green grass,
I hear buzzing bees and rain hitting the roof,
I taste soda, cookies, candy and cake.
I smell fresh air, flowers, cookies, and cake,
I feel warm and happy.
Michael Liebig, Grade 3
Granville Elementary School, NY

Spring Fever

Spring is coming,
Soon it will be here,
The smell of beautiful flowers is almost near.
Can't wait to go,
To the park and play,
Hope it's sunny not a rainy day.

Sheyla Martes, Grade 3
Public School 105 Senator Abraham Bernste, NY

If I Were...

If I were blue, I'd be a pretty, pretty sky.
If I were red, I'd be a beautiful rose.
If I were pink, I'd be a pretty flower.
If I were purple, I'd be a butterfly flying through the air.
If I were yellow, I'd be a sun sitting in the sky.
If I were green, I'd be the soft grass.

Preslie Coffman, Grade 1
St Clement Mary Hofbauer School, MD

Friendship

Once in a while,
You'll meet a person who is as beautiful as a dove.
Or you'll meet someone who is crabby and mean.
But whomever you meet,
Crabby or mean, or as beautiful as a dove,
You'll always be loved,
Once in a while.

Alyssa Gonzales, Grade 3
Acushnet Elementary School, MA

An Anxious, Spoiled Cat

The black, yellow eyed cat purring anxiously for someone to pet him.
Purring, purring, louder, louder!
So cute, so puffy, looking so lonely so sad.
Perks up when you pet him.
Such a spoiled little cat.
Yet determined to get your attention.
Such soft, low footsteps on the clean grey carpet.
Smell like pine on a winter day.
Such a silky, slim cat.
Hoping that he will get some ice-cream.
So tasty so fine.

Kayla Morkert, Grade 3
Fannie E Proctor School, MA

I'm White
I'm white.
I'm a ghost.
I'm an angel.
I'm a stripe.
I'm a cloud.
I'm a lily.
I'm paper.
I'm an egg.
I'm snow.
I'm the dove in the sky.
I'm ice.
I'm chalk.
Matthew Kordziel, Grade 1
St Madeleine Sophie School, NY

Scootering
Push, push, push!
Going faster
And faster
And faster!
Gliding down the street.
Feel the wind in your face.
Stop at the stop sign.
Turn around,
Push, push, push!
Faster, faster, faster!
Now you're back home.
Veronika Hughes, Grade 2
Milton Terrace Primary School, NY

The Ocean
In the ocean blue
the sun's glare makes the water
sparkle gorgeously
Lauren Juchem, Grade 3
Park Avenue School, NY

Ribs
R iot of food and tasty
I ntercontinental food
B orders to serve the food
S it and enjoy the wonderful meal
Thomas Horrigan, Grade 3
Sacred Heart School, MA

Sadness
Sad is blue
like a dead blue robin
and also like heaven.
It makes me feel very sad like funerals.
Chase Johnston, Grade 3
Somers Elementary School, CT

Things Helpful to America
They made a plane
They made cars
They made a train
They made a moon buggy
They made an elevator
They created a bus
They made a smart thing for our town:
It is the subway
Oscar Amaya, Grade 3
Trinity Christian School, VA

Flowers
Shiny
Beautiful
Roses
Daisies
Red color
Blue color
Pink color
Purple color
Any color, in the world
Needs a lot of sunshine
Water the flowers every day.
Maryam Ahmed, Grade 3
Public School 148 Ruby Allen, NY

Lindsay
L indsay is sweet.
I love her a lot!
N ot annoying!
D o not fight!
S he is a loving and considerate sister!
A shley and Lindsay are twins!
Y ou are the sweetest girl in our family!
Ashley Smith, Grade 3
Penn Yan Elementary School, NY

What Is Gold?

Gold is the earring in my special box,
It's the goldfish in my room,
It's the sun that shines through the window
And the ring that I wore when I was a flower girl

Gold is happiness when the sun sets
Gold is the feeling of sadness when my goldfish dies
Gold is shopping when I saw a gold dress
In the store
At Cape Cod

Ilana Skvirsky, Grade 3
Cabot Elementary School, MA

If I Was a Butterfly

If I was a butterfly, I would fly high in the sky!
I would talk to the birds.
I wonder how it feels to be a B
               U
            T
           T
          E
         R
         F
       L
        Y

Stephanie Arustamyan, Grade 2
Dr Samuel C Eveleth School, MA

Red

Red is like the sound of the Boston Red Sox fans
cheering as they win the World Series.
Red is like the smell of hot pasta sauce in the kitchen cooking for dinner.
Red is like the taste of a lick of a sweet red lollipop at the beach.
Red is like the feel of a hot summer day in your backyard
playing tag with your sisters.

Jack Rafferty, Grade 2
Long Meadow Elementary School, CT

Snowflakes

Snowflakes twinkle as they come down from the sky
They glitter on the brittle leaves
It looks like sprinkles coming down from the silver skies

Afton Burrell, Grade 3
Center School, MA

Spring

S uper fun!!!!
P eople sing!!!!
R ing ring the school bell's ring!!!!
I love fishing!!!!
N obody likes bee stings!!!!
G ood times with friends!!!!

Mark Kabbeko, Grade 3
Robeson Elementary School, PA

Sleep

I go to bed.
The owls wake up,
Bats and others too.
He goes to brush,
get PJs
and sleep.
He cuddles the sheets
and goes to sleep.
I wake up at 3 a.m.
Most unusual!
I see something in my bedroom.
I wonder, Who?
It is Cuddle Horse and Nick, too.
But how? I say.
I go back to sleep 'till 8 a.m.

Charlie Tanner, Grade 2
South Butler Primary School, PA

Spring

S is for shorts.
P is for play at the playground.
R is for running.
I is for ice cream.
N is for net.
G is for go to the movie theaters.

Beatrice Harris, Kindergarten
Fisher Hill Elementary School, MA

Black Cats

Black cats are so nice
Absolutely amazing
They are cute critters.

Autumn Michlovsky, Grade 3
Penn-Kidder Campus, PA

Linus

Linus was my cat,
I was very proud of that.
On January 23, 2005,
Linus was running around outside,
It was twenty-three degrees out there,
But he didn't care!
Linus was crossing the street,
He started to walk out,
But suddenly a car hit him,
Without a doubt.
We found him laying on the street
And brought him to the graveyard,
It was very, very hard
To say good-bye to my friend,
Linus was my best and only friend,
But now he was coming to an end.

Mia Patriacca, Grade 2
Cabot Elementary School, MA

Clock

Tick Tock
goes the Clock
going
to a
number

Tick Tock
goes the Clock
it makes
lots of noises
on the Clock

Tick Tock
goes the Clock
makes music
When you
want to hear
listen

Tick Tock
Tick Tock
goes the Clock.

Jackie Cortez, Grade 3
Public School 69 Jackson Heights, NY

Color

C olor is a rainbow standing truthfully in the sky waiting to be admired.
O range is the beautiful song birds sing when the flowers blossom and bloom.
L ight blue is a stream leading boats into the ocean.
O ak trees are the most beautiful brown no one can resist in the winter.
R ed is the deep sleep at the end of the day.

Claire Niesobecki, Grade 3
Middlebury Elementary School, CT

Coffee and Toffee

Can I get toffee with my coffee
Sure you can have toffee with your coffee
Coffee and toffee warm me up
Coffee and toffee you taste so good
Coffee and toffee I love you
I SURELY LOVE YOU!!!

Natalie Kolczynski, Grade 3
St John Neumann Regional Academy - Elementary School, PA

Summer

I smell a flower and fresh air,
I see the playground and the hills by rivers,
I hear kids on the swing and the swing is squeaking,
I taste the flavor of vanilla ice cream, Brrr!!
I feel the sand at the beach.

Sabrina Bishop, Grade 3
Granville Elementary School, NY

Ice Cream Cake

I cy
C reamy and smooth
E ven in different flavors

C ake with ice cream is great
R eally full of chocolate
E very piece is great
A ll of it is cake and ice cream
M ake it any way you want it

C reamy and cold
A ny ice cream is great but not as good as ice cream cake
K eep it away from your Dad.
E ven in the winter they are great.

Timmy Keohane, Grade 3
Sacred Heart School, MA

Diggin' for Fossils
Scientists
are digging
Deep, Deep, Deep,
searching
for fossils.
If they
have luck,
they
will discover
bones
and find out
the history
of our
world.
Sam Bernstein, Grade 2
Dr Samuel C Eveleth School, MA

Jack Frost
Jack Frost
Busy, chilly
Traveling, whistling
He makes a deal with a ground hog
Winter sprite
Thomas Flannery, Grade 3
Houghton Elementary School, MA

Spring Days
I see a bird
I hear a peck
I smell a flower
I taste the wind
I feel happy
I know it's finally spring!
Zoe Erme, Grade 1
Artman Elementary School, PA

A Monkey Named Fred
I once knew a monkey named Fred,
Who loved to eat raisin bread.
When he looked through a screen,
He yelled, "I want ice cream!"
And then he went right to bed.
Olivia Sothoron, Grade 2
Oakdale Elementary School, MD

Dogs
Barking, chewing
Playing, running
Having lots of fun
Dogs
Kathryn Bellavance, Grade 3
Plainfield Catholic School, CT

A Drop of Writing
A drop of writing
I do it when it rains.
I cry when I write
and when it rains
so I cry I cry I cry.
While I write this poem
I wish I didn't cry
when it rains.
Anthony Lauretti-Pereira, Grade 2
Willis E Thorpe School, MA

Spider
Up and down,
the spider bobs,
leaving a thin line
of thread behind it
When its web is finished,
it waits.
Finally a fly
flying by
gets stuck.
The spider leaps
into action…
and has a tasty meal.
Rebecca Tedeschi, Grade 3
Thoreau Elementary School, MA

Spring
S ophie loves flowers
P lant tulips
R ain falls for the flowers to grow
I love spring so much
N ew leaves on the tree
G rowing trees
Francesca Tesei, Grade 1
Frenchtown Elementary School, CT

Spring

Blue and yellow flowers blooming in the garden.
Red birds chirping on a tree.
Beautiful flowers blowing in the wind.
Delicious popsicles being licked on a stick.
Pretty flowers being touched on the ground.

Joshua Miles, Grade 2
St Mary Magdalen School, DE

My Blue Room

My room is magical,
it's a room made for me.
When I read a book,
I feel like I am part
of this blue,
magical place.

Karl Charles, Grade 2
Public School 152 School of Science & Technology, NY

Dance

D oing tap, jazz and ballet every day
A rtistically expressing our feelings
N imble, graceful feet
C ircling the globe doing performances for everyone
E xercising every muscle

Samantha Dubey and Haley Nicholson, Grade 3
Leicester Memorial School, MA

Silent Night

As the sky darkens and the sun sets in the west,
I lie in my bed and wait for something wonderful to happen.
My room grows dark and silent, but happy and peaceful.
My sister lies still in the bed by my side,
Soon I'll be asleep on that silent night.

Allison McGlone, Grade 3
Jamestown Elementary School, VA

My Football

I am a football.
I get thrown by people that I don't know.
I feel sad when you kick me.
I feel happy when you play with me.
I would like to change my color to gold and silver.

Eduardo Diaz-Carrera, Grade 2
Bensley Elementary School, VA

Ice Cream

Soft and fluffy
Light and creamy
All so delicious
I don't know what
To choose
I think I'll get
Mango Tango
Fruitie Tutie
Triple Chocolate Fudge Ripple
Bongos for Bananas
Vanilla Bean
And maybe a little bit of
Moose Tracks
Elise Ribaudo, Grade 3
Lincoln Street School, MA

Music

Music
is like
a tune
that tickles
your ear
as you
listen to
the gentle song
Aidan Dougall, Grade 2
Tashua School, CT

Teddy Bears

Curiously fun
curly, soft, live and squishy
unique toys that sing
Nicole Sciotti, Grade 3
Sacred Heart School, CT

I Like to Play

I like to play
we play all day
I climb a tree
or maybe three
with my friends
Sam and Bobby
Josiah David, Grade 1
Geneva School, PA

My Cat, Pat

Hi, I'm Matt, I'm a boy.
My heart is full of joy.
Matt, who I am has a cat.
I named him Pat.
He is one fat cat.
Sometimes, I put him on my mat.
Plus he likes my hat.
He likes it better than my mat.
He hides in it all day.
"Where is he?" I should say.
But this time, I didn't know where he was.
I looked in my room,
but he was not even behind my toy bus.
Then I saw something hiding under my mat.
Is it Pat?
I took out the mat.
It was Pat!
Carolina Ortiz, Grade 2
Public School 2 Alfred Zimberg, NY

Fish

The fish wiggles
It's jumping
jump, jump
It is a wiggle thing

The fish swims
It is splashing
splash, splash
It is a scuba diver

The fish fights
It is wrestling
wrestle, wrestle
It is a great boxer
Shivam Khatri, Grade 3
Public School 69Q Jackson Heights, NY

Halloween

Halloween is cool
People get to trick or treat
You get to dress up.
Nicholas Oertel, Grade 2
Fonda-Fultonville Elementary School, NY

Cars

Cars have motors and metal.
Cars have gas tanks we put gas in.
Cars have exhaust and smoke.
Cars have lights.
Malcolm Jones Jr., Grade 2
Bensley Elementary School, VA

Autumn

Fall is here it's finally come
Colored leaves are welcome
Summer is gone it's no longer here
School has started for its year
Bright leaves are a'falling
Mother Nature is a'calling
The trees hang bare against the moon
The winds are crisp and cool
Adira Balzac, Grade 3
Center School, MA

Toys

Toys, toys, toys
Everyone
Playing, playing, playing
When it's raining.
Always playing
Raining, raining, raining
Always playing
When it's raining.
Noooo!
The rain stopped!
Dylan Haraden, Grade 2
Milton Terrace Primary School, NY

Spring

S hining sun.
P laying outside.
R iding bikes.
I nteresting flowers.
N o snow!
G ood days!

Spring!
Maya Goldman, Grade 2
Dr Samuel C Eveleth School, MA

Flowers

Flowers, flowers
Have lots of petals,
They grow so slow,
As the sun goes by.

When they bloom,
Their petals grow,
They smell so good,
With full of joy.

Flowers, flowers,
Start from seeds,
Then they grow
into flowers.

Slowly, slowly,
The petals fall,
Then all the
flowers die.
Sikder Sakil, Grade 3
Public School 69 Jackson Heights, NY

The Middle of Spring

Flowers bloom
Butterflies fly
Kids play outside
Families go on picnics
The sun shines
Rainbows glow
Grass grows
Sometimes it rains
Everyone loves spring
Because summer's next!
Charlotte Cunsolo, Grade 2
Public School 122 Mamie Fay, NY

Spring

Pretty deer running in a meadow.
Amazing butterflies flying in a meadow.
Loud birds chirping out back.
Beautiful flowers blowing outside.
Funny squirrels running up a tree.
Samantha Davis, Grade 2
St Mary Magdalen School, DE

Snow

S ledding is fun, but you
N eed warm clothes
O r else you
W ill freeze outside

Thomas Parker, Grade 3
Houghton Elementary School, MA

Tomatoes

Tomatoes are like a clown nose
Honk! Honk!
Tomatoes are like a water balloon
splat splat
tomatoes are like a big cherry
YUM!

Kamryn Sarratt, Grade 2
Tashua School, CT

Spring

I look outside.
I see the trees, the sun
But wait —
there's something new.
It's SPRING!

Annie Wilson, Grade 3
Thoreau Elementary School, MA

Soccer

S cores a goal
O ut of bounds
C ool colored balls
C oach cheering you on
E quipment in bags
R eferees blowing whistles

Alysse Carpenter, Grade 3
Leicester Memorial School, MA

Soft Night

The night is so soft
with the sounds of crickets and wind,
Not everything is silent, but the
creatures of the night
are silent to me

Michael Grassetti, Grade 3
Somers Elementary School, CT

What Is Red?

Red is my tongue.
Red tastes like cherries.
Red smells like roses.
Red sounds like a heart beating.
Red feels like a ladybug.
Red looks like a valentine.
Red makes me feel pretty!

Lin Marie Vitarbo, Grade 1
St Rose School, CT

Jump Rope

"Jump!"
Jump the rope!
A summer sport of jumping the rope,
Jump rope is the game of the day.
Jump Rope!

Mikaela Jeffers, Grade 2
St Madeleine Sophie School, NY

The Moon

The moon, the moon.
It looks so white.
It shines so brilliantly,
Especially at night.

It lights the skies
So radiantly.
It watches over us.
It changes night by night.

In the morning,
We await its return
To watch it in the night sky.
Oh, the moon, the brilliant moon.

Christian Woo, Grade 3
Trinity Christian School, VA

Wind

Feel the wind in the breeze
You can feel it up to your knees.
Say hello to the trees,
Then you can be a trapeze.

Amelie Luegmayr, Grade 3
Evergreen Elementary School, PA

Hot Pink

Hot pink is like the sound of a long sharp colored pencil waiting to be used.
Hot pink is like the smell of wonderful roses in the summer garden.
Hot pink is like the taste of a cold ice pop on a hot sunny day.
Hot pink is like the feel of a soft hot pink puppy on my bed.

Rachel Donovan, Grade 2
Long Meadow Elementary School, CT

Spring

In the spring there are lots of new things
The birds like to sing
Flowers bloom and bells ding
And children like to sing.

Here in the nest the bird is seated
Keeping the eggs heated
Soon they will hatch and you'll see their little feet
So many new things in the spring to meet.

Now we hear the birds sing
The happy songs of spring
The flowers will wake up from their sleep
They will pop up from the ground and take a peek.

Now the winter is in the past
It's time to have a blast
It may be little windy but that won't last
Because spring goes by so fast.

Spring brings lots of new things
Birds singing
Windy days
The best of all it brings us summer!!!!!!!

Daphne Buzard, Grade 3
Chestnut Street Elementary School, PA

Winter

W hen I go snowmobiling I usually get snow in my pants from falling off it.
I n the winter I play outside while my dog is chasing me and biting me.
N ever stick your tongue on a light pole because you could rip your taste buds off.
T he snow is so cold you could get frostbite.
E at the snow because you could drink it.
R ide a snow mobile when it is icy out because you could slide all over the place.

Anthony Ralphiell Bernard, Grade 3
Granville Elementary School, NY

Millie
My dog
Plays fetch
In the afternoon
In my backyard
Because she loves me
Jack Cope, Kindergarten
St Christopher's School, VA

I Like Legos
I like Legos.
They are fun.
My favorite is Star Wars Legos
Lego City is so joyful.
Lego Bionicle is also a joy.
Lego fire trucks roll around!
Mark Kendziorski, Grade 2
St Rose School, CT

My Spring
Brown
Deer
Running Spring is here.
Reese Miller, Grade 1
Trinity Christian School, VA

My Sister
I like when
my friends share with me.
When they are mean to me,
I feel a little sad.
When my sister is born,
she will be my friend,
when she grows up.
Kayla Fuentes, Kindergarten
Agape Christian Academy, VA

I Like:
Animals that run.
Soccer; that's fun.
Baseball; yeah, we won.
Swimming; under the hot sun.
Basketball; I shoot a ton.
Andrew Zulli, Grade 1
St Joan of Arc School, PA

A Poet
A poet expresses his or her feelings.
They go out and discover the real world
and write about the real world.

Poetry is about spreading your wings.
Some people are not meant to be poets!
They say stuff like,
"My name is Jamie, I'm flamey, yo' word!"

No such thing! Those people are brainless.
They have no feeling.
Remember…think before you speak!
Nynetta Alexis Adams, Grade 3
St Gabriel School, DC

I Am an Eagle
I am an eagle,
flying so swiftly and bold,

I am an eagle,
staring down prey with a keen sense of sight,

I am an eagle,
so determined and fierce,

I am an eagle,
the bird of the country,

I am an eagle,
a free eagle.
Steven Porter, Grade 3
Meeting House Hill School, CT

Dear March
March, how glad I am to see you,
Your wintery goodness is getting warmer,
You bring us Easter and St. Patrick's Day,
You give us joy and wonder,
All of the families get together,
Giving each other presents,
Cold air drives by,
Making children go outside.
Kaela Hale, Grade 2
Roger E Wellington School, MA

Earth

The Earth is the birds that do solos in the beautiful morning that comes with the hot sun rising in the East and setting in the West. The birds sing like a beautiful la-la-by, and you wake up to hear all the wonderful noises that whisper in your ears, you are lucky to be alive in this amazing land that surrounds you with all your love ones and just regular people. The Earth is the tulips that grow in the hot hot summer day swaying from side to side. The Earth is a juicy peach falling from a thick, brown peach tree, an old, grandfather peach tree. The Earth is the grasshoppers that hop and hop all summer long. In the cooler Winter, the moose and deer come out to say hello but it's really just to eat you wonderful flowers. And if we don't take care of our Earth then all of that will go away and maybe us!

Jake Flecke, Grade 3
General John Nixon Elementary School, MA

My God Is Always with Me

When I look out my window, I look up in His kingdom and
I know He created me and will always be with me.
I know He loves me now and forever.
I know He cares for me now and forever.
I know He heals me now and forever.
I know I will be with Him now and forever.

Emily Torre, Grade 3
St Madeleine Sophie School, NY

Reaching for the Sky

I know what to do. I'll do it through the day,
With all of my friends. We run to the park,
And head for the swings, and try to reach the sky.

Always when I'm on my swing, I hear a whisper
From the wind trying to tell me something. Or
Sometimes I think it's wrapping me. Trying to lift
Me to another world.

I want to reach for the dazzle in the sun. I want
To grab it and bring it home with me and play
With it. Then soon we'll be best friends.

Always when I'm on my swing, I smell the fresh
Lovely air around me. But, when I smell closely
I can smell other things too like dirt, flowers, trees,
And even bushes.

Sophia Sabet, Grade 3
General John Nixon Elementary School, MA

Summertime
As hot as the sun.
As hot as fire.
As hot as hot cocoa.
It is summertime!
Gianna Cataloni, Grade 1
Artman Elementary School, PA

Blue Kangaroo
There once was a blue kangaroo.
Who hopped right over you,
Grabbed a green baboon
Was swept away by a typhoon.
Up! Up! Up! They blew.
Allison Marie Duffy, Grade 2
Geneva School, PA

My Bird
Birds are big
Birds are small
Cookie is the one I love most of all
Her head is red
Her body is blue
Look really close you'll see purple too
She is sweet
And oh so kind
A better bird is hard to find
Listen up and you will hear
A little hello in your ear
We have to go, we'll be back
It is time for cookie to eat a snack!
Lauren Beck, Grade 2
Fox Chase School, PA

About Me
My name is Krystal
I do not like to be tickled
Steak is my favorite food
Because it tastes so good
My favorite color is pink
Fruit punch is my favorite drink
I have many favorite things
It is hard to name just one thing
Krystal Leung, Grade 1
St Joan of Arc School, PA

Work Is Fun
I love work too much.
Work is fun and math is fun.
A work book is fun.
Jacob Alisauskas, Grade 2
Fisher Hill Elementary School, MA

The Pointer
The pointer
sits
on the edge.

I think
there's a piece
of
magic
inside.

I think
the magic
makes
the sparkly blue sand
and
blue confetti
float
up and down
the watery tube!
Elizabeth Janko, Grade 2
Dr Samuel C Eveleth School, MA

Crayons
Some crayons are red
Some crayons are blue
My favorite color is yellow and
I hope yours is too!
Red and blue make purple
Blue and yellow make green
Red and yellow make orange
If you know what I mean
Crayons are colorful
Crayons are fun
My favorite color is yellow
It's like the beautiful shining sun
Tara Conte, Grade 3
Public School 2 Alfred Zimberg, NY

If I Were 100
If I were 100
I'd be a number
If I were 100, I'd be a three digit number,
If I were 100, I'd be in 5's, 1's, 2's, and 10's.
If I were 100
I'd be a special number!

Jaybriel Lopez, Grade 1
Public School 105 Senator Abraham Bernste, NY

Blue Night
The sky is blue, the gateways are white as glue. See the sky? No clouds are
white, no kites are seen. Only morning days. Someone pays attention through
the garden window. The lights are bright like a diamond shines. The trees
stand still as stones. I see two trees. They are like clones. A house has many
eyes on their faces. I see that house someone paces, back and forth. The eyes
are glowing. I see three pies on that window. I see someone opening a door it's
the mouth of that house it is eating the person who is going in. I see a porch
where people are meeting. Now the sky is dark. And also the park.

Umme Hani, Grade 3
Public School 148 Ruby Allen, NY

Spring Is a Wonderful Time
It is spring outside.
As I look out the window.

The sun is shining bright.
And the sky is blue and white.

I see the flowers bloom
And a butterfly glides to the moon.

The cold snow and ice are gone.
And people are happy the winter is done.

The children are smiling and playing football.
And crowds start cheering when they score a goal.

My birthday party is very soon.
And friends are coming with balloons.

The students are happy the summer is near.
During the summer, school break is here.

Eugene Kochergin, Grade 2
St John Neumann Academy, VA

My Stomach Hurts

My stomach hurts
I don't really know why
For all I ate was
frogs covered in chocolate,
snakeskin pie,
octopus arms,
pizza ice cream,
turtle neck taffies,
rhinoceros tofu,
rotten cheese strawberries,
saliva spinach,
toe nail rice and
snail slime blend.
My stomach is still hurting
and I don't know why
Demetri Macioce, Grade 3
Westall School, MA

Sun

Sun
Bursting
Hot.
Sizzling.
Burning
Fire
Balls
Shooting
Light in
People's eyes.
Hot sweat
Dripping
Down.
Sun is a ball
Firing in
The sky.
Jethel Bayawa, Grade 1
Fulton Avenue School #8, NY

Spring

It is getting warm
Watching the snow melt away
Spring is beautiful
Jonathan Orce, Grade 2
Guilford Lakes School, CT

In the Sun

I like to play in the sun
I like to run
It is fun.
Francisco Lopez, Grade 1
Public School 1 The Bergen School, NY

Skates

Skates are beautiful —
Skates are as beautiful as the shiny ice
So icy, icy, icy
I feel like a penguin
Slip slide
Fall on my face
Fall on my hip
Fall everywhere
Slip slide
So slippy so slippy
Slip slide
No no no it is
Okay to fall, fall on my face.
Slide I think I am awaken like a penguin
From falling so much too much falling.
Parisa Vahid, Grade 1
Buckley Country Day School, NY

Snow

My house is warm all day long
We stay inside and listen to a winter song
Snow is falling
I hear snow calling
Snow is the best — like a nest
I go outside and go go go.
Adrienne Ruest, Grade 2
Willis E Thorpe School, MA

Winter

Winter is blue.
It tastes like hot chocolate.
It sounds like children playing in the snow.
It smells like ashes in a fireplace.
It looks like a blanket covering the Earth.
It makes me feel cold.
Ereni Christ, Grade 3
St Clement Mary Hofbauer School, MD

Spring My Favorite Time of Year
March, April, May, and June.
I wake up in the morning and smell the flowers bloom.

Daisies, Roses, Tulips, too.
The sun comes out and I see them bloom.

I look outside and see birds in the sky.
I wonder how quickly the seasons fly.

Playing sports and riding bikes.
No wonder why it's spring I like.

Spring is my favorite time of year.
Before you know it summer is near.

Zachary Appel, Grade 3
Willits Elementary School, NY

Money
M y favorite thing in the world
O n the job you get paid money
N ickels, dimes, and dollar bills are examples of money!
E xpensive things like "bling" are bought with money
Y ounger kids get money too.

Zachary Lakmany and Dan Powers, Grade 3
Brookside Elementary School, MA

Amelia Earhart
A woman who inspired other women to take risks
M arvelous and courageous woman
E njoyable daring adventures
L oved to fly
I n June 1937 Amelia vanished along with Fredrick Noonan.
A ble to fly solo across the Pacific Ocean

E arhart was determined to fly around the world
A ble to do exciting stunts and air show
R eady to attempt the impossible
H elped to create an organization of women pilots
A volunteer in a Red Cross Hospital during World War 1
R espected by other women through generations
T he first woman to fly across the Atlantic Ocean

Mrs. Betances' 3rd Grade Class
Public School 131, NY

Animal Sounds
Sssssssssnakes slithering
Rabbits chewing
Listen to the cow mooing

Sharks munching
Lobsters pinching
Listen to the waves splashing

Eagles wings flapping
Ducks quacking
Listen to the birds caw
Jack Thompson, Grade 1
St John Neumann Academy, VA

Bubble, Bubble Pop
Bubble, bubble, bubbly bubbles.
A rainbow color on a rainy day.
A stable with a sleeping horse.
It is going to be fun today.
Hip, hip, hurray, a rainy day!
I think I am going to play all day.
Mystic Higginson, Grade 2
St Rose School, CT

Christmas
Christmas,
Family,
Presents,
Tiny elves,
Pretty tree,
Big, sparkly, red ornaments,
Huge, fluffy, marshmallow snowman,
Delicious cookies,
Huge sleigh,
Soft, cold, snowy day,
Icy, white, winter snow,
White snow, too.
Flat ice
Green tree
Don't forget, chocolate cookies
Last of all, best of all,
I like Christmas trees!
Samantha Schulok, Grade 3
Stony Point Elementary School, NY

The Moon
The moon shines up in the sky.
It reflects in a shimmery lake.
It dances in the dark blue sky.
Until the sun wakes up
And the moon goes to sleep.
Amelia Dolce, Grade 3
Carlyle C Ring Elementary School, NY

Moss
Moss
In a dark forest
A springy patch of moss grows
Fearing to be picked
Waiting for someone to sit
In the cool damp and strange world
Allison Salwen, Grade 3
Cabot Elementary School, MA

Spring
S is for sun
P is for plants
R is for run
I is for ice cream
N is for no snow
G is for garden
Paige Bennett, Kindergarten
Fisher Hill Elementary School, MA

I Like Football
Tackle
Quarterback
Run with the ball
Pass the ball
Defense
I like football
Logan Machado, Grade 2
Milton Fuller Roberts School, MA

Bears
They are mean and big.
They will stand up on their legs.
They eat animals.
Stanley Tucker, Grade 2
Bensley Elementary School, VA

What Is Red...?

Red is like a juicy apple. As wet as a watermelon. It can be your lunch, and it's
as beautiful as a rose. Red is also a primary color, a feeling like love and
madness, also when you blush. It's as fun as holidays! And as bright as
Rudolph's nose, as jolly as St. Nicholas. Red is the color of Christmas and
sometimes gifts that bring happiness to others. Red is like respecting the
American flag at the Fourth of July, it's the loud sound of fireworks crackling in
the night. Red is also the bright welcoming of summer, the fox so sneaky to
surprise you in the dark forest. When you cross the street you see a stop sign
approaching with those capital letters.

THAT IS WHAT
RED IS!

Linnea Hummel, Grade 2
Shady Grove Elementary School, PA

Winter Night

The icy snow drips on my face.
I shake it off because my face gets cold.
As I walk, I'm wobbling like a penguin.
Whhhoooo, the wind blows past my face.
It makes me feel colder and colder by the second.
I go to my door, but turn around and say a little prayer for a snowday tomorrow.

Nicholas J. Troia, Grade 3
Munsey Park Elementary School, NY

My Friend

R uns every day
A lways gets into trouble
N ever quits
D oes nothing
Y ells a lot.

Justin Steele, Grade 2
Public School 152 School of Science & Technology, NY

If I Were a Rainbow

If I were a rainbow
I will have beautiful colors on me,
If I were a rainbow, I will be colorful.
If I were a rainbow, people will slide on me.
If I were a rainbow,
I will be in the sky!

Imani Cephus, Grade 1
Public School 105 Senator Abraham Bernste, NY

Pencil Sharpener

Pencil Sharpener
I think
there is one little mouse
inside of the pencil sharpener.
When I sharpen my pencil
the mouse nibbles on the tip
to make it sharp.
Erica Mariani, Grade 2
Tashua School, CT

Earth

Our world is so big,
things people have never seen,
lie here on Earth.
Braden Mayer, Grade 3
Saw Mill Road School, NY

Spiders

Hairy animals,
creeping in grassy gardens,
moving in the grass.
Ian Garrabrant, Grade 2
St Christopher's School, VA

Waterslide

I am on
a water
s
  l
    i
      d
        e
When I slide

D
O
W
N

it feels like
I am going down
a volcano.
Brent Nolan, Grade 1
St Rose School, CT

My Teacher

My teacher is so sweet
Like a chocolate treat
She cares and she shares
There's no doubt about it
I love my teacher!
Alana Yannone, Grade 3
Helen B Duffield Elementary School, NY

My Pencil Broke

I was writing with my pencil,
and then my pencil broke.
I was writing with my pencil,
and then I heard a croak.
I was getting really angry,
and now I'll tell you why,
I broke 32 pencils
and now I saw somebody starting to cry.
Sobia Shahab, Grade 3
Public School 48, NY

Leprechaun Len

There once was a leprechaun named Len.
He always carried a small pen.
So he got funny.
And saw a little bunny.
And then fell into a bear's den.
Stephanie Maurina, Grade 3
St Rose School, CT

Jets

Jets are my favorite
Jets are a good football team
I saw the Jets play
Adam DeSorbo, Grade 2
Fonda-Fultonville Elementary School, NY

Crazy Leprechaun

There once was a crazy leprechaun named Jake
He woke up and yelled, "My goodness sake!"
There was a dog
Who chased my frog.
He ran into the kitchen to bake them a cake.
Bridget Walsh, Grade 3
St Rose School, CT

Oak Tree

Oak tree standing tall
The leaves are spacious and broad
Bark crunchy and brown.
Jessica Wensus, Grade 3
St Stephen Regional School, PA

The Sea in Motion

The sea glides
from wave to wave.
You dive
and relax
and float.

When you can't hold
your breath
anymore
you stretch
and pull,
moving upward.

Suddenly
the sea splashes
your face.
The waves
grow so big.
You want badly
to get
out
but the sea
takes you in.
Emily Lamontagne, Grade 2
Dr Samuel C Eveleth School, MA

Vacation

V ideo games
A pples
C limb trees
A fter school ends
T emporary swimming lessons
I nnings of baseball
O utside fun
N othing is better
Evan Rysdam, Grade 3
Heron Pond Elementary School, NH

Frog from Space

There once was a frog from space,
He wanted to get out of the place.
His friends were mean,
He ate a jellybean.
And then he got out of the case.
Jack Laub, Grade 1
Mater Christi School, VT

Life

I lay down on a sunny day,
In a wide field of stalks of hay.

The sun on my face tells me
"It's not a race!"
To be great in life,
Take your time! There's not strife.

I run a lap
Around the field,
And do not stop,
Or do not yield.

I'm life
And life's mine
Then mom calls "It's time to dine!"
It ends there and then,
At a perfect time.
Nicholas Ornstein, Grade 3
James Russell Lowell School, MA

We Like to Bounce

Bouncing bouncing bouncing
you can bounce on 1 foot
I bounce on 2 feet
I feel like a kangaroo
you can bounce on your head
you can bounce on your pinky
I prefer to bounce on my 2 knees
Bouncing bouncing bouncing
I bounce on a trampoline
you bounce on a table
We both like to bounce!
Allie Casciano, Grade 3
Somers Elementary School, CT

A Windy Day

The wind blows so strong
The leaves fall
People stay indoors
I hear the wind whistle
From my bedroom
The window RATTLES
Scary sounds

Mark Novello, Grade 3
Public School 2 Alfred Zimberg, NY

Maysa

M y name is Maysa.
A dorable am I.
Y ou can be my friend.
S inging is my favorite thing to do.
A lways kind.

Maysa Poston, Grade 3
Penn-Kidder Campus, PA

Crunchy Foods

Crunchy foods
Yummy Yum
I like crunchy foods
Potato chips
Cheez-Its
Crunchy crunch crunch

Justin Hayward, Grade 2
Milton Fuller Roberts School, MA

Play a Game!

If you want to play
you have to take a game.
Read the directions
and follow the rules
so you can play.
Play, play, play
is the thing you can do all day.
Talk, talk, talk
you can't do all day.
Now I got the game
So now let's play, play, play
until the end of the day.

Albert-Daniel Shub, Grade 3
Buckley Country Day School, NY

School

S pelling
C reate
H ave to raise your hand
O ooh I like math.
O oo I like going outside.
L earn

Dae' Corey Williams, Grade 2
Bensley Elementary School, VA

My Life

My life is happy
because I have friends.
In my home I am playing
with my toys.
In EE. UU. is very fun
Because it's snowy
and I like the snow.
I don't like Paraguay
because it's very hot.
But with my friends
yes I like the sun.

Veronica Testi, Grade 3
Public School 148 Ruby Allen, NY

Summer

S chool's out
U mbrellas at the beach
M iracle warmth
M y pool comes out
E ach day is long
R ipe tomatoes

Alexandra Habekost, Grade 3
Edgartown Elementary School, MA

Apple

Apple, apple, up in the tree,
Ripe and juicy just for me.
Way up high —
in the sky…
Just waiting for me to pick you.
Apple, apple, up in a tree,
Ripe and juicy just for me!

Rachel Murphy, Grade 2
Milton Terrace Primary School, NY

If I Were...

If I were blue, I'd be a stream floating into a river.
If I were green, I'd be a tree swaying in the wind.
If I were pink, I'd be a beautiful flower.
If I were red, I'd be a really crunchy apple.
If I were purple, I'd be a butterfly flying through the air.
If I were yellow, I'd be a sun shining in the sky.
If I were orange, I'd be a really juicy fruit.

Lorelle Tribble, Grade 1
St Clement Mary Hofbauer School, MD

Spring Time

Spring! Spring!
All hot and warm spring!
Is fun and hot!
Come on, let's go outside and play tag!
Let's play jets and sit on a chair and have a drink!
Then we can go inside.

Keenan Murphy, Kindergarten
St Rose School, CT

White

White is what brings the soul to you,
It's the star not discovered,
The moon not yet born,
It's the word not written,
The dove that never flies.
White is the fool among the smart,
It's the difference between
A snowflake on your tongue and
Paper on a burning fire,
It's what makes you tired
When it's only noon.
It stops the sad from gaining power,
It's the friendship that only best friends can have,
It's that idea that's stuck in your head,
It's what keeps you going even when you're the
Smallest thing in the world.
White is the mother of peace,
It's why there's sunlight
Every time you wake up,
It helps you through every problem.

Louis Torracinta, Grade 3
Cabot Elementary School, MA

The Smell of Rain
The smell of rain in time
It smells like water and air and lime
in a room and dust and cold
and nothing.
It smells like a sandstorm.
Anders Pecore, Grade 3
Lincoln Elementary School, PA

Why?
Why can't I be perfect?
Why can't I have a pet monkey?
Why can't we stay in school?
Why can't I be rich?
Why can't people be nice?
That would be so cool!
   I'm rich
Destiny Bailey, Grade 2
Bensley Elementary School, VA

Movie Theater
lights dim
everyone comfy
darkness blankets

hush falls
eyes widen
hearts race

teardrops fall
gasps heard
whispers carried

lights blind
moviegoers sigh
reality almost forgotten
Ilana Albert, Grade 3
Sinai Academy of the Berkshires, MA

Truth
An icy sea cries, "I am frozen."
The sunny sky tells a summer lie
The frozen sea tells the truth.
Ian McKinnon, Grade 1
Dartmouth Early Learning Center, MA

Trees
Whistle in the wind
bend back and forth but don't break
leaves of all colors
Madison Powe, Grade 3
Sacred Heart School, CT

That Meat
I have a piece of meat
And it smells
like smelly feet
Gabrielle Higgins, Grade 1
Hebbville Elementary School, MD

My Room
My room is a mess,
as you can see.
My bed is trash,
I hope you're very pleased.
My books are all moldy,
you really don't want to see.
My clothes are untidy,
that's all up to me.
My desk has so many papers,
I can barely write on it.
So make this a lesson.
Make your room all neat.
That's how it goes,
before you get a treat.
Kayla Beyer, Grade 3
Thoreau Elementary School, MA

Scared
AHHHHHHHH!
A ghost is coming,
A ghost is coming,

I am so scared.
I jump and scream.

But when I stop
It's just my sister
Under my blanket.
Kristina Sanoulis, Grade 2
Buckley Country Day School, NY

Love

You have been away a long time.
Now you are here on Valentine.
It was a big wish,
now I am singing songs.

Marquis Maitland, Grade 2
Public School 152 School of Science & Technology, NY

I Am

I am mean.
I am sad.
I am special.
There are a lot of things I am, but there is some more things you don't know.
I am happy and I am God's friend.
I am God's child waiting to grow to be big and strong.
I am fun.
I am jumpy.
But hold your horses it gets better.
I am mean,
I am sad.
I am special.
I am happy.
I am God's friend.
I am God's child.
I am fun and jumpy.
So now you know about me.
So, I can't wait to hear about you.
So, I will see you tomorrow but not today.
So, goodbye, goodbye, goodbye!
I will see you tomorrow but not today.

Vishaan DeNobrega, Grade 2
St Mary's Primary School, MA

Purple

Purple as a butterfly going into a tree
Purple as the sky when it's looking at me
Purple as a tower going up high into the sky
Purple as a purple balloon in my hand ready to fly
Purple as a daffodil growing tall
When I try to pick it up, I will probably fall
Purple as a hat going up into the air
I will probably need a helicopter to catch it when I am there

Gabriella Mocheniat, Grade 3
Public School 97 Highlawn, NY

Page 157

The Mustang Convertible

It glides down the street
And you can feel the wind in your ears.
The steering wheel gleams brightly
Like the sun itself
Impatiently waiting for the rider.
The windshield is as clear
As a cloudy day
I feel like I am flying
When I stick my head out the window.

Jackson Barkstrom, Grade 3
St Christopher's School, VA

Fireworks

Yellow is happy like the bright sun
and also like fireworks bursting
in the air. It makes me
feel happy like playing outside.

Cameron Mackechnie, Grade 3
Somers Elementary School, CT

One Fish

Silently coming toward me
with no group,
Softly gliding in the water
turns
and swims away.

Isak Ring, Grade 2
Dr Samuel C Eveleth School, MA

My Fish Named Fire

Always swims and
Begs for food.
We play.
He chases my finger.
Tap, tap, tap!
On the glass.
Surprise!
Red, orange silky fins
Looks like a leaf
Floating from
The
Sky.

Justin Matzel, Grade 2
Milton Terrace Primary School, NY

My Big Dream

F antastic
A wesome
N early impossible
      not to have a dream
T errific
A wonderful place
S o independent
Y ours only

Ryan Flaherty, Grade 3
Heron Pond Elementary School, NH

Colors

Gray feels like I am crazy.
White is the color of sadness.
Brown is the color of being mad.
Blue feels like I am joyful.
Orange is the color of excitement.
Black is the color of being frightened.
Yellow is the color of happiness.
Red is the color of angry.
Purple is the color of boring.
Pink is the color of imagining.

Jacob Bornstein, Grade 1
Glover Elementary School, MA

If I Were the Amazon River

If I were the Amazon River
I would flow along
Checking and chatting
With each tree.
I would look up
And see a rainbow
Shining and sparkling
In the light of the sun.

Supriya Pandit, Grade 2
Heim Elementary School, NY

Waterfall

Water falls flowing down
Filling the pond below
With clear fresh water
Singing as it splashes

Matthew Perry, Grade 3
Dartmouth Early Learning Center, MA

The Most Beautiful Family in the World
The most beautiful woman in the world is my mother.
She has taken care of me and loved me, that's why she is so beautiful
    in her own way.

The most handsome man in the world is my father.
He has taken care of me and loved me, that's why he is so handsome
    in his own way.

The most wonderful family in the world is mine!
They have taken care of me and loved me. That's why they are so wonderful
    in their own way.

Valerie Ventura, Grade 3
Powells Lane School, NY

Swimming
S is for that surprising feeling of getting in the cold water,
W is for how warm you are when you start to swim around,
I is for all the power I feel when I'm jumping off the diving board,
M is for the miraculous cheering you get when you just made a wonderful dive,
M is for many hours in the pool,
I is for indoor or outdoor pools that you swim in,
N is for never wanting to leave,
G is for finally getting out of the pool.

Maggie Kishbaugh, Grade 2
Fishing Creek Elementary School, PA

Spring
Yellow and black bees buzzing from flower to flower.
Rain showers falling from the clouds.
Pollen on flowers with butterfly on them.
Cold ice cream melting in the house.
Flashing lightning bugs flying in the sky.

Andrew Kielar, Grade 2
St Mary Magdalen School, DE

Thank You
Thank you God for all the wonderful things you have done for me.
Thank you for my mommy and my daddy.
Thank you for my staff for all the good things they are doing for me.
I like all my friends and my cat Kit-cat.
Love, Melanie

Melanie, Grade 2
Kanner Learning Center, PA

Easter

Easter is almost here,
I am almost there.
Easter eggs are red,
And so is my bed.
Easter is very colorful,
And so wonderful.
I get Easter candy,
And watch a show called
Billy and Mandy.
Julia Mulligan, Grade 3
Our Lady of Hope School, NY

The Sun

The sun
hugging
the earth
and painting
the sky
yellow
and heating
up the earth
the earth
John P. Ligouri, Grade 2
Tashua School, CT

Hockey Hall of Fame

My name is Mark the shark,
Playing hockey is my game.
If I play hard and do my best,
I might be in the Hall of Fame!
Mark Sickler, Grade 1
St Joan of Arc School, PA

My Dog Is...

14 and a half years old
Medium sized
Yellow colored
Likes to bark at other dogs
Likes to go outside
Sleeps on the floor
Eats brown dog food
I love my dog.
Alex Brown, Grade 1
St Christopher's School, VA

Mysteries of the Deep

Magic
Power
Below the shimmering water
Down into the depths
The heart
The core
Of the ocean
Up above the water is still
It looks as if one touch
Would shatter it like glass breaking
Inside or out
It will be there
Until the end of the EARTH
Elizabeth Quinn, Grade 3
General John Nixon Elementary School, MA

Pink

When I go to the Topsfield fair
I always ask my mom or dad for cotton candy
it melts in my mouth

Pink bubble gum...
it pops in my mouth
I love it so much

Furberries are cute as little bunnies
You can cuddle with them

I always wear flip-flops in the summer
they go flip flop, flip flop

pink lipstick makes me very pretty
pink is almost my favorite color
Molly Pinho, Grade 1
Willis E Thorpe School, MA

Lollipop

Around I go in the white tasting like ice cream
Around I go in the pink tasting like bubble gum
Back to the white
Back to the pink
Yum

Shay Mahon, Grade 2
Buckley Country Day School, NY

A Rainy Day

On a rainy day you might say,
Why does it have to be raining today?
But I know what to do on a rainy day.
Maybe do something fun or play.
Maybe monopoly or some card games, too.
But just remember to have some chips and dip, too.

Nola McGuire, Grade 2
Greenock Elementary School, PA

Rainbow

Red, orange, yellow, green, blue, indigo, violet,
The colors of a rainbow,
Red, a sunset on a hot summer night,
Orange/yellow, the color of a pencil while we write our homework,
Green, the grass of a soccer field in spring,
Blue, the color of the sky that surrounds us,
Indigo, the sky at twilight,
Violet, the flowers in spring that smell delightful.

Benjamin J. Eglash, Grade 3
Weston Intermediate School, CT

The Angels of Winter

When winter time comes, one startstruck snow angel flies
down from the heavens and spreads her blanket of snow
Here on earth

By day the children full of laughter, frolicking in
The snow having a splendid time

By night, animals lurk in the shadows,
The snow is shimmering in the moonlight

Snowflakes fill the air. Walking outside it is dark,
yet peaceful

Snow falls to the ground, looking up, and the snow angels
In the sky dancing and spreading more blankets of snow

Go inside, look out your bedroom window, see these snow angels
Hear them sing their beautiful song,
The song of winter.

Sarah Milnamow, Grade 3
Lincoln Street School, MA

Spring

S is for sunflower.
P is for playing outside.
R is for roses.
I is for ice cream.
N is for nice weather.
G is for go to the movies.

Cynthia Kelly, Kindergarten
Fisher Hill Elementary School, MA

Feather

Swaying through the air
Gentle and swift like a bird
Gliding over top

Sam Pruden, Grade 3
Somers Elementary School, CT

Don't Take Your T-Rex to School

Don't take your T-Rex to school…
I think he'll want some meat —
If he sees YOU,
He'll start to drool —
And soon he'll want to EAT!

Gavin Vitarelle, Grade 2
Milton Terrace Primary School, NY

Spring

I love spring.
Because there is green grasshoppers
and butterflies too.
So don't stay home.
Come out of your house
and play with the green.

Amrit Singh Gill, Grade 2
Public School 2 Alfred Zimberg, NY

The Jungle

It is hot in the sun.
It was fun.
I saw a frog
Sitting on a log.
Then I saw a bear.
I found a rock that is rare.

Patrick Sidilau, Grade 2
Fisher Hill Elementary School, MA

Why Can't

Why can't we not move far away?
Why can't we behave every day?
Why can't we drive away?
Why can't we swim in our home pool?
Why can't there be no school?

Stephen Yachuw, Grade 2
Bensley Elementary School, VA

Birthdays

It's that time of year
so go on and cheer
It's your birthday
don't sit there and stay
It's your birthday
scream it so everyone will hear
It's your birthday! Hooray!

Calista Connors, Grade 3
St Rose School, CT

Summer

I see sparking pool water,
I hear people laughing,
I taste hotdogs,
I smell hamburgers,
I feel relaxed.

James Pawlikowski, Grade 3
Granville Elementary School, NY

Leaf

L eaves are falling
E arth is important
A pples falling from the tree
F alling all over the ground.

Danny Caswell, Grade 1
Milton Fuller Roberts School, MA

Spring

Spring, spring, spring is here.
Spring is everywhere.
Spring is high. Spring is low.
Spring is high and low.
Spring is everywhere in the air.

Reshma Davis, Grade 1
Joseph Greenberg School, PA

I Am

I am a sweet loving girl that always likes to read.
Sometimes, I am naughty.
Sometimes, I am caring.

I am a person with a heart and feelings.
I am a person with a brain.
I am a person who listens to my teacher.
I'm helpful.

OK, sometimes I get carried away.
Most of all, I'm a person with confidence in myself.
I am.

Julie Mason, Grade 2
St Mary's Primary School, MA

Fall

Pumpkins big and pumpkins small
Windy days and that is all
October is a pretty month
I enjoy the colorful leaves
It is sunny, then cold
It is fun to jump in piles red, yellow, orange, brown, and green leaves
Raking leaves is fun to do
People like to eat crispy apples and go on hay rides
There are many fun things to do in the fall
Fall is a great season!

Abigail Schmidter, Grade 2
Long Meadow Elementary School, CT

Summer

Summer is a time to go in the pool.
In summer, you can go to the beach and jump in the sprinklers.
Summer is a good time to have a birthday party in your backyard,
if you have a pool in your backyard.
You can go fishing in the summer and the ice cream truck comes.
Summer is fun and in summer you can go surf boarding.
  U
    M
    M
      E
      R...is FUN!

Averi Kaplowitch, Grade 2
Dr Samuel C Eveleth School, MA

Linus Project

L ove
I n
N eighborhood
U nited
S ervice

P eople
R esponsible
O bliging
J oy
E very
C hild
T hankful

Christine, Grade 1
Kanner Learning Center, PA

Shiny Rock

It is shiny
not like dirt
It is cool
not like sticks
It is like ice
not like boxes
It is like a mountain
not like sand
It is a remarkable
incredible
terrific
shiny rock

Noah Neville, Grade 2
Cabot Elementary School, MA

The Weather

Rain falls

down
   down
      down

Sun comes up
and makes
the world calm.

Chase Harper, Grade 1
St Rose School, CT

Spring

Spring when are you coming?
Spring how far are you?
Spring please come to me cause
I feel nothing if you are not here
Spring I am glad you came to me.

It's time to smell the sweet smell of spring.
It is time to hear the bird chirping.
It is time to go out and play with your friends.

Sylwia Wisniewska, Grade 3
Public School 131, NY

Friend

A friend will share
A friend will always care
A friend is always there

Delilah Pellot, Grade 1
Public School 1 The Bergen School, NY

I Am Water, I Am Sky

If I am water, I can play on the waterfall
I can be in the river; I can be on the stream
I can be rain falling down on the ground
I can be the ocean tide on the beach

If I am sky, I will have clouds; rabbit clouds
dog clouds, cat clouds, a lot of clouds
I can move wherever I want
because I am sky

Mel Jiang, Grade 3
Lincoln Elementary School, PA

Animals

Some animals swim some animals run
Some have fun
And others get caught
Some animals eat
And some animals are sweet
They lay their eggs while others give birth
They live in water and land
I can't tell the difference
I just can't understand

Jarol Navarro, Grade 3
Public School 2 Alfred Zimberg, NY

Spring
Pretty flowers growing in a field
Blue birds singing in a garden
Fresh air flying in the sky
Sweet hot dogs cooking in a house
Colorful leaves lying in a tree
Francesca Knoll, Grade 2
St Mary Magdalen School, DE

Lollipops
Different
sized lollipops,
sticky things
so sweet
not sour,
come in all
different
colors
red, purple
green, blue,
yellow and orange.
Lick
Suck
Melt.
Dana McKinnon-Tucker, Grade 2
Dr Samuel C Eveleth School, MA

Don't Take Your Octopus to School
Don't take your octopus to school —
She will cause some trouble…
If she sprays her bubble,
You'll be in extremely BIG trouble!
Morgan Relyea, Grade 2
Milton Terrace Primary School, NY

I Made a Friend
I have no friend and I sure needed one
When I got on the bus I sat right down
I had a frown
a little while I had a smile
because I made a friend
her name was Ashley
and that is when I made a friend.
Taylor Albano, Grade 2
Pomperaug Elementary School, CT

Christmas Day Dinner Party
Plan a party.
Put up lights.
Put up the tree.
Cook the food.
Danayja Sorel, Grade 2
Bensley Elementary School, VA

Kites
Dipping, diving
slowly, quietly,
gently gliding
in the air
through
the blue sky.

A change…

The sea breeze,
strong
and powerful,
swoop
them
into
the
Atlantic Ocean.
Mike Kagan, Grade 2
Dr Samuel C Eveleth School, MA

Seagulls
Seagulls live at the sandy cool beach.

They are laughable to watch while
They run up to the water.
When the water goes down,
The seagulls run up.
When the water comes up,
The seagulls run back.

They are hilarious to watch while
They catch small bites of bagels.

Seagulls live at the sandy cool beach.
Emma Duane, Grade 2
Hopewell Elementary School, PA

Poetry Is This

Poetry is like
a thousand stars
in the sky
twinkling above
your head.

Poetry is like
your little sister's
big blue eyes shining
up at you when
you play together.

Poetry is like
a loyal friend laughing
when you say something
hilarious.

Poetry is like
your father's big hug
and warm kiss.

Poetry is your mother
reading this poem
to you at bedtime.

Ella Goodwin, Grade 3
Slingerlands Elementary School, NY

Dark Pink

Dark pink, bubble gum, tasting
like fresh new strawberries

Dark pink fluffy cotton candy,
like a brand new fluffy pillow

Dark pink tropical bird, soaring
through the sky so gracefully

Dark pink rose blooming in
the spring so slow and peacefully

Dark pink leaves falling
from the sky in the fall

Cloey Houk-Salvati, Grade 3
Lincoln Elementary School, PA

Fishing

I go fishing when it's late,
I take my rod and my bait.
I cast and catch a big fish.
I am cold while I fish.

I make my fishing rod bend,
To give squid to my fish friend.
The squid's as squishy as slime,
It is only worth a dime.

Théo Guérin, Grade 3
Edgartown Elementary School, MA

Princess Crown

I am not a
princess or a queen.
I just wear this
thing on my head.

I am not royalty
or a clown
I just wear this
thing on my head.

I just like wearing it
for fun!
It is my favorite hat...
My Princess Crown

Clarissa Nascimento, Grade 3
Public School 69 Jackson Heights, NY

Jungle

In the jungle were monkeys
Swinging on the vines
That look like lines.

In the jungle were parrots
Cawing in the tree
Luckily they got free.

In the jungle were lions
That roar even more
Than before.

Madison Belli, Grade 2
Carlyle C Ring Elementary School, NY

Spring

Flowers are flying in the air
I can see a baby bear
For this season I have plenty of playing time to spare,
And the wind is blowing in my hair.

The deer are jumping in the grass
I tried to touch them, but they run too fast
The sun above is bright and vast
I wish that spring would last and last!

Nicholas Bartholow, Grade 3
Crossroads Academy, NH

Winter Is

Winter is smell of hot cocoa.
Winter is seeing snowmen dressed in hats and scarves.
Winter is the taste of hot soup slowly going to my tummy.
Winter is hearing the wind whooshing through the leafless trees.
Winter is happy!

Sunshine de Castro, Grade 1
St Teresa of Avila School, NY

Me

When I was a baby as I nuzzled close to my mom
I could feel that her love was as warm as the hot sun.
When she kissed me on my little fuzzy head I could tell
Her kisses were as sweet as candy whose flavor never melts away.
In all the old photos my mom used to take I could tell
I was like her little baby doll.
From the old video tapes of when I was little I can tell that
I was spoiled stubborn
Because I cried and wouldn't stop until my parents gave me a bottle.
It seemed that when I was with my mom I was as happy as a clam.

But now things are different. My mom is a lot busier than before.
I'm not as careless as I used to be.
I don't spend as much time with my mom anymore.
Sometimes I feel as if I can't touch her hand.
It feels like there is a magnet that pushes one against the other.
But as I grow older I know my path will grow harder
And that she will be the rock I lean on.
That will be how our bond will be cemented together again.

Georgia Neale, Grade 3
General John Nixon Elementary School, MA

Cranes

The cranes are pretty.
The cranes are very lucky.
The cranes are heroes.
Anna Giglio, Grade 3
St Joseph School, NY

Money Is...

Something to spend
Something to save
Money is dollars
Money is cents
I love money.
Ramsey Morris, Grade 1
St Christopher's School, VA

Spring

Waiting for the warmth.
The snow is melting slowly.
Bears are waking up.
Buds are beginning to bloom.
Many flowers are blooming.
Ryan Bolebruch, Grade 2
Wells Central School, NY

Beach

Waves crashing to shore
flowing waters called ocean
fascinating shells
Nathan Spicer, Grade 3
Sacred Heart School, CT

Drift Wood

It travels to a stream
Gets wet
and softer
and smoother
becoming a
diving board for a frog
It drifts to the shore
Lizards can lie on it
warming themselves
in the sun.
Vincent Bartoli, Grade 2
Tashua School, CT

The Three Butterflies

There are three butterflies in a tree.
Come and count them 1, 2, 3.
Some can be small.
Some can be big.

People watch them fly so high
People watch them low below

But now the butterflies are back in the tree.
Come and count them 1, 2, 3.
Julie Chou, Grade 3
Willits Elementary School, NY

Seasons

Fall is the time to play in the leaves.
Winter is the time to play in the snow.
Spring is the time to pick some flowers.
Summer is the time to play in the pool.
Eden Teska, Grade 1
Eagle Elementary School, NY

Basketball

B ounce the ball every time.
A ll of the players need to play a part
S ubstitutions take people out and people in
K ids and grownups can play.
E very time someone shoots it's 2 points.
T ake the basketball so it's a steal.
B asketball is really fun to play
A lec doesn't know anything about basketball
L ots of people cheer for you
L ike lots of people that play basketball.
Michael Odiana, Grade 3
Brookside Elementary School, MA

Birds

Birds make me think of flying.
Flying makes me think of butterflies.
Butterflies make me think of flowers.
Flowers make me think of mud.
Mud makes me think of worms.
Worms make me think of birds.
Katelyn East, Grade 3
Cambridge Springs Elementary School, PA

A Tree

The gentle sound of the trees rustling
Back and forth in the wind,
Swaying, but never making a sound
As if it were speaking but yet it is silent.
The cool breeze blowing and making the leaves fly all around,
Until the tree has disappeared till Winter's end.

Peter McGurk, Grade 3
General John Nixon Elementary School, MA

A Most Beautiful Moment

Dew dripping down a blade of grass
A silent trickle, a whisper only your eyes can hear.
I look closely as one drop of water
    slowly makes its way.
A spider spins its thread on the grass
    making a bigger moment in time.
Laying down I watch
One drop travels down the web
    onto a silky piece of grass
Trickling into the dirt
Making the most beautiful moment
    beyond your mind's dream.

Isaac York, Grade 1
Dartmouth Early Learning Center, MA

Here Comes Winter

All the birds are heading south,
Nice sweet s'mores going in our mouths.
All the leaves falling to the dry ground,
Quickly, quietly not a single sound.
All the trees are getting really bare,
So you just might not see one single kind of bear.
Bye dull fall, cold winter is here,
So let's go out into a big winter cheer!

Christine Chesnais, Grade 3
General John Nixon Elementary School, MA

Yummy Bunny

My funny bunny is yummy.
I like chocolate and chocolate is my favorite thing to eat.
But, my favorite thing to eat is the best chocolate ice cream.

Stephanie Albelo, Grade 1
Park Avenue School, NY

Penguins
I love penguin's feet
Because they are neat
They like to eat fish
Because that's their dish
Their feathers are black
They carry a pack
They have a weak beak
When they're scared they're weak
Dylsi Teo, Grade 3
Bensley Elementary School, VA

The City
the city is beautiful
It's full of shops!
And shoes
and shirts
and pants
and underwear!
Shops, shops, shops
have everything.
They have food like McDonalds
Wendys
Burger King
It like a lot of stores if you do…
Let's be friends!
And shop together
laugh together
do everything together!
Demetrios Goungoudis, Grade 2
Public School 2 Alfred Zimberg, NY

When I Said Achoo
When I said achoo,
my face turned all blue,
my mother said, "Do you have the flu?"
Then when I tried to leave I sneezed.
Here came that achoo,
my face got all blue,
my mother said, "Do you have the flu?"
I got up to leave, but then I sneezed.
Wait! Maybe I do have the flu,
my mother said, "I told you!"
Toni-Ann Wade, Grade 3
Holy Rosary School, NY

Ocean Art
I love art.
I love how
pretty colors
spread on
my paper.

I can smell
the waves
and see
the seaweed
wrap around
my ankle
and it goes on.
Michaela Bird, Grade 2
Dr Samuel C Eveleth School, MA

Tigers
They are very fast.
A tiger is colorful.
They are meat eaters.
Keeshawn Capers, Grade 2
Bensley Elementary School, VA

Basketball Court
Deserted,
except for a few children,
yelling at each other
and running around,
disturbing the awakening
of nature.
Shelby Brown, Grade 3
Thoreau Elementary School, MA

Fun in February
F un in the snow
E veryone is happy
B uckle on your boots
R ight now it's cold
U ntie your boots
A re you freezing?
R un inside for warmth
Y ou and I will do some crafts
Delaney Parker, Grade 3
Heron Pond Elementary School, NH

Story of Bloody Mary

Sitting in the darkness with candle light,
the moon shining bright.
She looks frightening with a black hearted soul,
there is no kindness, but a big hole.
The things she did were evil,
most people say they were unbelievable.
She murdered, and it was really bad,
it made people sad.
Every Halloween night kids chant her name three times in the pitch black,
after she was gone, some thought it was wack.
Be careful of what she would do,
all she would say was boo!

Joey, Grade 3
Kanner Learning Center, PA

Rap-n-Rock

Rap is fun
It has a good beat
Makes you jump out of your seat
Makes you move your feet

Everyone likes a good tune
The crowd goes crazy when the drums go boom
Takes you to the moon

Rock and roll makes you do flips
Makes you feel good
Makes you eat chips
Makes you move your hips

Mrs. Melissa Scott's Class, Grade 2
Henry Clay Elementary School, VA

What I Like About My Mom, Michelle Washington

Michelle Washington — she is my mom. She is very talented.
She always provides food for us. She puts clothes on our backs and takes care
of us. She runs a great program named, the United Front Youth Organization.
She teaches at schools about their group and how to stay out of gangs. She is a
blessing to me.
We're lucky we don't have to walk to school and back home, know why, because
we have a mother that cares. I am really happy that I have a home to live in.
That's what I like about my mom. I am glad that I have a mom!

Ameian Washington, Grade 3
St Casimir Regional School, NY

Orange

Orange oh orange
so tasty
and yummy
I take a bite
squirt ow
Harrison Yoguez, Grade 2
Tashua School, CT

Baseball

I like baseball,
and I always have fun.
I always play baseball
and always slide,
and I don't get hurt.
Almost every day,
I watch the Yankees play
baseball on TV.
My favorite team
is the Yankees.
I always wear my Yankees cap
and I always tap it
for good luck.
Nick Randazzo, Grade 3
Holy Rosary School, NY

Adina

My loyal puppy
a labrador and poodle
one labradoodle
Cameron McCarthy, Grade 3
Sacred Heart School, CT

Daisy

Magnificent
standing tall
yellow and white
in the sunshine
like a lion
with its fluffy mane
gently flowing in the breeze
it is queen
of the garden.
Madison Wirth, Grade 2
Tashua School, CT

Valentine's Is Ick

Valentine's is ick
it makes me really sick
I saw some candy on the teacher's desk,
I took it
and made a huge mess.
The teacher yells
I scream
"Ooh a jellybean"
"Too much candy," says mom.
"Too bad," says Dad.
And then somehow it ends up with me
and my dad locked me in my room
cause mom was mad,
and we were bad.
Garrett Warren, Grade 3
Penn Yan Elementary School, NY

Dancing

Dancing
Fun, creative, tutus
You need to practice very hard!
Hard, practice, learning hard, dancing bars
Tap shoes
Morgan Reed, Grade 2
St Madeleine Sophie School, NY

How I Remember You

I remember I was small,
and I was playing basketball.
I remember you let me lose my temper,
and I know it was November.
I was so blue,
I felt I was glue.
You were still so glad,
that you had made me mad.
I am glad at the end,
we became friends.
I can't wait to see you,
because I will always remember you.
Yes I remember,
You remember,
We all remember.
Malaika Johnson-Bey, Grade 3
Al-Rahmah School, MD

Winter Is

Winter is the smell of apple pie in the oven.
Winter is the taste of brownies and hot chocolate.
Winter is the touch of snowmen.
Winter is the hearing of bells at church.
Winter is seeing a snowball fight.
Winter makes me excited to play outside.

Jose Caneta, Grade 1
St Teresa of Avila School, NY

Rabbits

Hear the rabbits wish when they go up swish
When they go through the air
They are fast when they see an enemy
They lick their babies and kick the enemy
Hear them sprinkle the dirt and scrape the ground
Hear them hit the ground
And that is how nice rabbits are.

Alex Hoy, Grade 3
Mohawk Valley Christian Academy, NY

Karate

Karate,
Karate,
Karate is fun.
On Saturdays,
I practice sparring
and sometimes it can be hard.
But I'm glad that I go.
By summertime,
I will be moving on to the
next belt.
Karate is fun.

Mecca Washington, Grade 2
Public School 152 School of Science & Technology, NY

Winter Is

Winter is the smell of pipe smoke and food.
Winter is the touch of snow, soft and white.
Winter is seeing snowmen and snow plows.
Winter is the taste of soup, cookies and popcorn.
Winter is the sound of laughter, crunchy snow, and music.

De'Ante Randall, Grade 1
St Teresa of Avila School, NY

Welcome to the Candy Shop
Candy sour, tart yumm.
Mints are good, yumm.
Delicious candy canes.
Coffee candy is for adults, yuck!
Green mints are my favorite.
White mints are my aunt's favorite.
Candy is so good.
I want to eat it for a whole year!
Hot candies, wow they are hot!
I like sugary, sweet candy.
Sweet, sour, tart, sugary, minty.
Yumm, delicious!!
Isabella Jimenez, Grade 2
St Rose School, CT

Leprechauns
Silly, sneaky
Working, playing, tricking
Leprechauns are very silly
Tricky people
Luke Zdankiewicz, Grade 2
Long Meadow Elementary School, CT

Gema
Fun
Love
Joy
Sad…
Crying
Death

"Mom, death is the worst."
"It was her time to go."
God take care of her please.
Travis Weiler, Grade 3
Robeson Elementary School, PA

Frogs
They hop and they leap.
They swim and they sleep.
They seem very fun.
I really want one.
Sophie Mikkelsen, Grade 3
Heron Pond Elementary School, NH

Everything Green
Green is beautiful!
Green tastes like broccoli.
Green smells like a flower.
Green feels like the grass.
Green looks like Ireland.
Green sounds like Irish music.
Green makes me feel like dancing!
Connor Dunn, Grade 1
St Rose School, CT

The Farm
Peaceful, happy, free.
Catching tadpoles, sledding down hills.
Bees, dogs, chickens, family.
Beautiful, quiet, green.
My home.
Anna Stefanou, Grade 3
Seton Catholic School, NY

The Street
The street is filled with people,
places, houses and stores
It has cars and parks
and everything that I love!
Mostafa Teleb, Grade 2
Public School 2 Alfred Zimberg, NY

Flower Ballet Dance
Like a ballet dance
their nectar resting in bed
and their stem swaying
Lorenzo Manuali, Grade 3
Buckley Country Day School, NY

Grace
I have a sister
Her name is Grace
She likes to put makeup
On her face.
She likes to play with me
And I like to play with her
We always get along together.
Alana Pessolano, Grade 3
Somers Elementary School, CT

Spring
Spring is light blue,
Like the bright sunny sky,
Or a garden full of wildflowers sparkling and dancing,
And birds with babies hatching, chirping wildly,
While teaching them how to fly.

Spring is green,
Like the tall grass swaying in the cool wind,
Or trees ready to bloom but waiting
For some big creature that was waiting there to get them
And gardens full of flowers and vegetables ready to be picked
From their green plants.

Spring is brown,
Like the warm, gooey mud,
Or the rough, dark brown branches, and trunks of trees,
And the soil that brings every plant and tree back to life
When the snow melts away.

Caroline Davis, Grade 3
General John Nixon Elementary School, MA

Hello Beach, My Old Best Friend
Hello beach, my old best friend
It's that time of year again!
I see the color blue
Like a never ending mirror.
I hear the rustle of sails and gulls that squawk in the silver sky.
I feel the salty waters that taste like tears.
Good bye beach, my old best friend.
I hope these days will never end!

Thorin Doerfler, Grade 3
Regional Multicultural Magnet School, CT

The Best Season
The air is getting warmer.
The grass is turning green.
The crocuses coming up are the prettiest I've seen.
You can hear the sounds of children coming out to ride their bikes.
Roller skating is something I like.
I open the window and I can hear the birds sing.
Oh, spring is a wonderful thing!

Elizabeth Cini, Grade 3
Willits Elementary School, NY

With You

I think I
could walk on
water with you
there.

I think I
can walk through
walls with you
holding my hand.

I think I can
walk on air with
you by my side.
What would I do
without my mom?
Vanessa Smith, Grade 3
Westall School, MA

Seasons

Spring flowers are
blooming blooming
Summer sun is
shining shining
Fall leaves are
falling falling
Winter snow is
falling falling
I love seasons!
Melissa A. Pippim, Grade 2
Tashua School, CT

Spring

The sun is rising
It is getting very warm
Spring is on its way
Emily Ciocca, Grade 2
Guilford Lakes School, CT

Tornados

Spinning cone feels like
a painful fan that destroys
cities and houses.
Jane Im, Grade 2
Killingly Memorial School, CT

A Friend

A friend is someone who cares for you.
A friend is someone who plays with you.
A friend is someone you will always be with,
your whole whole life.
Of course, a friend most of all, plays a role.
They are always deep in your heart.
You could never, EVER live without a friend!
Nefes Pirzada, Grade 3
Buckley Country Day School, NY

Autumn*

Orange leaf, Orange leaf how do you do?
Where did you come from?
What did you do?
Why did you turn orange?
What happened to you?
How do you feel?
What could you do?
I have no clue.
Brian R. Garfield, Grade 3
Our Mother of Perpetual Help School, PA
*Dedicated to my family and friends

Shattered Raindrops

Shattered raindrops falling from the sky
Ice shining as gentle as the stars
The clouds cast shapes
Pods of rain fall down
The quiet,
    silent,
        looming,
            flickering, peaceful
            tempting moon
            shines in the sky.
Emma A. Graham, Grade 3
Lincoln Elementary School, PA

Angelo

I'm as athletic as a sports player
I'm as hyper as a monkey
I'm as fast as a cheetah
I'm as smart as 100 computers combined
Angelo Bonvino, Grade 2
Buckley Country Day School, NY

Flower

F lowers are so pretty
L ike little planets
O h where is the
W ater
E xtravagant!
R eally cool
Quinton Horning, Grade 3
Penn Yan Elementary School, NY

The Monkey

The monkey
swings vine to vine
in the trees,
makes its
way
through
the deep
dangerous jungle.
Luke Fobert, Grade 2
Dr Samuel C Eveleth School, MA

A Crayon Is a Crayon

A crayon is a crayon
you know that's true
A crayon is a???
What is it???
A hat, scarf, leg.
No
A crayon is a crayon
Alejandra Vidaic, Grade 2
Public School 2 Alfred Zimberg, NY

Lizard

fast runner,
high jumper,
cool colors,
deep darkness,
very hungry,
hears a cricket,
waiting nicely,
munch munch,
away!
Christopher Ruediger, Grade 3
Thoreau Elementary School, MA

Polar Bears

Polar Bears, I hope they keep cool,
swim in a cold pool.
Do not keep hot,
find a nice spot.
Please help.
Antonio, Grade 1
Kanner Learning Center, PA

What Is Poetry?

A poem is like
a lollipop dancing around,
hopping into
your mouth,
the white stick
sticking out
like a pretzel stick

A poem is like
a light bulb,
sparkling around you,
everywhere;
then you get an idea,
the light bulb pops
over your head

A poem is like
a pencil,
filled with grips
hugging the pencil,
the tip kissing
the paper,
nonstop
Abby Young, Grade 3
Slingerlands Elementary School, NY

Spring

S is for sun.
P is for popsicle.
R is for rose.
I is for ice tea.
N is for no bugs.
G is for go to Game Stop.
Todd Chiasson, Kindergarten
Fisher Hill Elementary School, MA

Talented Pig

There once was a talented pig
And he knew how to dance a jig
He did other tricks
Like juggling sticks
But he couldn't juggle a fig

Connor Collins, Grade 3
Memorial School, NH

Springtime

Spring is here!
We like to play outside!
The sun shines in our faces
I love you spring!
Stay with me forever!
You make me so happy!

Tanzila Zomo, Grade 2
Public School 122 Mamie Fay, NY

The Nature of Rain

I hear rain
Outside in the drain
   pitter patter
   pitter patter
Rain falls in the junkyard
And hits the old broken down crane.

I see water flow
Where it goes I do not know
   swish swish
   swish swish
Perhaps it makes the worms grow.

I feel the splashes
When the rain hits my glasses
   splat splat
   splat splat
Now I can't take classes.

   pitter patter
   swish swish
   splat splat

Tanner Mikus, Grade 3
Home School, VA

Starry Starry Night

Pitch black except for the light
of stars twinkling
High in a land that
we can only dream of

Aaron Fishbein, Grade 2
Dartmouth Early Learning Center, MA

Mrs. Politidis

Kind, nice
Beautiful, loving
Caring, teaching
Full of love
Sprouting out
You may be strict
But I don't blame you

Anna Dimitriadis, Grade 2
Public School 122 Mamie Fay, NY

May

May
Warm, flowers
Celebrate, play, rolling
Flowers are blooming outside
Fifth month

Sabrina Roberto, Grade 3
Evergreen Elementary School, PA

Spring

Spring is on the way,
So we can go out and play,
We have to wait a week or so,
It's worth the wait, don't you know?

Jack Manzo, Grade 3
Our Lady of Hope School, NY

Fun in the Sun

I go to the park to have fun.
We like to swing and run.
I run really fast.
It's really a blast,
To laugh and play in the sun.

Jordan Brown, Grade 2
Oakdale Elementary School, MD

Violet
Violet is like the sound of a hair band popping up and down and all around.
Violet is like the smell of perfume with beautiful flowers that make it smell so good.
Violet is like the taste of a juicy lollipop with good flavor
that everybody would like to try.
Violet is like the feel of a smooth dress with nice stunning flowers on it.

Arielle Francis, Grade 2
Long Meadow Elementary School, CT

The Clock
Tick tock
I hear a clock.
It has a big noise
but it is not a rock.
I hear it in the day
and
I hear it in the night.
I hear it everywhere
And it is not polite.

Lydia Holder, Grade 2
Public School 152 School of Science & Technology, NY

Music
The way it feels flowing through my head
The loud thumping of the electric guitar being strummed by Keith Richard's
Or the soft gentle sound of the acoustic being played by Taylor Swift.
The D.J spinning the records to it's own new beat.
Or the sound of Louie Armstrong playing the trumpet.
The sound of Bruce Springsteen singing one of his number 1 hits,
"Born in the U.S.A."
All of these different sounds have one thing in common
they're all music.

Sydney Wry, Grade 3
General John Nixon Elementary School, MA

Ben
My name is Ben and I like to play
soccer at Sports City every Saturday.
I'm number 3 on the gray team — we win every week.
So far we have a winning streak!
This Saturday is our last indoor game.
Come cheer for us and call out my name!

Benjamin Almond, Grade 1
St Joan of Arc School, PA

Children

C alling to their mothers
H eights are different
I ntelligent and awesome
L ike to eat chocolate
D on't always like school
R unning, skipping and hopping
E ver so playful
N ice and sometimes naughty
Edward Guenette, Grade 3
Leicester Memorial School, MA

Snowy Day

As cold as ice.
As cold as rain.
As cold as wind.
Is snow.
Elizabeth Hamilton, Grade 1
Artman Elementary School, PA

Birds

In my wood birdhouse
Birds are chirping a sweet song
Every spring morning.
Madeline Brown, Grade 3
St John Neumann Academy, VA

Rain

Rain falls in a pond
Making ripples all around
It continues day and night
Paige Franklin, Grade 1
Dartmouth Early Learning Center, MA

Stripy Snowy White Seashell

lots of stripes on the top
lots of hearts on the bottom
ovally shaped
the Stripy Snowy White Seashells
we all collect
we find them at the beach
and in the sand
Maggie Quigley, Grade 2
Cabot Elementary School, MA

Snow

Snow is falling,
It is all around,
It's on my head,
It is on the ground.

Big wet snowflakes,
Sign of a short storm,
Small fluffy snowflakes,
Sign of a long storm.

Snow formed in spring
Turns into rain
When it's melting,
I love watching.
Talene Pogharian, Grade 3
James Russell Lowell School, MA

Flower Clip

Very,
   very,
      pretty.
Beautiful flower.
Pink and purple
and sparkly too.
Diamond in middle
that looks like a mirror.
Very,
   very,
      pretty,
flower clip.
Nuzhat Khan, Grade 3
Public School 69 Jackson Heights, NY

Spring

Spring is so calm.
All animals come out.
The sun is bright,
Lets go in the bright light.
Spring is so calm,
We will have so much fun…
When spring is here.
Helene Hoxha, Grade 3
James Russell Lowell School, MA

Dandelion Yellow

Dandelion yellow is like the sound of crackling fire on a cold winter night.
Dandelion yellow is like the smell of a beautiful flower in the meadow
Dandelion yellow is like the taste of a piece of banana in your mouth.
Dandelion yellow is like the feel of the hot sun beating down on you on a summer day.

Michaela Quinn, Grade 2
Long Meadow Elementary School, CT

Red

Red tastes like juicy, delicious strawberries
in the springtime, with juice running down my chin.

Red smells like spicy, hot sauce on wings
in the kitchen on Sunday afternoon.

Red looks like crunchy, sweet apples
on a cool fall day.

Red feels like smooth, long ribbons
in a girl's hair.

Red sounds like screeching, huge fire trucks
going to put out a fire.

David Lugo, Grade 3
Watsontown Elementary School, PA

Growing Up

Step by step we move with strides,
Lessons learn as we go by.
New friends, new schools, new books new tools,
Come on David grow with me
Soon we'll be able to reach the sky.

Michael Johnson, Grade 2
Great Oaks Elementary School, NY

A Garden

I see a garden with a beautiful flower.
There is a tree as tall as a tower.
Lots of fruits and vegetables. Apples, pears, lettuce and peas.
But there are no foods like cereal and cheese.
You could see some bugs
Like butterflies and maybe slugs.

Kaya Doyle, Grade 2
Clarksville Elementary School, NY

I'm a Little Pencil

I'm a little pencil —
I'm a little pencil, pencil
I love to draw,
Draw, draw
I have lead inside
So I can write
I'm a special pencil
I only work with righties.

Yusuf Meghji, Grade 1
Buckley Country Day School, NY

My Sister

My sister
is the
meanest
in the
world
She pulls
my hair
every time
I sleep
She kicks
me but
I love
my sister
because
I always
wanted a
sister.

Angelica Mejia, Grade 3
Public School 69 Jackson Heights, NY

The Birthday Piercing

On my seventh birthday
I went to Claire's,
I chose a pair of earrings
that I wanted to wear.
I sat in a chair
and the ladies pierced my ears,
it hurt a little bit
but there were no tears.

Madie Solomon, Grade 1
St Joan of Arc School, PA

Pets

Pets are there to comfort you, love you,
And play with you. You may have
A dog, cat, bird, gerbil, hamster,
Guinea pig, fish, turtle, or lizard,
But no matter what,
They love you and you love them.

Sarah Mancini, Grade 3
Somers Elementary School, CT

Cats

Cats are nice, cats are neat
Cats are also really sweet.
To see my cat is a special treat,
I love cats!

Juliet Isselbacher, Grade 2
Cabot Elementary School, MA

Ice Skating

Everyone is on the ice
Having fun because skating is so nice!
Skating here, skating there,
People falling everywhere.
Some little kids are using crates,
Some big kids, just on skates
Skating is so much fun,
Why don't you try it everyone?

Amy Freed, Grade 2
Willis E Thorpe School, MA

The Appley Soury Excitement

A green and red paint bomb
that booms
boom kaboom
boom kaboom
boom kaboom
crackle
sizzle-z-z-z-s-s-s
Poof
the soury
excitement
is over

Matthew Rivnak, Grade 2
Tashua School, CT

April

A pril fools!
P ranks on April 1st.
R ain, so much rain.
I n April everything is fun.
L eaves are finally starting to appear, spring is here!

Ben McCarthy, Grade 2
Dr Samuel C Eveleth School, MA

All About Football

Football is my favorite. I always love to play it.
When you play football you will enjoy it.
Every time you get tackled, it doesn't feel so good,
but when you tackle somebody
or when you get a touchdown, it feels great.
Especially when you win a game,
your feelings get even better,
you feel so happy you want to do it again.
But you better watch for when you lose,
you want to scream and shout, but trust me,
that happened to me,
deep down inside, I felt like a bomb exploded,
and it did not feel so good.
But one day I won a game
and I think my heart got bigger, it felt very good.
It doesn't matter if you win or lose,
because it's all about fun.
But when you play football,
you will enjoy it and have fun.

Frank Morganti, Grade 3
Holy Rosary School, NY

In the Night Sky

I look up
it's so dark,
Stars are glowing,
nothing like the morning sky.
I wish that I could
touch the sky.
Oh, why is it so high?
How I wish I could
touch the sky!

Israt Islam, Grade 2
Public School 152 School of Science & Technology, NY

Winter Day

The fire is crackling
and we are snacking.
It starts to snow
Outside I go.
We will build a snowman.
Until spring it will stand.

Brenda Torres, Grade 3
Penn-Kidder Campus, PA

Chocolate

Chocolate, chocolate
I love chocolate,
When it is white or brown
Or even chocolate lollipops!
I love chocolate!
Mmmmmmmmmmmmm
Chocolate!

Emma Barake, Grade 2
Cabot Elementary School, MA

Snake

Ssst
slithering across the floor
sssst
sliding carefully
sssssst
hissing loudly
sssssssssst
ow it bit me!

Josh David, Grade 2
Tashua School, CT

Ants

Ants are gross,
Ants are ewww
Ants are crawling
In my shoe!

Ants are icky,
Ants are gross,
Ants are crawling
On my toast!

Sophie Spector, Grade 2
Cabot Elementary School, MA

Eels

Slithery, slimy at the bottom of the lake,
Eels, I think you are great!
No legs, no arms, just one long tail.
Eels, I think you are great!
Stay in the sand all day long.
Eels, I think you are great!

Nicole Palmieri, Grade 2
St Rose School, CT

Rainbows

Rainbows make me think of colors.
Colors make me think of flowers.
Flowers make me think of the sky.
The sky makes me think of rain.
Rain makes me think of rainbows.

Michael Mosconi, Grade 3
Cambridge Springs Elementary School, PA

Anne Frank

Anne Frank wrote every day in her diary,
Well you know what? She's just like me.

The Germans wanted to destroy the Jews.
So Anne's family had to pull through.

In March of 1945 Anne died of typhus,
So she left her diary for all of us.

Adriana Martinez, Grade 3
Oakdale Elementary School, MD

A Mouse Who Lived in a House

I saw a mouse who lived in a house
His friend Ned woke up from bed.

He played with his toy jet
then sent his dog to the vet.

Now the mouse is resting
fluffing his nesting.

Settled for the night
he is in flight.

Brandon Cay, Grade 3
Seaford Central Elementary School, DE

Rain

R ains a lot in the rainforest
A rmadillo has a hard body to keep it safe
I nsects like to crawl on the forest floor
N ight time is when the hungry caiman and the bats come out

Max Barile, Kindergarten
Montessori Development Center, PA

Snow

The season is winter the snow is everywhere. I can see the snow falling from
the sky, and the clouds seem dark. Then the smell of snow was in the air. I
throw myself in the snow to make a snow angel. I stomped in the snow. I liked
the feeling of the snow on my toe. I made a snow ball and threw it at my
friends. We played in the snow until my mom calls, "come inside!" I love snow.

Caija C. Clarke, Grade 3
Pat-Kam School & Early Childhood Center, NY

If I Were...

If I were blue, I'd be a bird sitting in a tree.
If I were green, I'd be a frog hopping on a hat.
If I were pink, I'd be a pencil box holding my crayons.
If I were yellow, I'd be the folder that has my papers in it.

Emily Dietz, Grade 1
St Clement Mary Hofbauer School, MD

Winter Is

Winter is the smell of cold air making my nose freeze.
Winter is the taste of mommy's warm pheasant soup.
Winter is the touch of snow freezing my fingers.
Winter is when you see icicles on houses.
Winter is the sound of wind howling outside my window.
Winter is a cold time of the year.

Marcello Fazio, Grade 1
St Teresa of Avila School, NY

Winter Is

Winter is the smell of fresh air, clean and good.
Winter feels cold when I touch the snow.
Winter is the taste of chocolate chip cookies, sweet and crunchy.
Winter is the sound of parties in my house.
Winter looks like families together in their homes.
Winter is exciting!

Christian Espigadera, Grade 1
St Teresa of Avila School, NY

David's Slingshot

David had bought a brand new sling,
But he did not go ling, ding, ching,
He tended sheep among the hills;
His slingshot brought him many kills.

The ugly lion snapped and growled,
and skinny, sneaky, coyotes howled.
David was too small for battle
But his God knew he could rattle.

Goliath was a giant man —
He did before the army stand.
But David trusted in the Lord,
He did not fear Goliath's sword:

He twirled the sling above his head,
The big tall giant was now dead.
Bryce Histand, Grade 3
Union Valley Christian School, PA

An Alien from Outer Space

There was an alien from outer space,
He said his base was only a suitcase.
Last night he had a nightmare,
He talked to a bear.
The bear went into the alien's base.
Corwin Riordan, Grade 2
Oakdale Elementary School, MD

Love

Love is a beautiful thing
Love is too great for words
Love is God
God is love
Love is wonderful
So please come spread
Love throughout the world
By setting an example of love —
Love everyone and everything
Then you will see how great
Love is
Sarah Gruhn, Grade 3
Trinity Christian School, VA

Tears

Are like tiny
Drops of rain
Running down
Your cheeks
Rain to the ants,
Feeling blue…
Must be a bad
Day for you
Zoe Baker, Grade 1
Buckley Country Day School, NY

Winter

The cold winter air
blows through
your hair.

The snow comes
down the color
of a polar bear.
C. Blair Marine, Grade 3
New Canaan Country School, CT

Yummy Gummies

Squiggling squirming gummy worms
Color splashed in my mouth
Oozing sugar
Gummy yummy
in its giant taste.
Chewing up and down
all around
I ate way too much.
So so sick!
Sarah Solomon, Grade 2
Dr Samuel C Eveleth School, MA

Funny Bunny

There was a leprechaun named Brian.
He was so funny that he was flyin'!
He hopped on honey
The bee got money
He was so sad he was cryin'.
Christopher Mok, Grade 3
St Rose School, CT

If I Were...

If I were purple, I'd be a kite flying in the air.
If I were white, I'd be a book from the library.
If I were yellow, I'd be the stars up in the sky.
If I were blue, I'd be a bird flying in the sky.
If I were green, I'd be grass that people would walk on.
If I were red, I'd be the heart beating in a body.

Danielle Zacierka, Grade 1
St Clement Mary Hofbauer School, MD

Purple

Purple is a flower pretty and fine, purple is a crayon who drew a neat squiggly line.
Purple is a nice poster or two, purple is a purple library book over due!
Purple is a friend to be by your side, purple is fog who always glide.
Purple is a ghost who give you frights, purple is a buddy to say goodnight!

Lucy Shin, Grade 3
Weston Intermediate School, CT

A Clear Rock

Shiny and clear
you can see through it
look closely and you can see a rainbow
you can see purple, blue, orange, pink, yellow, zigzags

It looks like magic
move it around and the colors change
the zigzags move
it has dots on the bottom

It is like a moon sailing through the sky
there's magic in the sky

Sophie Natale-Short, Grade 2
Cabot Elementary School, MA

Creatures of the Night

In the nighttime you might think it's quiet and peaceful.
But out in the world there are creatures awake,
playing and dancing until daybreak.

These creatures are special.
These creatures are different.
These creatures are nocturnal.

Claire Dettelbach, Grade 3
Thoreau Elementary School, MA

America

Our nation is free
Fifty stars upon our flag
Love is in the air.
Julie Waller, Grade 3
Sacred Heart School, CT

Bunnies Are Cute

Blue whales are cute
But turtles are cuter.
Turtles are cute,
But bunnies are the cutest!
Ian Erickson, Grade 2
Cabot Elementary School, MA

Spring

April breezes blow
Rain is falling on us now
Rainbows over me
Philip Kramer, Grade 2
Guilford Lakes School, CT

Ghost

G ray
H alloween
O ld
S cary
T ricks
Alexis Sager, Grade 2
St Joseph School, NY

Pink

Everywhere I look
I like it on my backpack
My favorite color
Grace Poe, Grade 3
Sacred Heart School, CT

My Friend Emma

Emma is my best friend.
We like to play pretend.
We have a lot of fun,
when we run in the sun.
Riley Gilmore, Grade 1
St Stephen's School, NY

Animals Around the World

Strong, soft, stripes, spots
Slow, slither, scales
Furry, fuzzy, fluffy feathers
Fast feet, tails

Wild wings, wet nose
Wimpy, woolly, wiggly
Loud, little, long leap
Jumpy, lumpy, jiggly
Ms. Kate Schoonmaker's Class, Grade 2
Henry Clay Elementary School, VA

Blue

What is blue?
The sea that comes out of your imagination
It goes by so fast
A fish can't ever swim in it
The flowing waves go through your mind
Blue covers the lonely passing by
It's the sky with lots of spots
Of white
It burns out raging fires
Jacques Klapisch, Grade 3
Cabot Elementary School, MA

A Rainy Day

A very very rainy day.
Spit-spat.
The rain is falling down out of the clouds.
I know that I'll surely get pretty wet.
Brennan McAvoy, Grade 1
Hyman Fine Elementary School, MA

Football

F ans always vote for their home team.
O ffensive line is the hardest place to play
O ffense is fun to play.
T eam players should be friends.
B enches are for football players.
A fumble has been received.
L inebacker is another hard place to play.
L oyalty is the best to give.
Zachary Venezia, Grade 3
Brookside Elementary School, MA

Outdoors Today

I like the hot sun
and to run with a chill
through my body
and music running
through my ears
the wind makes
a whistle in my ears
but I will run till
   the wind
slows me down

Kayleigh Edwards, Grade 3
Washington Elementary School, PA

Snow

Snow is on the go,
In the winter so.
It might cause a snow day,
Then kids go out to play.
At five o'clock I hear a plow,
I wake up now.
And here I stand,
Looking at this bright dreamland.

Katie Bachli, Grade 3
Craneville School, MA

School

S ometimes really cool
C orrecting the papers
H elps you learn
O ften is hard work
O nly five days a week
L earning with your friends

Marcus Rodriguez and Tyler
Jefferson, Grade 3
Leicester Memorial School, MA

A Tree in a Forest

A tree in a forest blowing in the wind
   While nature flows everywhere.
   Sky's so blue clouds so white,
I just might fall asleep here at night.

Rebecca Pinho, Grade 3
Willis E Thorpe School, MA

Things to Do if You Are a Tiger

Eat other animals
Sleep in the forest
Live in a shady forest
Have stripes and orange fur
Have sharp teeth
Drink from a lake

Joey Ferrucci, Grade 1
Glover Elementary School, MA

Pop It Up Ball

Colors spinning in the air,
   moving fast,
   keep it up,
   keep it moving,
   light finger touch.
Count the pops.
POP IT UP!

Ashley Nye, Grade 2
Dr Samuel C Eveleth School, MA

A Very Good Day

It was a sunny day.
So we went out to play.
We went to the park.
Until it became dark.
I went home and did my math.
Before my mommy gave me a bath.
I then went to sleep.
Without making a peep.

Maria Milonas, Grade 2
Public School 2 Alfred Zimberg, NY

December

D ecorating the tree
E ating lots of goodies
C hristmas parties
E xcited for Christmas Day
M essy wrapping paper
B est time of the year
E ating lots of turkey
R eading Christmas stories

Jacqueline McQuaid, Grade 3
Houghton Elementary School, MA

Winter Months

Movingly cold, yet kids play in them.
What is there about it, what magic?
How is it that a thousand families
have died in it, yet lots survive?
How can kids play but not adults?
What is there about this strange time?

What?

Why?
Eleanor Mancusi-Ungaro, Grade 2
Dr Samuel C Eveleth School, MA

Twilight Star

Bright star, bright star
Twinkling high above so far
They'll twinkle
Right above the moon
Those big, beautiful twilight stars
Twilight star, twilight star
Twinkling high above so far
Those big beautiful stars
Might even twinkle
Right past Mars
Twilight star, twilight star
Olivia Permatteo, Grade 3
Lincoln Street School, MA

Ocean Life

Dipping
Diving
Fish,

Seagulls
In the
Sky,

One little starfish
on a rock,
and the lighthouse
is dark.
Kyle Pettinelli, Grade 2
Dr Samuel C Eveleth School, MA

Summer

Hooray! Hooray!
Summer is here!
It is time to have some fun.
Playing outside, waterslide.
Going to the beach.
Having fun.
Playing games, and lots of other things!
David Ducharme, Grade 2
Dr Samuel C Eveleth School, MA

Billy Madison

B ully
I magines penguins
L ikes his third grade teacher
L ikes his go-kart
Y ucky language

M ountain Dew
A bsolutely silly
D unce
I nto pop
S ometimes uses not nice words
O h so weird
N ot smart
Niko Kaliszuk, Grade 2
Klein Elementary School, PA

Petals

Jumping around
Dancing joyfully now
In the darkness of the cold night
Weakness
Julia Kadis, Grade 3
Cabot Elementary School, MA

Fall

Fall, fall it has it all
Leaves falling
Nature calling!
Yellow, orange, green and red
Goodnight! As the flowers go to bed
Mary Clare George, Grade 3
Seton Catholic School, NY

Blakeley

Blakeley rang the doorbell.
Then she rang the school bell.
She slipped on an eggshell.
Then on a nutshell.
Her feet started to smell.
Then her nose began to swell.
And now it's time to say farewell.

Adrian Willis II, Grade 1
Magnet School of Math, Science and Design Technology, NY

I Am Billy Babcock

I am a great athlete and a good fisherman.
I wonder if war will go on in the future.
I hear people screaming in the stands.
I see people walking the earth for peace.
I want Arnold Schwarzenegger for President.
I am a great athlete and a good fisherman.

I pretend that I am in the army fighting for my country.
I feel someone is always behind me helping me with everything.
I touch the red, white and blue flag of the United States.
I worry that someone is going to wreck my house.
I cry because some people don't do the right thing.
I am a great athlete and fisherman.

I understand that war is going on in the world.
I say stand up for what's right.
I dream that there is world peace.
I try to do my best in baseball and school.
I hope that I get into the military.
I am a good athlete and a good fisherman.

William Babcock, Grade 3
Stony Point Elementary School, NY

Bubble Bath

In a bubble bath
smooth and soapy,
clean and nice.
Blow bubbles under water,
take a bubble bath until night.

Abel Antoine, Grade 2
Public School 152 School of Science & Technology, NY

My Brother

shooting the ball
passing the ball
blocking the player
stealing the player's ball
defending the goal
kicking the ball
soccer is cool!
Renzo Rosales, Grade 2
Tashua School, CT

Toasty Hug

I hear footsteps
Thump! Thump!
They're getting louder
Thump! Thump!
They're getting closer
Thump!
They're here
Is that you Mom
Yes
Give me a hug!
Maggie Ameer, Grade 2
Tashua School, CT

Winter

Summer is done
But winter is fun
Having snowball fights
We will stay up all night
Riding my sled
Then going to bed
Billy Steen, Grade 3
Penn-Kidder Campus, PA

Wind

Wind
fast like a cheetah
strong like the Hulk
sounds like a ghost
opens my door
boo aaaaa
run under my bed!
Matt D'Amore, Grade 2
Tashua School, CT

Robber/Cop

Robber
sneaky, feral
stealing, running, startling
bank, house, patrol car, badge
rescuing, working, helping
charming, bold
cop
Carlee Walker, Grade 3
Bradford Township Elementary School, PA

I Am Julia

I like to collect spoons
and I like pink balloons.
I like to comb my hair
and I play fair.
I love gymnastics
and I think Hannah Montana is fantastic.
Someday I hope to write
a book that's out of sight.
Julia Vargo, Grade 1
St Joan of Arc School, PA

Seasons

Fall hit the spot
and summer ran away
Then it was a day to find my way
I used the day yesterday
To find my way
Then winter wrestled fall
and winter won
When winter came I slowed down
I sat at the window trembling
as I looked at the shamed snow coming down.
Another day to find my way
Then I put myself on top of the bay.
Jackson Rheault, Grade 3
Somers Elementary School, CT

Love

Love is important
Mommy and Daddy love me
Love is in our hearts
Katie York, Grade 2
Fonda-Fultonville Elementary School, NY

Dinosaurs

Dinosaurs are creatures that we don't really know
All we know is that they lived millions of years ago.
Some ate plants, some ate meat
T-Rex can eat us to our feet!
Dinosaurs can't swim
Dinosaurs can't fly
All they do is walk and run by
Dinosaurs are amazing, you know
Paleontologists have a lot of digging to go.

Zipporah Diaz, Grade 3
Public School 105 Senator Abraham Bernste, NY

A Desk

I am a desk.
I hold onto books and journals.
I feel sad when my owner keeps me dirty.
I feel sad when I am raised higher.
I wish I could move to third grade with my owner.
I would tell my owner to keep me clean every day.

Brian Balcarcel, Grade 2
Bensley Elementary School, VA

Spring

In the spring, the sun begins to get hot.
I start to sweat in the hot sun.
I see the beautiful flowers.
They are blue, yellow, and red in color.
You can see more fish, whales, sharks, and plants in the water.
Crocodiles live in the water to keep themselves warm.
There is so much to see in the spring!

Desmond Allen, Kindergarten
Agape Christian Academy, VA

A Welfin

This is a Welfin.
A Welfin lives in wishing wells with whimpering wolves.
A Welfin eats wooden wheels, worms, and wrapping paper every day.
A Welfin likes wands, witches, windmills, and the wilderness.
A Welfin is a wonderful, whimsical creature on very windy Wednesdays.
My Welfin tried to waltz wonderfully with a walrus and me.

Michaela Seay, Grade 3
St Clement Mary Hofbauer School, MD

I Am Like a Lion
I am like a lion
Brave with courage
Working hard every day
I am a lion
With bravery in every stitch

Julie Kim, Grade 2
Buckley Country Day School, NY

Summer
S unny.
U ntil the flowers pop up.
M usic of the birds.
M aybe it is a hot day.
E njoy the sun.
R ain.

Andrew Carreon, Grade 1
Hyman Fine Elementary School, MA

Rain
D   d   d
r   r   r
o   o   o
p   p   p

    rain
pops
   down
     on
      my
       head
it sounds like the wind

Georgia Ring, Grade 1
Glover Elementary School, MA

Playing with Legos
You can build with them.
You can play with them.
You can take them apart.
You can make things with Legos.
Legos come in many shapes and sizes.
Lego sets have Lego guys in them.

Jack Starbird, Grade 1
Glover Elementary School, MA

Spring
S is for sun.
P is for puddles.
R is for running.
I is for ice cream.
N is for nest.
G is for go to the ball game.

Deven Patch, Kindergarten
Fisher Hill Elementary School, MA

The Raindrop
The raindrops fall.
They hit the ground.
The drops sink in the ground.
The rain stops.
Out comes a beautiful rainbow.

Evan Carling, Grade 1
Hyman Fine Elementary School, MA

Spring Is Coming
Spring is coming!
In like a lion
Out like a lamb
From snowy days
To sunny bays
Cold winter freezes
To warm summer breezes
Spring is here!

Jordon Clibbens, Grade 3
Concord Elementary School, PA

Awesome Dog!
Soft
4 legged
Big nose
Sharp teeth
Sports playing
Smart
Furry
Awesome
Great name:
Yellow Lab

Ryan Fronheiser, Grade 3
Washington Elementary School, PA

Mars

M ars is the fourth planet and was discovered in prehistoric times.
A round Mars the diameter is 6,974 km or 4,222 miles.
R ed is the color that Mars appears to be.
S tar of death named by the Babylonians.

Isabella Silverheels, Grade 3
Brant Elementary School, NY

Dads

Dads —
dads workout,
dads are smart,
dads are good,
dads are funny,
dads are brave.

Payten Valmont, Grade 2
Public School 152 School of Science & Technology, NY

Earth

Earth is where my mom gave birth.
Earth is where I live and work.
Earth is where I like to play.
Earth is my favorite place.
Earth is where I want to stay.

Khalycza Rosario, Grade 3
Public School 105 Senator Abraham Bernste, NY

Red

Red is like the sound of flames and wood crackling in the chimney.
Red is like the smell of juicy watermelons in the beautiful garden.
Red is like the taste of the apples crunching in my mouth in the backyard.
Red is like the feel of sunburn on my soft skin on the beach.

Spencer Jenney, Grade 2
Long Meadow Elementary School, CT

Horse

H ooves pounding on the ground.
O utstanding animals.
R unning in the woods.
S tallions running everywhere.
E yes see in two directions.

Kristin Gascot, Grade 3
Public School 105 Senator Abraham Bernste, NY

Winter

The fireplace smells fine
When it is burning pine.
School is out
Let's all shout.
Tons of snow fell everywhere
So we're not going anywhere.
Zeb Kleintop, Grade 3
Penn-Kidder Campus, PA

My Spring

Black
Horses
Galloping
Spring is here
Genevieve Pietrzak, Grade 1
Trinity Christian School, VA

My Dog Ate It

My dog ate it
My dog ate my homework
My dog's name is Terk
He only eats homework
And maybe some jerky
He may eat some turkey
But that's all.
Julianne Cobb, Grade 3
Trinity Christian School, VA

Happy

I love God.
He is my friend.
God makes me happy.
He is always with me.
Alina Hollister, Kindergarten
Agape Christian Academy, VA

I Need You

Roses are red
Violets are blue
Can you do me a favor,
And pray for me too?
James, Grade 3
Kanner Learning Center, PA

I Am

I am a child of God.
I am a member of the church.
I am a good kid at my house.
I am not a tattletale.
I am Italian and Portuguese.
I am an older brother.
I am 8.
I am a good helper and aide.
I am a good computer person.
I am Paul Rodrigues son of Paul Rodrigues.
I am very special
Paul Rodrigues, Grade 2
St Mary's Primary School, MA

I Am

I am 7
I am a year older every May 3rd.
I am a happy girl
And a fun one too.
I am funny well I think so
I hope people will think that I am funny too
I am almost 8
I am nice, I know you are
I am stopping now, so bye.
Victoria Vecchiarello, Grade 2
Willis E Thorpe School, MA

I Am

I am good at being a good friend.
And being a good son.
I am very good at schoolwork.
I do not like it, but I will do it any ways.
I am very good at playing the drums.
But the best thing I'm good at,
Is playing baseball.
And I am an expert at playing video games.
But the most important thing is that I'm
A child of God.
I am good at predicting the weather.
And I am Kyle.
Myself.
And the last thing is I am kind.
Kyle MacKnight, Grade 2
St Mary's Primary School, MA

Spring

I see colorful rainbows fading away in the blue sky.
Blue birds singing in the trees.
Pretty flowers growing in the earth.
Yummy ice cream licking it off a cone.
Green grass growing greener by the second everywhere.

Abigail Brackin, Grade 2
St Mary Magdalen School, DE

If I Were a Pizza

If I were a pizza,
I'd be covered with cheese,
If I were a pizza,
I'd be yummy
If I were a pizza
I'd be Yum, Yum, Yum!

Amber Gonzalez, Grade 1
Public School 105 Senator Abraham Bernste, NY

White

White is kittens
White is milk
White is a spark of an idea
Writing it down on white paper
White is life, but also death,
On a white road to heaven
White is a hallow feeling, but soft and squishy, too
White is twinkling stars at night
It's a vanilla cone with white cream on top
White is a nurse's coat while in the white hospital room
White covers up the bad at night
While having white dreams
White is nothing, but also many things
White is that color on our proud flag,
Flapping in the white wind
White was the beginning
It shall also be the end
White is your breath standing in white snow
White is Grandad's beard, soft as fur,
And white is when you look up at night
And feel freedom in the air

Julianna Lakomski, Grade 3
Cabot Elementary School, MA

Don't Take Your Puppy to School

Don't take your puppy to school.
He'll eat all the playground logs.
If the teacher sees him —
I'll get in trouble...
Oh Milo, don't act like a hog!
Taylor Zegers, Grade 2
Milton Terrace Primary School, NY

Stars

Twinkling bright
Through the night
They will guide you out of fright
They are gems that can't be mined
They are lovely
You can't deny
Helen Crosby, Grade 3
Center School, MA

March

On a windy day.
Then thunder and lightning starts!
A wicked rain storm!
Connor McNerney, Grade 2
St Rose School, CT

When My Grandpa Died

When I was six
My Grandpa died
I've cried ever since
Now I keep his model ships
And he remains in my heart
Justin da Silva, Grade 3
Acushnet Elementary School, MA

Nature

Nature is beautiful. Nature is grand.
Nature is a beauty and a brand.
The birds soar.
The bears roar.
The deers run through the sun.
And the hummingbirds hum and hum.
Rhiannon Mattingly, Grade 2
Walker Memorial School, ME

My Ball Buddy

With my friend Tina, I play ball.
With my friend Tina, I call.
With my friend Tina, I go on a boat.
With my friend Tina, I share a coat.
Bethany Phillips, Grade 2
Trinity Christian School, VA

A Crayon Is Pink!

A crayon is pink as
houses,
sunsets,
pigs,
and soap.
A crayon is as pink as
poodles,
flowers,
eraser,
and shirts.
A crayon is pink!
Avery Roberts, Grade 3
Granville Elementary School, NY

Colors

Red is an apple.
Orange is a carrot
Yellow is a sun and...
You know all your colors...
So watch out for your colors!!!
Ally Wells, Grade 1
Carlyle C Ring Elementary School, NY

The Dark Scary Night

It's scary and dark,
You're all alone,
The wind whistles,
Owls hoot,
Leaves silently fall to the ground,
All of a sudden...
Boom! Bang! Bam!
THUNDER!
You start to cry all alone.
Nicoletta Tachtchouk, Grade 3
Public School 48, NY

Turquoise

Turquoise flowers can be found only in Hawaii
Miners find turquoise gems in abandoned caves
I really like swimming in the turquoise ocean water
Turquoise rocks are just beautiful
I like painting rocks
I really, really, really want a turquoise bike!

Timothy DeCoff, Grade 1
Willis E Thorpe School, MA

Familiar Colors

Pink is the color of a beautiful rose
Or the color of a blanket when you are in a doze

Gray is the color of fog in the sky
Away is where we want them to fly

Blue is sad on a horrible day
Or the color of a couch on which I lay

Green is grass in the middle of spring
Or the vibrant color of an emerald ring

Brown is the color of an old oak tree
And it seems like a very dark color to me

Red is the most known color for Valentines Day
Or the color of a beautiful flower in May

Black can be the sky at midnight
When the moon is not shining very bright

Erin Umlauf, Grade 3
Stall Brook School, MA

Recycle

Recycle, reduce, reuse what you use.
Recycle, reduce, reuse what you use.
Turn plastic to elastic.
And glass into brass.
Recycle, reduce, reuse what you use.
Recycle, reduce, reuse what you use.

Evan Cantone, Grade 3
Susquehanna Community Elementary School, PA

The Attack!
S hhhh!
H elp me!
A hhhhhhhh!
R oar!!!!!!!!!!!!!!
K ills other sharks!
Reece Ferguson, Grade 2
Klein Elementary School, PA

The Beach
The beach,
I like the sand in my toes.
The beach,
I like the wind in my hair.
The beach,
I like the water on my legs.
Because,
It all feels good!
Skyla Bunnell, Grade 2
St Mary's Primary School, MA

Wag! Wag!
My dog
named Molly
has my
dreams
and life.
She has
my love.
I have
her love.
We both
love
each
other.
Adelaide Meier, Grade 1
St Rose School, CT

Puppy Dog
My dog is black like
outerspace and she runs in
the woods behind trees
Hannah Ames, Grade 2
Killingly Memorial School, CT

Starry Night
One night, a very starry night,
I went to sleep on a blanket on the beach.
The waves crashed up against the shore wall.
I counted the shiny stars in the sky.
I dreamt of jumping from star to star and
sleeping on the moon.
Suddenly I woke up in a flash to see my
Dad carrying me into the car.
Away I went.
Phoebe Walker, Grade 3
Weston Intermediate School, CT

Green the Leprechaun
There once was a leprechaun named Green.
He wanted to touch a bean.
It was so tall.
It made him fall.
And then he had to get clean.
Lauren Cirone, Grade 3
St Rose School, CT

Spring
Blue and red birds flying in the clouds.
The warm wind blowing everywhere.
Beautiful flowers swaying in the air.
Delicious water ice fresh out of the freezer.
Wet rainbows gliding in the sky.
Daniel Deckers, Grade 2
St Mary Magdalen School, DE

The Domino
The domino sounds like a zebra galloping
It feels like one too!

It is black and white
like a zebra
but
I
wish
it
had
stripes

Leah Navin, Grade 1
St Rose School, CT

Baltimore*

B aseball rules!
A nybody who sees a home run cheers!
L oving baseball.
T ejada was traded to the Astros.
I slands south of Florida play baseball.
M ascots can make people laugh.
O rioles play in Baltimore.
R unning the bases.
E very game makes lot of memories.

Jackson Payne, Grade 2
Kent Gardens Elementary School, VA
*Dedicated to the city of
Baltimore, Maryland

Clock

The clock
Ticks
Like
The crickets
At
Night.
A wolf's howl
Matches the
Moon
At
Midnight.

Kimmy Amash, Grade 2
Milton Terrace Primary School, NY

Whale Sharks

I studied whale sharks,
Baby sharks are cool.
They grow inside eggs.

Whale shark's not dangerous.
They're not whales they're enormous
Lazy, slow, fish, very rare.

Whale sharks are covered with scales
Greenish gray with yellow dots.
Symmetrical dot designs.

Gregory Kazanjian, Grade 3
James Russell Lowell School, MA

A Rainy Day

Drip drop! Drip drop!
The drops land on the ground, plop!
Tip tap! Tip tap!
They fall on the ground, splat!
The clouds make the rain come.
That's where it comes from.
The rain sounds like a drum.
While it's raining, let's hum.
Oh, I love the rain.
Falling on the windowpane.

Karen Jorgensen, Grade 3
Heron Pond Elementary School, NH

Angels Fly

Angels, angels everywhere
One is here, one is there
Angel, angels everywhere
Angels fly, dazzling bright,
They fly till the morning light,
Angels, angels everywhere
One is here one is there
Angels, angels everywhere.

Rachael Nelson, Grade 3
Heron Pond Elementary School, NH

Puppies

Funny and playful
love to chew their squeaky toys
small, terrific pets

Jennifer Lussier, Grade 3
Sacred Heart School, CT

Birds

Birds, birds are flying, flying.
In the store.
Ruining everything
Everything.
We are out of luck.
How many times
Did they peck?
Maybe 20, 30 or 100.

Sean Michael Meyre, Grade 2
Milton Terrace Primary School, NY

My New House

I want to build a new house
It's not going to allow a mouse
It will look like a bunker in the ground
and there is camouflage all around
it's going to have a lot of army stuff
it is going to look very tough
you have to have the code to get in
you have to type it again and again.

Ian Potter, Grade 3
Ellicott Road Elementary School, NY

Daschunds

Dogs barking.
About to jump under the table.
They run.
Ruff…ruff!
Every once in a while
There is a Daschund race.
Daschunds rule!

Corinne Hill, Grade 1
Hyman Fine Elementary School, MA

Flowers

Roses are red
Violets are blue
don't you like these flowers too.

Some flowers are purple
Some flowers are peach.
Some grow so high
that I cannot reach.

In the winter
no flowers bloom
but in the spring
the scent fills my room

I like flowers
Yes, I do
I like flowers
How about you?

Janai Toney, Grade 2
Great Oaks Elementary School, NY

The Three Little Puppies

When they were born
They didn't do much
Their eyes were not open
And we could not touch
Every day they would grow
Learning how to walk and run
They have lots of energy
To jump and have fun
They are so cute and furry
I could hold them all day
The most fun thing to do
Is take them outside to play
The don't know a lot
And sometimes they act crazy
They get into everything
Even my Mom's daisies
They can be very noisy
Like when they bark and whine
But it doesn't bother me
Because they're all mine.

Jessie Johnson, Grade 2
Mary Walter Elementary School, VA

My Teacher

Mrs. Galenda
Teacher, sunshine
Writing, thinking, teaching
School, classroom, chair, desk
Sitting, talking, driving
Rose, great name
Wife

Angel Martinez-Mendoza, Grade 3
Brant Elementary School, NY

Winter Is…

Winter is white.
It tastes like hot chocolate.
It smells like Christmas trees.
Winter reminds me of snow
And sounds like icicles breaking.
Winter feels very, very cold.

Andrew Francioni, Grade 2
Curtisville Primary Center, PA

Dragon Flight

I have a pet dragon.
His name is Twagon.
My dragon was four heads and he has four beds.
He breathes orange fire that can burn your tires.
My favorite thing with my dragon is flying on him.

David Moss, Grade 3
Trinity Christian School, VA

Winter

In the winter, children run to the kitchen as hot chocolate warms them.
All the snowmen look like soldiers with long carrot noses.
All snow angels dance around.
The birds say goodbye and leave the last sight.
Trees are still.
Children laugh and play.
Winter vacation comes.
The clean and beautiful snow is white.
But shhh, the long white blanket covers the earth.
Shhh the earth is asleep.
The animals hibernate.
But take your time because March is on its way.

Rebecca Yunusova, Grade 3
Queens Valley School of the Arts, NY

Waiting, Wishing, Wondering

Rustling in the wind,
with the sounds of happiness falling off branches.
The leaves glisten like emeralds.
Rubies burst out of carnations like a caterpillar and its cocoon.
When lightning strikes, you feel it is nigh but it is far.
The thunder rumbles
like a herd of elephants shaking the rubies off the flowers.
Warm wind brings me orange thoughts.
With bells of joy mixed with the bird's song,
we have an orchestra.
The drums of excitement pound in my ears,
telling me, "Look at the season, what do you see?"
I just listen intently.
I wander through the field of colors,
waiting, wishing, wondering.

Caleb Martin-Rosenthal, Grade 3
General John Nixon Elementary School, MA

So I Went Skiing

It was winter
So I couldn't go in my pool
So I went skiing instead
It was very cool.
Bailey Smith, Grade 2
East Hill School, NY

Tulips

Tulips start as a bulb
Grow into pretty flowers
Lovely to look at
Emma Rand, Grade 2
Guilford Lakes School, CT

We Are Outside

Leaves are coming out
Soccer and baseball start now
We fish in the spring
Jacob Walker, Grade 2
Guilford Lakes School, CT

Pizza

Hot or cold anywhere
pepperoni or cheesy
dinner in a slice
Lucia Guzman, Grade 3
Sacred Heart School, CT

The Horse

When I
was riding
on a
horse
I felt
a leap of joy
in my heart
because the
horse was
very calm
I felt very happy
in my heart.
Paige Simms, Grade 1
St Rose School, CT

Love Day No Way

Love day no way.
I can't believe it's here.
I don't know what to say.
Everybody is kissing.
That is so gross!
And they aren't missing.
Our teacher isn't hissing.
There is a boy that loves me
and I don't want to know who it is.
Something I don't like is the love delight.
Brianne Coon, Grade 3
Penn Yan Elementary School, NY

Spring

Spring is orange.
It tastes like jelly.
It sounds like bird songs.
It smells like fragrant flowers.
It looks like butterflies.
It makes me feel happy.
Matthew Zacierka, Grade 3
St Clement Mary Hofbauer School, MD

The Fourth of July

The Fourth of July is my favorite day
when everybody comes out,
the fireworks pop out of nowhere,
and there is one firework
that is called the American.
It is a flag of the United States of America.
Everyone sings when that firework comes out.
Matthew Stazzone, Grade 3
Holy Rosary School, NY

My Dog

Black and white,
Brown or gray,
All different colors.
Once he ate a pen,
Now he's pinkish reddish on his chin and nose.
I laughed and so did my sister,
My mom was mad, but then she laughed too.
Maria McGlone, Grade 1
Jamestown Elementary School, VA

Let's vs That Team

The crowd sits quietly as the game begins.
The players go to their spaces and hope to win.
Dribble, dribble, dribble the ball goes down the court.
The player shoots the ball in the hoop, he is a good sport.
Two points, ten points, we win, we win!

Frankie Geraci, Grade 3
Our Lady of Hope School, NY

If I Were a Kapok Tree

If I were a Kapok tree.
I would spread my beautiful branches in the sunshine.
Rainforest animals live in my limbs and other parts of me.
I am sky high — or even higher!
Sharp thorns stick out of my cortex.
And my buttress roots help me stand up.
Bumble Bee will pollinate my flowers
Making fibrous fruits grow.
I love being a Kapok tree!

Harshita Devisetty, Grade 2
Heim Elementary School, NY

If I Were in Charge of the World*

If I were in charge of the world,
I'd cancel wars, homework, books
And also boarding schools.
If I were in charge of the world,
There'd be robots to do your homework,
Layer cars, schools, sports and lots of art.
If I were in charge of the world,
You wouldn't have jails.
You wouldn't have thunder.
You wouldn't have tsunamis
Or police.
You wouldn't even have snakes.
If I were in charge of the world,
There'd be lots of peace
And a person who sometimes forgot how to drive,
And sometimes forgot how to build,
Would still be allowed to be in charge of the world.

Henry Robinson, Grade 2
St Christopher's School, VA
*Patterned after "If I Were in Charge of the World" by Judith Viorst

The Rain

Drip,
Drop,
Drip,

The rain
outside
makes
everybody glum

The sun
is hiding behind
the dark, gray
clouds

With nothing
to do
I sit down
and wish
the sun would
stay
Isabella Bitar, Grade 3
Public School 69 Jackson Heights, NY

Space

Space
The stars and the sun.
Space
The white on paper.
Space
A room without furniture.
Space
The air around you.
Space
An empty place.
Matthew Leon, Grade 3
Carlyle C Ring Elementary School, NY

If I Were a Snowflake

If I was a snowflake,
I would fly up and down like a leaf.
I would be white like a freezing icicle.
Jacob Palmer, Grade 1
Hyman Fine Elementary School, MA

Spring

Colorful butterflies flying in the zoo.
Pretty birds chirping in the trees.
Blue flowers waving in the grass.
Tasty fruit growing in the garden.
Green clovers blowing in the meadow.
Jenna La Pira, Grade 2
St Mary Magdalen School, DE

Nature

The sky is blue.
The clouds are white
The sun is bright
The water is shiny
The ants are tiny
The cars are loud
Everything from sky to ground
This poem is about
Daniel Castano, Grade 2
Public School 2 Alfred Zimberg, NY

Train

All aboard howled Miss Nash
everybody sprints on
like cheetahs
everybody's JOLLY!
everybody's on the train
"Next stop, music," says Miss Nash
HOORAY
everybody gets off
like
CRAZY
New Yorkers!
Allison Hazen, Grade 2
Tashua School, CT

Girl from Saturn

There once was a girl from Saturn,
Who wanted to learn how to burn.
She made a fire,
It got higher,
And then she made a pattern.
Alexandra Landry, Grade 1
Mater Christi School, VT

Stars!

Have you ever seen stars up close?
They just make you want to roast!
Just like butter on a piece of toast.
The wolves howl at the stars.
Maybe they came from big old Mars?
Stars, stars, and stars again,
they are such pretty words that I can't comprehend.
They are white and glow in the night.
They never give me a fright.
In the morning I cry and cry
and I really try,
to make the stars come back to me.
Finally, night comes and my tummy roams
so I think of the Moon like a big pizza pie,
on the side the stars are little pieces of cheese.
I fall asleep
without a peep
and in the morning I don't cry
I just lie
and watch the beautiful sky.

Jamie Quinzi, Grade 3
Holy Rosary School, NY

Lady Bugs

Lady Bugs have warning colors
Red, orange, yellow, black, gray, white
So other animals like different kinds of birds don't eat them
Lady Bugs like flowers and like to eat aphids

Abby Stratton, Grade 3
Evergreen Elementary School, PA

Paw Island

Have you ever been to Paw Island so very far away?
If you have, you probably had preferred to always stay.
You'd meet my Little Cutie Pie in her pretty hut.
She might tell you the story of Old King Tut.
You might sleep over
In a giant clover.
Oh my!
I have to say good-bye.

Jessie Yu, Grade 2
Trinity Christian School, VA

Watery Beach

Water crashes on
The beach, wetting the sands
It is soft and cold
So you can make sandcastles
With a bridge and moat too
Matthew Swain, Grade 3
Cabot Elementary School, MA

As Smelly as My Mom

Sometimes my mom
smells like a nice perfume.
Sometimes she smells
like a wonderful rose.

As beautiful as perfume
you can smell the
scent for six miles away
As if she is on the red carpet.
Brandon Gervasio, Grade 3
Westall School, MA

Natasha and Michael

Smart, intelligent, kind
and pretty is Natasha.
Intelligent, smart, kind
and cute is Michael.
We both like red.
Happy Valentine's Day!
Natasha, Grade 3
Kanner Learning Center, PA

Snowflake

like a star floating
in the sky
swirling in the sky
spinning
spinning
swirling swirling
in the sky
the snowflakes mix together
and stay next to the moon
Jeremy Heitsman, Grade 2
Tashua School, CT

Nature

In the forest,
where the animals roam,
There are many tourists
Who carry cleansing foam.
There are millions and millions of trees,
and the butterflies fly,
where you don't have to pay fees,
some baby animals may even cry.
Please don't wake my Baby!
Samantha Cotten, Grade 3
Seaford Central Elementary School, DE

Friends

With my friend Eleanor, I play.
With my friend Eleanor, I play with clay.
With my friend Eleanor, I eat an apple.
With my friend Eleanor, I go to chapel.
Ana Maria Ron, Grade 2
Trinity Christian School, VA

Reading

Reading is such fun for me
In the books I soar
My dad comes in and says "Go to sleep!"
I ask "Five minutes more?"

Reading is like a show for me
That never ever ends
Once I finish my book
I look at the clock
It says five minutes to ten!
Taylor Drew, Grade 3
Saw Mill Road School, NY

Flowers

I love flowers
Flowers in towers
The rain falls in showers
Do flowers have powers?
I can look at them for hours
They're always sweet,
They're never sour.
Bryant Zavala, Grade 2
Public School 1 The Bergen School, NY

Raindrop

Raindrop, raindrop
Splishing, splashing, plop!
Dripping and dropping you never stop
You help the colorful flowers grow
Where you will land, I never know!
Whether I'm under an umbrella or running free;
Little raindrop, you are a beauty to me!

Corinne Walker, Grade 3
Vassar Road School, NY

My Brother's World

My brother Logan is just like me,
Except that he sees things differently.
He likes to tell jokes, he likes to pretend,
I wish I could find him the perfect friend.
I try to guide him and hold his hand,
His days don't always turn out how he planned.
Later on we'll try our best to reach him,
But in the meantime we'll continue to teach him.

Ashley Van Horn, Grade 2
Klein Elementary School, PA

A Flataflower

This is a Flataflower.
A Flataflower lives on a filthy fingernail floating in the forest.
A Flataflower eats falling fruit and fish from a fantastic fairy.
A Flataflower likes fabulous fenders, fiddlers, flags, and fleas.
A Flataflower flew to Florida to follow four freckled foxes.
My Flataflower flipped on my furniture and frightened my frog.

Kayle Lytle, Grade 3
St Clement Mary Hofbauer School, MD

If I Were...

If I were red, I'd be an apple outside on a picnic table.
If I were green, I'd be a frog standing on a hat.
If I were black, I'd be the shirt that I like to wear.
If I were yellow, I'd be a piece of paper being crushed for trash.
If I were gray, I'd be a crayon that I use to color.
If I were blue, I'd be a kite flying in the sky.
If I were pink, I'd be a crown for a queen.

Joseph Kulikowski, Grade 1
St Clement Mary Hofbauer School, MD

Salmon in School
I found a salmon
I brought it to school
My teacher said P-U
But the kids all said woo-hoo!
Ryan Fox, Grade 3
St Madeleine Sophie School, NY

Summer
No work.
No school.
No teachers.
No cold.
No, No, No, No, No, No snow.

I like summer because it's fun.
Just playing all day in the sun.
Alex Ciprut, Grade 1
Our Lady of Good Counsel School, NY

Rain
Wet, moving, pouring
Clear, rainforest, rain, moving
Clear, moving, cold, rain.
Ashley Nadeau, Grade 2
Long Meadow Elementary School, CT

Music Tape
sometimes a music tape
looks like
a really long black railroad
that goes on and on
and on
and on
and never stops
and, well, you walk on it
you will feel so tired
tired as can be
you walk
and you can only see the railroad
but it is
just the music
Willy Hodgson, Grade 2
Cabot Elementary School, MA

Seasons
I love the seasons,
I'll give you more than one reason.

I love the Summer,
When it leaves it is a bummer.

I love the Fall,
It is my favorite of all.

I love the Winter and the falling snow,
Then making snowballs to throw.

I also love the Spring,
and how the birds sing.

That is why,
I like the seasons passing by.
Maggie Scanlon, Grade 3
Ellicott Road Elementary School, NY

Bunny's Money
My funny bunny
One day the bunny
Came out from his hole.
It was so sunny she said
She will hop to the store with money.
Then she will buy some honey.
Ibania Cardoza, Grade 1
Park Avenue School, NY

In My Dreams
In my dreams,
I am a race car driver.
I travel around the world.
I see famous racers.
They want to race with me.
I beat them all and say Hurray!
In my dreams,
I am an astronaut.
I float in outer space.
I see different planets zooming past.
Jamal Akhund, Grade 3
Al-Rahmah School, MD

Mrs. Schwartz

I miss you so,
Please never go!
On day one I wasn't having fun!
On day two I was really missing you!
On day three I could not say "yippee!"
On day four I missed saying "au revoir" at the door!
Please, please, I can't take it anymore!
I need you!
I love you!
I miss you!
Margaret Badding
Your loving second grade student!
PS:
Please come back as soon as you can!
I miss my loving friend!

Margaret Badding, Grade 2
Campbell-Savona Elementary School, NY

If I Were...

If I were blue, I'd be a blue bird in the sky.
If I were red, I'd be a red bird in a nest.
If I were pink, I'd be a crayon.
If I were brown, I'd be my sister's two big eyes.
If I were white, I'd be paper as pretty as the snow.
If I were yellow, I'd be the sun up in the sky.
If I were orange, I'd be a juicy orange.

Savannah Hunter, Grade 1
St Clement Mary Hofbauer School, MD

Grandma's Sweetness

My grandma's very nice,
I love to eat her rice.
My grandma is very sweet,
She gives me lots of treats.
I love her the most,
because she gives me French toast.
My grandma's lots of fun,
she smells like cinnamon buns.
When my grandma goes away,
I wish, I wish, that she could stay.

Maya Merced, Grade 3
Public School 105 Senator Abraham Bernste, NY

Lucky

Lovable hedgehog
my terrific, tiny pet
eats cat food
Ashley McFadden, Grade 3
Sacred Heart School, CT

My Mom

Makes dinner each night
is there till the morning light
our love is endless
Amanda Luther, Grade 3
Sacred Heart School, CT

Wolf

If I were a wolf
I would howl all night.
I'd be soft as a pillow.
I'd be BIG and brave.
I'd eat a lot.
I'd look cute,
But I would not be a pet.
I'd run far away and
I'd live in the woods.
Teddy Hill, Grade 1
St Christopher's School, VA

Spring Is Windy!

green
trees
swaying
Spring is windy!
Grace Wagnblas, Grade 1
St Rose School, CT

Winter Is Great

Winter is great
So don't be late
Go out and run
And have some fun
It will go away
But I hope not today!
Louis Gleason, Grade 2
Willis E Thorpe School, MA

Winter

The best season is Winter!
Outside I have fun with my Sister.
We have fun in the snow,
building our friendly little snowman!
We bundle up with scarves, mittens and hats!
Off we go, down the hill on our mats!
Bailee Galinski, Grade 1
Christ the King School, NY

My Best Friend

A person who comes to help
when the world will not
Someone who will not laugh at me
when the world does
Someone who tries to solve the problem
when the world makes it
That someone is my best friend
Alexander Scott, Grade 3
Clover Street School, CT

Flowers

Flowers make me think of plants.
Plants make me think of trees.
Trees make me think of leaves.
Leaves make me think of clouds.
Clouds make me think of rain.
Rain makes me think of flowers.
Jordan Leandro, Grade 3
Cambridge Springs Elementary School, PA

Seasons

In the warm spring, you'll feel a cool breeze,
But in the winter I think you'll freeze!

I love the summer and the pool,
I think that summer is very cool.

In autumn the leaves do fall.
In autumn you can play basketball.

Sometimes in winter you drink hot cocoa.
If there's enough sugar it'll drive you loco!
Meagan Perro, Grade 3
Leicester Memorial School, MA

Sleepover

Why do they call it a sleepover
if no one ever sleeps?

We just eat junk food
and hang out.

So,
Why do they call it a sleepover?
Emma Deutsch, Grade 2
Buckley Country Day School, NY

Spring

Beautiful flowers growing in a meadow.
Loud Woodpecker pecking on a tree.
A burning barbecue
Cooking on a grill.
Yummy ice cream
I'm licking on my porch.
Little puppies barking in the woods.
Dillon Coughenour, Grade 2
St Mary Magdalen School, DE

Spring

Spring is a beautiful time
the flowers come back
with wonderful colors
and it rains a lot.

The birds sing
the trees grow leaves
and I go to the park.
Oscar Guevara, Grade 2
Public School 2 Alfred Zimberg, NY

Cotton Candy

Cotton candy
like the clouds.
Soft as a dogs fur.
Sweet like a cherry.
Cotton candy
Cotton candy.
Sebastian Montenegro, Grade 3
Public School 69 Jackson Heights, NY

Summer Is...

Summer is green.
It tastes like lemonade.
It smells like grass.
Summer reminds me of an oven
And sounds like lawnmowers.
Summer feels like water from the pool.
Brady Groves, Grade 2
Curtisville Primary Center, PA

Pumpkin Pie

We got a P
We got a U
We got an M P K.
We got an I
We got an N
So what do you say?
Pumpkin, Pumpkin, Pumpkin Pie!
Brendan Ho, Kindergarten
Milton Fuller Roberts School, MA

Football

Football
Tackle
Gain
Pain
1st down
Hit
Sweat
Football
Anthony Leo, Grade 3
Plainfield Catholic School, CT

Flower

Flower, flower, flower
I'm a flower
I live in the dirt it is so fun
Because I have my own secret place
Flower, flower, flower
I eat the dirt it is delicious
I'm allergic to seeds
I like being a flower
Alexandra Ferdinandi, Grade 1
Buckley Country Day School, NY

Where Are Poems?

Poems are everywhere
Inside a shaggy-skinned
Elephant
Everywhere
In an atom
That's so small
Everywhere
In Albert Einstein's
Crazy, out-of-control hair
Everywhere
In a pyramid that looks
Like crystal against the sand
Everywhere
In a hockey stick
Handling, shooting
Everywhere
Especially inside a wonderful pencil
Poems are everywhere

Andrew Kopplin, Grade 3
Slingerlands Elementary School, NY

Up at Bat

I was up at bat.
I got so nervous
I called time out just for a moment.
The pitcher was
        throwing
                balls.
NERVOUS.
He threw that
one
strike
I hit it
It went through the short stop's legs
It kept on rolling
I said
HOORAY!
I
won
the
GAME!

Willie Arena, Grade 3
Buckley Country Day School, NY

Where to Find a Poem

A poem is something
that can be found
in a purple horse's blue mane,
blowing in the harsh wind,
whipping it back into
its dull gray stable.

A poem is in a tiny bug
crawling on a silver
drop of liquid,
like a pool
to the tiny bug.

A poem is something that
can be combed out of a
girl's silky
black hair.

A poem can be in a sentence,
A poem nobody notices,
A poem is in a poem.

Emma Walsh, Grade 3
Slingerlands Elementary School, NY

My Body Parts

Fingers to snap
Hands to clap
Toes to wiggle
Or tap, tap, tap!
Eyes to open
Eyes to close
Wiffer sniffer
That's my nose
Legs to run
Feet to walk
Arms to swing
Ears to hear
All my parts
As you can see
Fit together
To make me!

Ayah Abdelghany, Grade 3
Cameron Elementary School, VA

The Day of Death

My mom said she had something to tell me about my Grandfather
"He died?" My sister guessed
"Yes" my mom said in a small and dreary voice.
The warm air turned cold
I tried going on the monkey bars,
I slipped
The monkey went out of me
The slide was now sticky
I didn't even try the swing
The park was empty
My throat was dry,
The only things that was wet were my tears
That rolled down my cheeks.

Esme Thompson-Turcotte, Grade 3
Public School 69 Jackson Heights, NY

Polar Bears

Polar bears live in the icicle arctic.
They live on chunks of ice.
They swim in frosty waters.
They look like regular bears.

Polar bears have dark black skin and snowy white fur.
Their warm fur keeps their own body heated all the time!
Sometimes their cheeks blush because it's cold.
Their white fur can camouflage in the snow.

Polar bears eat blubbery whales for energy during deep hibernation.
Big fat seals or walruses are their favorite food.
They are very speedy when they are hunting.
Their bites are very bloody.

Fiyi Adebekun, Grade 2
Hopewell Elementary School, PA

Outside

Outside it's a lovely day to jump and play!
It's a lovely day to play and say, "Hip, hip, hooray!"
Sometimes we play in the snow,
or sometimes we play in the rain,
and when my brother comes outside he drives me insane!

Anna Tyrrell, Grade 2
Dr Samuel C Eveleth School, MA

You Have Been Minimized

The world goes spinning round
Don't make a sound
Hear the petals of the flowers slowly
Move to a different size,
As the gorgeous morning rise and then
You realize, that you have
Been minimized.

I don't like it one bit. Neither do you,
Neither do I
All I do is sit, sit, sit.
Fatema Lovely, Grade 3
Public School 131, NY

Funny Story About Reptiles

Reptiles like to stay dry.
They may turn into a French fry.

Then they will cry.
Away they will fly.

Then they'll meet Tim.
Will they eat him?
Justin Lewis, Grade 3
St John Neumann Academy, VA

Noises of the Ocean

Woosh, woosh
Goes the ocean through a dark path
It comes to shore
And leaves a big ROAR
Shhhhh
A boat passes by
CLICKETY-CLACK
Two seashells attach
Now...
The sea comes back,
The boat goes away,
The shells unattach
We all go home
Goodbye Ocean!
Veronica Paulino, Grade 3
Public School 69 Jackson Heights, NY

Stars and the Sun

Stars are like a million night lights
In the dark, dark sky
When it's morning
The sun shines
And those night lights go off.
Arel Pirzada, Grade 1
Buckley Country Day School, NY

The Guitar

It is strapped to the neck
of the person waiting to play it.
The amp beams out music
like church bells when they ring.
The metal strings are
as smooth as sour cream.
I feel like a rock star
when I play my guitar.
Buck Mitchell, Grade 3
St Christopher's School, VA

Pink!

Pink is the color of a beautiful sunset
Pink is the color of Valentines
Pink is the color of a summer day
Pink is the color of a pink marker
Kirana Marksohn, Grade 1
Buckley Country Day School, NY

Lizard

Little lizard on a rock
Tries to sleep till one o'clock.

Then along comes a fly
It goes bye bye.
Colin O'Brien, Grade 3
St John Neumann Academy, VA

I Love You

We know that roses are red.
We know that violets are blue.
But did you know that I love you?
Logan Perez, Grade 1
Calvary Chapel Christian School, NY

If I Were Hair
If I were hair
I would be pretty.
If I were hair
I would be straight
If I were hair
I would be with snow on it.

Dea Ganaj, Grade 1
Public School 105 Senator Abraham Bernste, NY

Winter Is
Winter is the touch of white and cold snow.
Winter is the taste of warm, hot soup.
Winter is hearing kids ice skating outside.
Winter is seeing boots in the hall and trees with no leaves.
Winter is the smell of spaghetti and meatballs.
Winter makes me happy.

Trishia Serrano, Grade 1
St Teresa of Avila School, NY

Summer Fun
Come waves, come wind, come sun, and come fun.
Swim with glee
Tan like bacon on a pan
I want fun for everyone here come people
So come waves, come wind, come sun, and come fun.
Hear the waves splash quickly on the sand
Feel the sun burn and burn on your skin
The fun is coming and so is laughter

Lani Mai-Nguyen, Grade 3
Somers Elementary School, CT

Love Is Always Stronger
When you hear a window break,
    it was hate who threw the brick.
When you hear a fight break out,
    hate began to kick.
Love is when your friend laughs or grins,
    when you ally with friendship your side wins.
When you hear a gunshot or you're angry to the core,
    love is always stronger and peace will win the war.

Fiona Mackenzie, Grade 3
Thoreau Elementary School, MA

The Colorful Autumn

The leaves on the autumn trees
are filled with color.
As the pretty leaves fall from the trees,
the ground is full of colorful leaves.
It made autumn so much fun,
to jump in the piles of leaves,
the colorful leaves in the air.
Fall is over. Now it is winter.
Mary Feeney, Kindergarten
Our Lady of Assumption School, CT

Basketball

Basketball
Sport, professional
Shooting, dribbling, running
Net, backboard, foul line, court
Tipping, rebounding, bouncing
Fun, exciting
NBA
Raymeer Boyette, Grade 3
Brant Elementary School, NY

Football

F ootball can be a fun sport
O r even played in the dirt
O n highways and the roads
T o a far field, here we go
B alance while you run the ball
A ll of us will do our best
L et's go, work real hard
L ose or win it's still great
Dylan Fagan, Grade 3
Heron Pond Elementary School, NH

Spring

S uper weather
P retty flowers
R ainy days
I nsects like butterflies
N o snow, I think?
G reat days almost every day
Mary R. Morano, Grade 3
Edgartown Elementary School, MA

Spring

Spring is fun when you play in the sun.
Spring is nice to go out and play.
Spring could be fun every day.
Spring could be special every day.
Going outside under the sun.
Going outside for a walk.
Spring is fun, fun, fun.
Tamara Jaljouli, Grade 2
Public School 2 Alfred Zimberg, NY

The Mouse

I have a mouse
That lives in my house

He ate my goldfish
Then took a nap in a dish

In the pantry, he leaves a mess
That little mouse is such a pest

I chase him around with a bat
I really wish we had a cat!
Andrew Gardner, Grade 3
Mary Walter Elementary School, VA

Spring Was Made for Happiness

Spring was made for happiness —
It warms me inside,
and outside as well.
The rain gives me a sign
that spring is here,
and — the rain also
spreads my cheer.
Spring mixes my
happiness and sadness,
It's like the smell touches my heart.
My arms and legs
twiggle and wiggle to the
happiness
of my heart.
Spring was made for happiness.
Lacey Williams, Grade 2
Public School 235 Lenox, NY

Recycle

R ecycle
E arth
C ans of soda you can save.
Y ou can recycle.
C an you recycle stuff.
L ights you can turn off when you're done
E nvironment

Jack Avery, Grade 3
Susquehanna Community Elementary School, PA

Bugs

Some bugs are big and small,
Some are hogs.
Some sting when birds sing,
high in the sky as they fly.
Bees buzzing
with yellow and black stripes.
While others enjoy spots and dots
on their back.
As some fly and some crawl,
spinning webs in corners of barns.
Bugs can be yellow, black, red and blue.
They will always love you.
Bugs are nice, so in night
when crickets chirp and moths fly
way up in the dark sky
with the stars up far.
When the moon is full, kids aren't at school.
Instead they are home resting their head in bed.

Raivyn Jefferson, Grade 3
Seaford Central Elementary School, DE

Recycle

R ecycle, reduce, reuse
E veryone can help
C ollect litter and put it where it belongs
Y ou can help stop pollution
C lean the air
L itter is bad
E ven planes pollute

Austin Chisek, Grade 3
Susquehanna Community Elementary School, PA

Spring

Beautiful flowers
Blooming tulips
Bees collect nectar
John Lemoine, Grade 2
Guilford Lakes School, CT

Stars

Stars in the sky,
for
miles
and
miles!

Big and small
shapes
and
sizes!

Masters of the sky!
Quinn McCusker, Grade 2
St Mary's Primary School, MA

Spring Rain

Rain is wet.
Rain is warm.
Rain is heavy as hail.
Pitter patter all around.

Rain is little waters
Very soft.
Pitter patter all around.
Jemma Petit, Grade 2
St Rose School, CT

Squirrel

Squirrel in the bird feeder,
Gray and black,
Squirrel in the bird feeder,
Coming out for a snack,
Squirrel in the bird feeder,
Please come back!
Jonathan Violette, Grade 2
Memorial School, NH

The February Vacation

Oh what a joy!
It's a celebration!
For one whole week
We have vacation.
We'll play, we'll sleep
We'll visit friends
We'll visit Grandma and Grandpa
There is no end
To the fun and good times
Hooray, Hooray!
To every girl and boy!
Citlally Gonzaga Ramos, Grade 2
Public School 1 The Bergen School, NY

Heart

A heart is a piece of love
Bright, pretty, lovable heart
Good for loving
Don't squeeze me or I'll burst into pieces
Megan Nash, Grade 3
Evergreen Elementary School, PA

Butterflies

Butterflies make me think of colors.
Colors make me think of rainbows.
Rainbows make me think of storms.
Storms make me think of clouds.
Clouds make me think of flying.
Flying makes me think of butterflies.
Krista Kelyman, Grade 3
Cambridge Springs Elementary School, PA

Rain

I hear rain, it's cozy and quiet inside,
then BOOM goes the thunder.
Pitter-patter as the rain splats on the ground.
It is peaceful and beautiful,
I love rain.
It's stormy and wet outside,
Lightning catches my eyes.
I feel sleepy and quiet,
I love rain
Brielle Correia, Grade 1
Dartmouth Early Learning Center, MA

A Jigglyjumper

This is a Jigglyjumper.
A Jigglyjumper joyfully joins other jiggles in Juneau.
A Jigglyjumper eats jelly donuts, jumbo shrimp,
    Juniper bulbs, and Jewish apple cake.
A Jigglyjumper likes jets, jewels, juices, and jackets.
A Jigglyjumper is sometimes juvenile, jealous, jolly, and he jogs.
My Jigglyjumper jerked me, jumped on me, jeered at me,
    and he jolted a robber and blamed it on me.

Joshua Podczaski, Grade 3
St Clement Mary Hofbauer School, MD

My Family and Pets

My dad teaches me soccer
My mom provides my family's food
And my sister makes me laugh till I cry
Most importantly, my brother is nice to everyone

Now, I covered everyone I'll tell you about my pets
I love my dog Max because he plays with me
I adore my cat Tiger because he is fun to cuddle up with
That is all I have to say.

Jessica Park, Grade 3
Trinity Christian School, VA

Beary and Lily

Once there was a bear named Beary Li (Lee).
She likes to play with her best friend Lily.
Beary reads and writes a book called Beary Land.
Lily Li and Beary Li play instruments in a band.
They play with very silly and funny hats.
They jump on many ugly, black mats.

Gabrielle Li, Grade 2
Trinity Christian School, VA

Who Am I?

My trip begins up high in the sky.
Twisting, turning, upside down, soon I will splash on the ground.
Watering grass, flowers, and trees
Scaring off a swarm of bees.
Who am I?

Marc Figueroa, Grade 3
Trinity Christian School, VA

Hearts

My heart is beating
Faster and faster
Thump! Boom!
Red, pink, and white
All different colors
Kind, loving, caring
All different things
Can be used in a heart

Christiana Psyllos, Grade 2
Buckley Country Day School, NY

My Dog

My dog is like wind
She howls at night
I think she gets a fright
I know I will see her again
Because, like the wind,
She will
Eventually
Stop!

Brooke Boulds, Grade 3
Acushnet Elementary School, MA

The Cat in the Hat

The cat is so hot.
He lives in a pot.
He played with some bats.
Instead of a hat.
He begins to frown.
And then he sat down.
And then he will grow.
Into a crow.

Jennie Garcia, Grade 3
Bensley Elementary School, VA

Shoot Out

The F-22 can fly very high.
The B-17 can bomb very hard.
The P-51 Mustang can shoot very far.
The Spitfire MKV is very famous.
Oh, yes!

Wesley Scriven, Grade 2
St Rose School, CT

Mabel

Mabel
Fast, pretty
running, jumping, swimming
is a loyal friend
Mae

Olivia Knight, Grade 3
Chilmark Elementary School, MA

Rain

Rain falls
Rain stops
Rain goes
Sometimes a rainbow
Will show
The kids get muddy
And icky
All through the day
People play in the rain, anyway

Jack Dobbins, Grade 3
Lincoln Street School, MA

Easter

Spring is so much fun.
Let us color Easter eggs
Let's plant flowers too.
Easter bunny please come here.
Bringing baskets filled with eggs.

Michael G. Shea, Grade 3
Penn-Kidder Campus, PA

What Poetry Is to Me

Poetry is like the wind
blowing through my hair
without a care in the world
and the magic of it just happens
like it is on the tip of your pencil
taking over it
without even thinking
you just
write

Olivia Fottrell, Grade 3
Slingerlands Elementary School, NY

Spring, Spring, What a Wonderful Thing!

Spring, spring, what a wonderful thing!
It makes me laugh, it makes me sing.

Beautiful butterflies fluttering by,
Blue birds flying so high in the sky.

Eggs are hatching with great delight,
I watch a robin start to take flight.

Now spring is over because of Earth's rotation,
But at least it's time for summer vacation!

Jessica Holt, Grade 3
Seton Catholic School, NY

White

White is the color of heaven and snow,
The clouds and a frosty night,
White is soft and snuggly, an angel's dress and kindness,
White is cold and the ruler of all,
White is calm and light

Caroline Safran, Grade 3
Cabot Elementary School, MA

Scissors

Scissors are purple, red, orange, green and blue,
They come in other colors too!
They are big and small
I love them all!

Angeline Marsh, Grade 2
Ewell School, MD

Summer Shopping

Going out to play. Having cook outs and shopping all day. Getting skirts,
dresses and necklaces and earrings, too. Shopping for games, toys and other
things. We can surely play. While shopping all day. Going to the mall and
shopping while we play. When we go home we can take a nap and eat a
chocolate fudge cake and call it a day.

Victoria Bean, Grade 2
Bensley Elementary School, VA

My Spring

Spring is here.
Spring is fun!
I love spring!
It is very fun!
Bees are buzzing.
Flowers are budding.
I love to feel the breeze!
Spring is excellent!
Anna Carnahan, Grade 1
Trinity Christian School, VA

Puppies

Puppies are cute.
Puppies are nice.
Puppies are awesome.
Puppies are lovely.
Puppies are awesome.
Puppies are pleasant.
Puppies are cuddly.
Puppies are charming.
Cullen Moore, Grade 2
St Rose School, CT

Rain

Rain is fun.
Rain gives you puddles.
Rain lets you splash.
Rain is wet.
Rain makes boats float.
Rain plops on my umbrella.
Rain is fun.
Sage Mikus, Kindergarten
Home School, VA

Spring

S un
P ool
R ainbow
I ce cream
N ewspaper outside
G rapes
Kylie Nash, Kindergarten
Willis E Thorpe School, MA

The Joys and Memories of Summertime

S plashing in the pool
U mbrellas not needed.
M oments to remember.
M om, dad, and family time.
E ating summertime fruits and treats.
R iding bikes with friends.
T imeless moments together.
I n school now, I don't think so.
M elodies from famous musicians
E ndless fun and memories with others.
Grace Hamilton, Grade 3
St Madeleine Sophie School, NY

Peeps/Ducklings

Peeps
Cute, fluffy
Swimming, waddling, playing
Peeps are really cute.
Ducklings
Mackenzie Thayer, Grade 3
Chestnut Street Elementary School, PA

It's Time for Love

Love is in the air
It's going everywhere
With kisses and hugs.

I have a special person
Who likes me the most
Boys think it's icky
Girls think it rocks.
I think it's the best in the entire world!

It's fun to get Valentine's cards
People ask me why I like Valentine's Day
I say I just love hearts that love
And flowers that are sweet!

Valentine's cards to all the boys
They all say "Be mine" or "I love you" and
"Happy Valentine's Day!"
I love Valentine's Day!
Kamryn Moravec, Grade 3
Penn Yan Elementary School, NY

Scary Island

Desert Island
Tall forest trees
Hot and humid
Beaches all around
Not so scary

Big bugs
Wild boars
Smugglers, and
Atomic bombs
Scary Island
Devon Nantais, Grade 3
Plainfield Catholic School, CT

Summer

S ummer is here
U nder the umbrella
M ore and more people
M artha's Vineyard is ready
E astville Beach is full of seaglass
R ed, white and blue
Amelia Durawa, Grade 3
Edgartown Elementary School, MA

Spring

S is for sun
P is for popsicle
R is for rose
I is for ice cream
N is for nice weather
G is for go to the baseball field
Austin Faneuf, Kindergarten
Fisher Hill Elementary School, MA

Puppy

Puppy
Cute, adorable
Cuddles, fetches, hunts
She listens to me.
Beagle
Sophie-Mae Scott, Grade 3
Granville Elementary School, NY

Skiing Double Black Diamond

On a cold winter day I skied
I skied the hardest trail.
It was getting steeper down the slope.
The ice was sticking to the snow
and then I started to panic.
When I got to the bottom of the slope
I was happy to get down the hill.
Matt Zackin, Grade 2
Pomperaug Elementary School, CT

Halloween

Halloween,
Halloween,
A deadly,
Holiday,
A time,
And place,
People die,
And monsters,
Come alive,
Let's say,
In Halloween,
I'm going to,
Dress up as,
Jason,
He's in
Friday the 13th,
But!
Beware!
This trip won't,
Come to an,
END!!!
Nikhil Shetty, Grade 3
Public School 69 Jackson Heights, NY

Winter

Let's go in the snow I want to say hello
To the snowman hello man
I see a snowman smile
while playing in a snow pile.
Alexys Naranjo, Grade 3
Penn-Kidder Campus, PA

A Germ

I am a germ.
I travel through the body.
I feel sad when white blood cells
try to eat me.
I feel happy when I escape from them.
I will not make people sick.

Zane Allen, Grade 2
Bensley Elementary School, VA

Spring

Spring, spring
rainbow and flowers
coming out in rainbow showers

Spring is in the air
I can feel it
everywhere
Everywhere I go

I smell
the fresh air
and that
reminds me,
Spring is in the air!

But when I trudge
through the flowers,
I don't know what to do
don't want to
step on the flowers
Does that happen to you?

Connyr Lu, Grade 3
Public School 69 Jackson Heights, NY

Spring

Spring is God's love
Spring is kids playing
Spring is love
But most of all
Spring is a time to love God

Colleen Denault, Grade 1
St Rose School, CT

The Five W's

Who
What
When
Where
Why
When they rhyme
They come to your mind.

Kelsey O'Sullivan, Grade 1
Buckley Country Day School, NY

Springtime

Springtime
Is when birds start singing
Springtime
Is when everyone plays
When does spring come?
Where is spring?
I saw
The colorful rainbow up in the sky
I guess spring is here!

Takuma Nishiya, Grade 2
Public School 122 Mamie Fay, NY

The Golden Retriever

G olden
O bedient
L oving
D ogs
E asy to train
N ice

R etrievers
E njoy them
T aught to find
R eady to listen
I n your heart
E asy to play with
V ery reliable
E nough in your heart
R eady to play

Carly Fernandes, Grade 2
Long Meadow Elementary School, CT

What Is Pink?

Pink is a nice, new, shiny pink car.
Pink is a pig that has mud on it.
Pink is a book that's not so shiny.
Pink is a nice coat that I use.
Pink is a nice worm that lives in the earth.
Pink is a card.
Pink is a yo-yo that moves up and down.
Pink is a tulip that grows.
Pink is a book bag.
Pink is a lunch box.
Pink is a chair that you sit on and play on.

Abigail Schaefer, Grade 1
St Madeleine Sophie School, NY

Mr. Superhero

There was a man,
he was the color tan.
He saved the day,
everyone said, "Hooray!"
There was a girl,
she helped save the world.
The man was bad,
and he was always sad.
Everybody hated him,
his name was Jim.
Mr. Superhero did the right thing,
he was like the third king.
He destroyed that man,
he also broke his hand.
This is the end
as they are my friends.

Stephon Short, Grade 3
Seaford Central Elementary School, DE

Spring Is...

S pring is going to the park
P laying baseball at school
R eading books at school
I ce cream with friends and family
N ew flowers in the yard
G oing to Boy Scouts

Brandon Dominguez, Grade 3
Helen B Duffield Elementary School, NY

Snakes

snakes
green, slimy
eat, slide, slither
sneaking through the woods
reptiles
Lauren Adams, Grade 1
St Rose School, CT

Paint

Look what I'm making
Yellow   boom
Blue   splat
Red   boom
Green   splat
I'm not done yet
Purple   boom
Brown   splat
Black   boom
Look what I've made!
Colby Miller, Grade 2
Tashua School, CT

Spring

The snow is melting,
The wind is blowing strongly.
Trout fishing begins.
Flowers are starting to bloom.
Birds flying back to the North.
Robert Zemken, Grade 2
Wells Central School, NY

I Love Skiing

I love skiing,
you feel like
a feather.
When you go on
fresh snow,
you feel weightless.
You go fast
so hold on
tight to your poles.
Victoria Scala, Grade 2
Tashua School, CT

Chicken-n-Jail

Once a chicken went to jail.
It wasn't really fun, because he got no mail.
Because everyone thought he was very bad
That made him very sad.
He really wanted to get out
So he started to pout.
Rachel Hantz, Grade 2
Trinity Christian School, VA

Spring

Beautiful flowers growing in grass
Chirping birds singing in the tree
Red roses growing in the garden
Smooth rain drops falling from the sky
A brand new ball being thrown in the air
William Hoffman, Grade 2
St Mary Magdalen School, DE

Where's the Perfect Place to Fly?

Flying high, flying low
Where's the perfect place to go?

Shall I fly to the fountain?
Shall I fly to the mountain?

Maybe I'll fly to my home
Shall I fly to the dome?

Where's the perfect place to go?

I found it! I found it!
It's on a cloud in the sky
That's where I'm going to fly.
Hannah Engel, Grade 3
Our Mother of Perpetual Help School, PA

Old Man

There was an old man with a bride.
"I hurt my back," he cried.
He ran into brick,
He got very sick.
Now he's stuck with his eyes opened wide.
Braden Lockard, Grade 2
Oakdale Elementary School, MD

Dolphins

D oes funny tricks
O ften makes clicking noises
L ives in the ocean
P layful porpoise
H appy blue creature
I s our favorite sea mammal
N ice to kids and adults
S wims fast like an eel

Reece McLeod and Ryan Greaney, Grade 3
Leicester Memorial School, MA

Winter

I need my hat
I need my coat
I look like a stoat.
I need my scarf
I need my mitts
I need warm socks
That really fit.

Alexis Solano, Grade 2
Public School 1 The Bergen School, NY

I'm an Alligator Snapping Turtle

Snap, snap, snap
The back of my shell is black.

Snap, snap, snap
I can grow to be 220 pounds.

Snap, snap, snap
I'm two feet long and very strong.

Snap, snap, snap
Fish, birds, snakes and frogs can be a snack.

Snap, snap, snap
North America is where my habitat is at.

Snap, snap, snap
That's the end of my song
So run along!

Cody Schnur, Grade 2
McQuistion Elementary School, PA

School

School is a national pool,
That fills my mind with water —
When I change to a subject;
The water splashes.
Nedia Thompson, Grade 2
Public School 235 Lenox, NY

Poetry Is Like a Lollipop

Poetry is like a lollipop.
The words stick to the paper
and you don't know what flavor it is.
But you lick it anyway.
Poetry is like a word river
flowing down the page.

Poetry is like a flower.
So many different smells
you just can't decide.
You think and think
and then just pick again and again
until you have a beautiful bouquet.

Poetry is like the sun.
Oh so bright bringing light
to our world.
Raina Briggs-Abrams, Grade 3
Slingerlands Elementary School, NY

Drawing

Drawing, drawing
Birds
People
Houses
Drawing everything!
When I draw
It makes me
Feel like I could
Draw more
More
More!
Sierra Lederhouse, Grade 2
Milton Terrace Primary School, NY

Spring Song

I like spring
because the birds sing.
I like the flowers.
It rains in spring.
I like to sing in the spring.
Tony Galdamez, Kindergarten
Agape Christian Academy, VA

The Four Seasons

Hmmm hmmm hmmm
goes the wind in winter

Bzzz bzzz bzzz
goes the bee in spring

Whew whew whew
goes the people
because it's so hot in summer.

Crunch crunch crunch
goes the leaves
when people step on them in fall.
Michael Manu, Grade 2
Buckley Country Day School, NY

Wind

Wind is a silent cat
It whispers and whispers
No one can hear it
But it's there
Nathan Davis, Grade 3
Acushnet Elementary School, MA

My Brother Carlo

Makes a mess
always active
oh why
is he so happy
I'll
never know
Steven Garcia, Grade 3
Public School 69 Jackson Heights, NY

A Kangaroo

A kangaroo looks as orange as a clementine
A kangaroo sounds as loud as a rock falling
A kangaroo smells as sandy as a desert
A kangaroo tastes as sweet as fresh tomatoes
A kangaroo feels as soft as a stuffed animal
A kangaroo is the bounciest animal ever

Kalle Weik, Grade 3
Sunrise Drive Elementary School, NY

My Grandma

I love my grandma
I love her so
I love her more
than you could know.

Jeffrey Osorio, Grade 1
Public School 1 The Bergen School, NY

Spring

Pretty birds flying in my backyard.
Beautiful chirping sounds outside my window.
Lovely fresh air blowing in the wind.
Sour lemonade being sold out front.
Flower petals swaying in the field.

Kevin Wierzbowski, Grade 2
St Mary Magdalen School, DE

Cats

We once found a cat
And we named it Jat
It was lean
And not clean
And we gave her a home
And let her play with some foam
We fed her cat food
Which got her in a good mood
She ran from the dogs
And hid behind the hogs
She was nice
And chased mice
My dad is happy
And played some mappy

Preston S. Budd, Grade 1
Thomas Jefferson Elementary School, VA

Easter

Easter is so cool,
There is a Easter bunny,
Who fills your basket.
With a lot of stuff,
I just can't wait 'til Easter!
Christian Gorbea, Grade 3
Penn-Kidder Campus, PA

Rain

Drip drop
the sound of rain
beating down
tear drops
fall from the sky
    splat
        splat
            splating
like a
faucet
dripping down
Elizabeth Cuevas, Grade 2
Tashua School, CT

About Me

My name is Paige.
Six is my age.
Vacations are fun.
I like the beach and the sun.
Music is fun to hear
In my ear.
Paige Fehl, Grade 1
St Joan of Arc School, PA

I Am a Kite

I am a kite
that flies in the sky
I fly so high
up to the sun
Then the wind stops
and I fall
I look like a queen
Anna Johnston, Grade 1
St Rose School, CT

Halloween

Witches on brown brooms
Vampires with black bats
Skeletons in trees with treats in their teeth
Wind is whistling on Halloween
Kelsey Harmon, Grade 2
St Joseph School, NY

Winter

Winter is coming, winter is coming.
I can't wait until winter,
can't wait, can't wait until winter!
Winter, winter, with the snow and snowmen,
can't wait, can't wait, that's right!
Gabrielle Zalzman, Grade 1
Joseph Greenberg School, PA

The Olympics

The Olympics started in Greece
The Olympics have many sports

Basketball, football, handball, volleyball
Wrestling, boxing, swimming, diving

This year the Olympics are in China
Their stadium is called the Bird's Nest

Tennis, gymnastics, archery, tae kwon do
Hockey, track and field, shooting, judo

The Olympic torch is carried around the world
They light it when the games begin

The athletes come from all over the world
They get medals when they win
Ms. Pam Kensinger's Class, Grade 2
Henry Clay Elementary School, VA

My Many Colored Days

On green days I run around my sister, Kaelin.
On blue days I like watching
the blue waves with my friend, Sophie.
On pink days I like seeing my friends.
Darcy O'Sullivan, Grade 1
Glover Elementary School, MA

You and Me

Lost inside your beautiful eyes,
I think that perhaps that I have died.
I see how beautiful you really are,
And realize you are worth more than every star.

As we spend every day together,
I believe our love will last forever
Happiness takes away every tear,
And you take away all my fear.

You are the love of my dreams,
And I don't understand what this means.
I guess it's trying to show,
That Cupid shot me with his bow.

You are my soul, my love and my heart,
This love will never split apart.
As the angels watch us from above,
We'll sing and laugh and fall in love.

Lindihana Mehmedi, Grade 3
Public School 69 Jackson Heights, NY

Spring Has Sprung!

"Spring has come! Spring has come!"
Colors colors everywhere!
Yellow, red, pink and blue
Flowers flowers blooming everywhere!
Cheerful, birds singing songs all day long...
"Spring has sprung! Spring has sprung!"

Azka Chaudhry, Grade 2
Public School 2 Alfred Zimberg, NY

St. Patrick's Day

In the Emerald Isle
Fields of Shamrocks grow
Glowing green in the sun
Where the lads and lassies like to run
Under the mushrooms leprechauns hide
Dancing their jigs with great pride
Grab your shillelagh and come along
We'll sing a happy Irish song!

Rachael Deakin, Grade 3
Court Street Elementary School, NY

Snakes

S ome snakes are poisonous.
N o snakes are scary to me.
A rattlesnake is cool.
K ing Cobra spits venom.
E ggs are what some snakes like.
S ome snakes are harmless.

Justin Reynolds, Grade 3
Brookside Elementary School, MA

Camping

I see campers and brooks,
I smell camp fire and grass,
I hear dogs and cows,
I taste marshmallows and hot dogs,
I feel grass and fur.

James W. Shaw III, Grade 3
Granville Elementary School, NY

My Dad

A hard working man
helps me with my math homework
takes good care of me

Angel Condeza, Grade 3
Sacred Heart School, CT

Husky

Husky
Nice, friendly, neat
Panting, running, leaping
Likes to rescue people sometimes
Snow dog

Chloe Tolderlund, Grade 3
Houghton Elementary School, MA

Girl from France

There once was a girl from France,
Who didn't know how to dance.
She clapped her hands,
And ate a rubber band,
And then she had a ranch.

Taylor Chatoff, Grade 1
Mater Christi School, VT

I Love Books

I love books because they are fun
Some books teach you about a bun
I think books are daring
Sometimes books are boring
But, most of the time books are happy
I wish there was a book about taffy
I love books
No matter how it looks

Madison Yon, Grade 3
Trinity Christian School, VA

Baseball

When you go on the field,
you smell the grass,
you feel a breeze,
you hear the crowd cheer,
it is the best time of the year,
if you're lucky, you will hit a homerun,
it would be the best day ever!

Andrew Wenzler, Grade 3
Our Lady of Hope School, NY

Dogs

Black dogs running fast
Digging up bones in the ground
Happy for a crunch.

Edward Anderson, Grade 3
St Christopher's School, VA

Valentines

V iolets are pretty
A special day
L ife's best day
E verybody together
N ever lonely
T ell the person you love them
I ncrease projects
N ever shy
E ven in love
S omeone might love you

Devin Stahlman, Grade 3
Penn Yan Elementary School, NY

Spring

Brown foxes running in the woods.
White rabbits jumping in my backyard.
Colorful flowers moving in the breeze.
Crunchy sunflower seeds waiting to be picked.
Green grass standing tall in my front yard.

Luke Dell'Oso, Grade 2
St Mary Magdalen School, DE

Nottoway

N ice celebrations
O utstanding work
T errific classes
T errific teachers give good grades
O utside is for kids to learn how to play
W ait your turn
A wesome work Cougars!
Y oung kids learn

Jamarr Brooks, Grade 2
Nottoway Elementary School, VA

Valentine's Day in My Class

Valentine's Day is coming, what should I do?
Off to the store to buy hearts and candy too.

But what would Mrs. Weir say about that?
"Candy in my class, I can't have that."

Mrs. Weir is right, candy is bad,
But I didn't want my friends to be sad.

I sat down to think about the right thing to buy,
I didn't want Mrs. Weir to sigh.

So, back to the store to buy something for you,
Candy and hearts just wouldn't do.

I searched the store up and down,
Hearts and pencils are what I found.

Hearts with a pencil is what I made,
For my whole class in the third grade.

Kirill Riesinger, Grade 3
Fawn Hollow Elementary School, CT

Video Games
Video games
are fun.

Video games
aren't near the sun!

Video games
don't make me bored.

Video games
make my dad snore!

Video games
are easy to find.

Video games
can make you blind!
Ryan Wheeler, Grade 2
St Mary's Primary School, MA

Skating
Skating's fun
It's number one
It's a fright when you fall
Going back to the wall
Come on, everyone
Doesn't it sound fun?
Little kids using crates
Other kids on their skates
People falling everywhere
There to there
Like a penguin
Slip slip slip
Everywhere
Mae-Lou Zaleski, Grade 2
Willis E Thorpe School, MA

Spring Flowers
Flowers are pretty
Popping and blooming
In spring so beautiful new
Lauren Porretta, Grade 2
Guilford Lakes School, CT

Water
I love cold water
Water is something to drink
Water is healthy
Zachary Guiffre, Grade 2
Fonda-Fultonville Elementary School, NY

Looking into a Mirror
Looking into a mirror,
Made a smile spread across my face
Like ripples in a pond.
As if reviving my past as a baby
I see a different face
I see my future and past
I feel a sudden desire to touch my past
My happy past,
Trying to remember my happy memories
But when my finger touches the mirror,
It comes to a stop.
As disappointment washes over me,
But because of mirrors deep in my soul,
I still know myself, and myself still knows me.
Julie Peng, Grade 3
General John Nixon Elementary School, MA

My Family
I have a sister, she really likes to play,
She won't stop until done for the day.
She will put up a fight,
If she can't play all night,
She will just stay and play.
All night and day!

I have a mom, she will go away,
And not come back to stay,
Until she is done getting coffee,
Going to the bathroom,
And getting dressed for play.

I have a dad, he likes to study,
Not play with silly putty,
But sometimes when he has enough time
He will be all mine.
Kendra Claire Valerius, Grade 3
James Russell Lowell School, MA

Monkeys
Monkeys are brown
Monkeys move fast
Monkeys live in trees
Monkeys eat bananas
Monkeys are cute
Cade Zolkos, Grade 1
Richland Elementary School, PA

You Can Find Poetry Anywhere
When a poem is an idea,
It's a bolt of lightning hitting me.
You can find a poem
In a woman's
Silver, jingling earrings.
Jingle, jangle, jingle, jangle.
You can find a poem
In salty, buttery, crunchy popcorn,
Popping in the microwave,
Waiting, ready for me to eat.
You can find a poem on your tongue
Lap-lap-lapping
Vanilla ice cream.
A poem is like a brush
Streaking through my hair.
A poem is like a soccer ball
being kicked
in different directions.
Poetry is like skis
Flying down a mountain.
Poetry is a gift.
Lauren Namkoong, Grade 3
Slingerlands Elementary School, NY

The Sun
The sun is awesome,
bright, shiny and warm.

I have fun in the sun!
Every summer day I go to the beach,
sand, wet, hot!
Hailey Cederquist, Grade 2
St Mary's Primary School, MA

Hockey
The Taylor's are good at hockey!
Hockey is cool,
Excellent work Daniel!
Andrew rocks at hockey!
We like to play!
Daniel Taylor, Grade 2
St Mary's Primary School, MA

Annie My Cat
Annie is a tiger cat
She is strong as can be
Her claws are sharp and clean

Annie is a tiger cat
She has glass sharp teeth
And I love Annie!
Jacqueline Leduc, Grade 3
Acushnet Elementary School, MA

Hockey
Hockey is a great sport.
It's spectacular and fun.
Whether you're short or tall,
You hit the ice and run.
Sometimes we get checked or tripped.
It's easy to get hurt.
Sometimes your team gets whipped
And ends up in the dirt.
Nylan Raggiani, Grade 3
Berkley Community School, MA

Movement
M ake your body move
O verture of Beethoven
V erbs
E motions
M ove around
E nergetic dancing
N ot to stay still
T ime to play
Owen Hess, Grade 3
Edgartown Elementary School, MA

The Moon

The moon came
I say
And it's shining
with a bright light
So it's almost
end of the day
My friend and I
run away
We come home at night
And I hope
tomorrow
the sun
will be
shining bright
Tasfia Rahman, Grade 3
Public School 69 Jackson Heights, NY

Space

Planet Mercury is hot
It is like a burning pot
Jupiter is dusty
The soil is hard and crusty
Pluto is small
If you go to Pluto you will fall
Andrew Sexton, Kindergarten
Montessori Development Center, PA

Roses

Beautiful, curvy
Colorful petals of red
Thorny and lovely.
Hefferson Lemus, Grade 2
Bensley Elementary School, VA

Easter

Easter! I can't wait!
When it comes we'll go outside
We'll go Easter egg hunting
I'll have fun with my family.
I just can't wait for Easter.
Alexandra Kowar, Grade 3
Penn-Kidder Campus, PA

City at Night

The city is bright at night
It looks so nice and bright
because the lights shine and glow
So nice and bright
like the shining stars at night
What a beautiful sight

When the lights glow at night
It is so pretty at night
Jose Arteaga, Grade 3
Public School 69 Jackson Heights, NY

Christmas Day

We went to buy a Christmas tree
Except for my sister and me
We had to put the Christmas lights
Because they were colored so bright
We had to go to our gray car
Because we left our Christmas star
We had to go to the big mall
To buy some Christmas colored balls
Maria Cabrera, Grade 3
Bensley Elementary School, VA

Spring

S hining sun in the sky
P lants grow fast
R aining makes flowers grow
I nside is not a place to be
N ature is back
G reatest time of the year!
Xavier Corkins, Grade 2
Washington Elementary School, MA

Nutty Banana

Nutty banana is yellow
Nutty banana smells icky
Nutty banana feels smooshy
Nutty banana sounds terrible
Nutty banana tastes good
Aidan Shilling, Grade 1
Richland Elementary School, PA

Spring
S now is melting
P lants start growing
R ain falls down
I like to swing
N ew bird nests are built
G rass begins to grow and get green

Shyanne Blankenship, Grade 3
Chestnut Street Elementary School, PA

Flowers
F lowing in the breeze
L aying in the grass
O pening up to get fresh air
W atching the bees
E ntering each spring day
R eturning from last spring
S prouting all about

Alyssa Zampogna, Grade 3
Chestnut Street Elementary School, PA

I Am Melissa Grall
I am cheerful and pretty
I wonder why there are so many stars in the sky
I hear the cries of my cat
I see the beautiful sun
I want a white kitten
I am cheerful and pretty

I pretend I can see gold in the leprechaun's pot
I feel my nonna's hand touch me
I touch a white puffy cloud
I worry about my nonna because I love her
I cry if somebody has to go to the hospital
I am cheerful and pretty

I understand my nonna when she speaks Italian
I say people can't push me around
I dream that I am really special
I try to stay away from bad people
I hope my nonna will be healthy forever
I am cheerful and pretty

Melissa Grall, Grade 3
Stony Point Elementary School, NY

Crystal Rocks

Crystal rocks
shine in
the night
just like
glass reflecting
on light.
They shine
so bright
like a glowing
city light.
So crystal
rocks you
are bright!

Melanie Saturnino, Grade 3
Public School 69 Jackson Heights, NY

Stars

Look at all the stars,
Sprinkled upon the vast spans of space.
Anything as beautiful as a starry night,
With colors red, white, or even blue,
They twinkle like morning dew.

Daniel Seitz, Grade 3
Trinity Christian School, VA

Spring

Sun melting the snow.
Warm sun birds come from the South.
Newborn life has come.
Grass starts to grow here again.
Bradyn playing in the mud.

Sheyenne Beach, Grade 2
Wells Central School, NY

Teachers!

Teachers
Teachers are fun.
Teachers have lots of pets.
Teachers have lots of fun projects.
So cool!

Taylor Pumphrey, Grade 2
St Madeleine Sophie School, NY

The Boy in the Barn

A little boy went into the barn
And lay down on some hay
An owl came out
And flew about
And the little boy ran away.

Dina Abdalla, Grade 3
Public School 2 Alfred Zimberg, NY

Worms

Worms are slimy,
Worms are free
But they're not for me.

Worms are tiny,
Worms are whiny,
Worms have shiny skin.

Worms are sticky,
Worms are tricky
They make me sicky.

Aaliyah Dunstan, Grade 3
James Russell Lowell School, MA

Changes

The slick movements
of the stillness on
the pods of rain.
Cool breezes sweep the smell
of pine onto the leafy vines.
The sun glows
its shadow on
the bits of corn
broken from the
glowing and
fresh corn stalks.
The fall leaves come and
go and the glimmering
of the fresh
corn stalks turn to
a crispy brown.

Yumeng Zhang, Grade 3
Lincoln Elementary School, PA

Fall

Fall brown, green and red.
It tastes like candy.
It sounds like people knocking on the door.
It smells like trees.
It looks like bare trees.
It makes me feel excited.

Stacie Kerbel, Grade 3
Evergreen Elementary School, PA

Sadness

Sadness feels like your heart is broken.
It sounds like glass shattering.
Sadness smells like salt.
It tastes like a flagon of poison.
It looks like gloomy dirt.
Sadness feels like your heart
 has been stabbed with a sharp knife,
  and it will *never* heal.

Nathaniel Casper-Miller, Grade 3
West Branch School, PA

Jupiter

Jupiter
60 moons, jumbo
Enticing, rotating, exploring
Red in the sky, biggest planet, fifth from the sun
Interesting, orbiting, fading ring
One ring, great red spot
Planet

Tealynn Twoguns, Grade 3
Brant Elementary School, NY

My Legos Army Strikes!

Legos, Legos, roam my room,
soon my sister will meet her doom.
They're like an army in rows of ten,
(my sister will never annoy me again!)
They attack with power, it's really cool.
Now she'll see that I'm no fool.
They are an army, heavily armed.
When my sister surrenders, she'll be disarmed.

Adam Ziccardi, Grade 3
Ellicott Road Elementary School, NY

Spring

S pring is beautiful
P lants are pretty
R ain is sparkly
I see blooming signs of spring
N o more icy snow
G rowing flowers is fun

Logan Waters, Grade 1
Frenchtown Elementary School, CT

It's Spring

When a cool breeze blows
my heart is pounding!
Everything inside me
feels like dancing!
I dance to the rhythm
of the wind.
A sweet smell from the tree makes me
feel like I'm in another world.
As everything is blooming, I feel
so happy in my soul.
Peace is all around me! It's spring!
When rain comes and washes,
there's a beautiful rainbow.

Amika Jacob, Grade 2
Public School 235 Lenox, NY

Springtime!

I look at ponds,
I walk in the sun.
Spring is fun including outside!
Springtime!

Kiersten Janis, Grade 2
St Madeleine Sophie School, NY

Colors

Colors, colors
I like colors
Colors on a rainbow
Colors on a wall
I like colors.

Chelsea Aviles, Grade 2
Public School 148 Ruby Allen, NY

Go to Sleep

Go to sleep don't wake up
Just close your eyes
And you'll be fine through the night
But turn out the light
Don't forget to turn off the TV
So you can snooze some ZZZ's

Skylar Reddington, Grade 3
Danville Elementary School, NH

Spring

S un is here
P lant a garden
R un around your home
I like spring
N o more cold
G row your vegetables

Michael Mizak, Grade 1
Frenchtown Elementary School, CT

Snowflakes

Snowflakes are pretty to see
and when you eat them they're cold
but they're tasty to eat.
Don't eat yellow snow…
it's yucky to eat.
I like them because
different sizes make me happy!

Morgan Darby, Grade 2
Pomperaug Elementary School, CT

Penguins on the Ice

Penguins are cute
Penguins are nice
I like penguins
Because they live on the ice

Penguins are happy
Penguins play
Penguins wear tuxedos every day
No way!

Devin Rooney, Grade 2
St John Neumann Academy, VA

Santa's Elves

Santa has many elves,
They work on putting toys on shelves.
They work all day,
They don't care for pay.
They make such cool little toys,
For all the good little girls and boys.
When Santa says it's Christmas Day,
They scream and shout and yell, "Hooray!"

Caroline Fredericks, Grade 3
Ellicott Road Elementary School, NY

French Fries

I like french fries
I like it so much
and I wish for a talking french fry
until I saw a magic french fry guy
in a costume with a boy.
He made a french fry talk
and turned me into a french fry guy.
So then he said don't eat yourself
but I did.

A'Keel Jones, Grade 2
Public School 205 Alexander Graham Bell, NY

Bottle Man

Bottle man, Bottle man.
He is full of water.
He is full of water.
Please don't drink me,
Please don't drink me.
Yes I will. Yes I will.

Kevin Fourman, Grade 2
Public School 205 Alexander Graham Bell, NY

Summer

Beach visits
burning days
running
playing
tanning
swimming

Taylor Sharp, Grade 3
Bradford Township Elementary School, PA

The Sky

The sky so soothing
so soft to touch and gentle
so bright with the sun
Sean McGrath, Grade 3
Saw Mill Road School, NY

Starbursts

Starbursts are yummy,
Starbursts are great,
Starbursts are yummy,
Whenever they're ate!
James Swomley, Grade 2
Cabot Elementary School, MA

In My Dreams

In my dreams,
I'm in an adventure.
I wander through
Different places.
Sometimes I fly
Above the sun.
In my dreams,
I live in houses
That are huge
And amazing.
In my dreams,
I travel in far
Off places.
Where people
And places
Appear, and
Then go away.
Saba Khan, Grade 3
Al-Rahmah School, MD

Dorothy

Dorothy
little, red
swimming, floating, splashing
blowing bubbles in her bowl
fish
Catherine Herrick, Grade 1
St Rose School, CT

Butterflies

I saw a butterfly so cute,
I wondered if it was a beaut.
I saw colors on its wings,
and I wondered if it had a lover.
They're so smooth when flying,
I think they're doing the groove.
They are so small,
I seem so very tall.
Butterflies are big,
I'm wondering how they can land on a twig.
They can be pink and blue,
I think I saw one fly by you.
Treasure Robinson, Grade 3
Seaford Central Elementary School, DE

The Rain

Plip-plop! Plip-plop!
The rain is gripping on the window pane.
It is hard to see outside.
Plip-plop! Plip-plop!
More rain.
Nickolas Brown, Grade 1
Hyman Fine Elementary School, MA

Christmas

Christmas time is almost here
so let's all cheer!
There will be lots and lots of toys
for lots of girls and lots of boys.
There will be fun
for everyone.
Natalie Cordova, Grade 2
Public School 1 The Bergen School, NY

Recess

Tariq banged his elbow,
Bilal skinned his knee.
Usaamah tore his sweatshirt,
Diata fell off a tree.
Malik got a bee sting and the girls ran away.
Now you know why we have recess…
Once a day.
Abdullah Williams, Grade 3
Al-Rahmah School, MD

Juice

Juice is tasty, it's very good.
I just love it.
I have it at night
with all my might.
I don't really like any other drink.
Juice, juice, I can't resist juice.
It's juicy.
It's good.
I can't get enough of it.
I love how it's so juicy.

Farrah DeRoss, Grade 3
Holy Rosary School, NY

Professor Crazy

I know a guy who is a professor.
He is very funny.
He has a pet called
Little Puffy.
His pet is so puffy white
that when I see it,
he blends in
with a thing that's white.
He wanted to die the cat a different color,
but all he got was a nice color.
I know how
it happened,
he put in the wrong ingredients.

No wonder why he
is so crazy!!!!

Michael DeRoss, Grade 3
Holy Rosary School, NY

Mud

Mud makes me think of smoothies.
Smoothies make me think of vanilla pudding.
Vanilla pudding makes me think of clouds.
Clouds make me think of the color white.
The color white makes me think of socks.
Socks make me think of kids.
Kids make me think of mud.

Kenny Shugerts, Grade 3
Cambridge Springs Elementary School, PA

December
D ecorating the tree
E ating cookies
C elebrating Christmas
E verybody has fun
M y birthday
B e happy
E mpty stockings
R est at night
Benjamin Arsenault, Grade 3
Houghton Elementary School, MA

You Can Find a Poem
You can find a poem
at the sunset every day

you can find a poem
in a dark and endless sea

you can find a poem
at the waterfall sounding like thunder

you can always find a great poem
inside your heart
Mahnoor Amir, Grade 3
Slingerlands Elementary School, NY

The Flag
The flag has red stripes.
The flag is blue with white stars.
Our flag is special.
Ash Shaw, Grade 2
Fisher Hill Elementary School, MA

Spring
S pring is here
P retty flowers
R ain is coming down
I love spring
N ow it is warmer
G row your flowers
Samantha Pollock, Grade 1
Frenchtown Elementary School, CT

Colors
there are colors everywhere.
there is black and white and yellow
and blue and many others too.
there are colors here and there.
there are colors everywhere.
Dalia Loughlin, Grade 1
Glover Elementary School, MA

Winter
Winter is white
It tastes like snow
It sounds like snowball fights
It smells like Christmas
It looks like playing
It makes me delighted
Rahul Krishnan, Grade 3
Evergreen Elementary School, PA

Friends
Beautiful long black hair
Skinny brown skin Mexican
Playing together loving each other
Never fighting
Helping each other
Sharing things and
Secrets sometimes
Staying over at her house
Special friend.
Staying together for a long,
Long, long time.
Vanessa Portilla, Grade 3
Public School 2 Alfred Zimberg, NY

Monday
M opey days
O ut of it
N ot completely awake
D ay dreaming
A bad day
Y ay! It's all over with
Patrick Reagan, Grade 3
Penn Yan Elementary School, NY

Snow

Snow is so cold
It is everywhere I go.
I go outside and make a snowman
And lick the snow off my hand.

I go inside to drink hot chocolate,
it warms my body, and
keeps me warm all day.
I love the snow.

Destiny Daley, Grade 3
Pat-Kam School & Early Childhood Center, NY

Candy

C andy is so sweet
A piece will make me satisfied
N ow I have to brush my teeth
D id you like the candy
Y our chocolate bar looks so good to eat.

Caitlyn McGrath, Grade 3
Sacred Heart School, MA

Tubing

Tubing is fun
I think it is number one
I think you should try it — come on everyone
Let's try it everyone
Come on come on it's fun.

Max Currie, Grade 2
Willis E Thorpe School, MA

Prairie Dogs

A prairie dog's fur is best,
Without it they're a total mess,
And what about prairie dog's teeth,
These bones help prairie dogs eat,
What do you think of their strong jaws,
That helps them when they need to gnaw,
These little rodents can be found,
In a tunnel under the ground,
So look around and you will see,
Next time you walk around prairies.

Danielle Schwalm, Grade 3
James Russell Lowell School, MA

Summer

Summer
Sunny, hot
Swimming, jumping, splashing
Fun in my cool pool
Season
Catherine DiMaria, Grade 1
St Rose School, CT

Birds

Fly high in the sky
singing grand, beautiful songs
colorful creatures
Shelby Poitras, Grade 3
Sacred Heart School, CT

Sun

Steaming hot sun
Fireballs melting to the ground
Drip-drop little flames
Come out of the fireballs
They come
Down
Down
Down
To the ground.
The sweat from
The sun drips
Down
Down
And down.
The sweat scatters at you
When the sun goes down
The sun is sad.
Chelsea Cascio, Grade 1
Fulton Avenue School #8, NY

My Dog

My dog is named Lady,
She is still a pup.
She is a Rottweiler,
And she is really wound up.
Victoria Pottorf, Grade 2
Klein Elementary School, PA

Snow

I love to walk in the snow
Crunch, crunch, crunch I'll go
But when there's a flurry
Home I'll hurry.
Diana Ashley Cubero, Grade 2
Public School 1 The Bergen School, NY

Baseball

I'm up to bat at a baseball game…
I'm scared I'm scared
I won't hit any baseballs
at this baseball game.
I hit a baseball so far it flew,
I ran around the bases so fast I flew too.
Eric Schwarz, Grade 3
Robeson Elementary School, PA

Webkinz

I have a lot of Webkinz,
a dog, a bear, a horse.
You don't know what a Webkinz is,
I'll tell you then of course.
A Webkinz is an animal,
you care for it on your computer.
They eat and sleep and play,
and don't have to worry about a shooter
you can buy different Webkinz at any store
There are so many available,
you will always want more!
Morgan Cooper, Grade 3
Seaford Central Elementary School, DE

Blooming Bluebells

Blooming bluebells! What a wonderful sight!
They sparkle when you look at them at night.
Spring is springing look at the flowers.
I sit and watch them for hours and hours.
Bluebells blooming here and there.
Bluebells blooming everywhere!
Now it's summer
Yes it's true
But there's still a drop of springtime dew.
Madison Fulton, Grade 3
Seton Catholic School, NY

Rain
Falling from the clouds
Drops of water, cold, freezing
Dripping down, splashing
Zachary DiMeglio, Grade 2
Long Meadow Elementary School, CT

My Grandma
I watch TV.
My grandma loves me.
I read.
My grandma loves me.
I play game boy.
My grandma loves me.
My grandma will always love me.
She will, she will.
Teddy Whiteman, Grade 2
Tashua School, CT

Valentine's Day
V alentine's Day is really fun
A bunch of candy yum, yum, yum.
L ove and joy
E veryone gets flowers
N o one gets left out.
T ell Mom you love her a lot.
I t's time to keep a secret
N ot a day to be mean
E veryone gets hugs
S mile, smile, smile.

D ad gives Mom a rose.
A fun time
Y eah, it's Valentine's Day!
Tyler Hurlbert, Grade 3
Penn Yan Elementary School, NY

Spring
In the flower tree
A bird is sweetly singing
In the morning time.
Claire Morris, Grade 3
St John Neumann Academy, VA

Hamsters
Hamsters are
soft,
and cuddly!

Hear them gobble down their food,
munch,
crunch,
munch!

I love to watch them run
side to side,
back and forth,
round and round!

I wish I had one!
If I did I would read to it and
flip
flip,
each page.
Lauren Tracy, Grade 2
St Mary's Primary School, MA

The Cabin
A log cabin in the woods.
Deer running in the trees.
Tiny frogs jumping in the leaves.
Swimming in the river.
Fun in the sun.
Fire in the fireplace.
Toasting coconut marshmallows.
Special times with my family.
Good memories forever.
I love the cabin!!!
Marilyn Voxakis, Grade 2
Public School 2 Alfred Zimberg, NY

My Robot
big and cool
climbs shoots jumps
I love it a lot
Dallis Jones, Grade 2
Nottoway Elementary School, VA

Skateboards

Skateboarding is easy.
It is very fun.
You could do tricks
and other things.
How could you think it's boring?
It is like fun to me.

Noah Taylor, Grade 2
Pomperaug Elementary School, CT

Meadow

M errily, I leap in an
E normous sea of grass.
A nimals and nature
D rift by, while butterflies flutter
O n their rainbow
W ings, above and around me.

Angelique Simeone, Grade 3
Buckley Country Day School, NY

Dance

D ance is really fun!
A wesome costumes to wear!
N ot cool to have a ripped costume!
C ool to dance with my friends!
E ach of us wear makeup!

Olivia Gomez, Grade 3
Brookside Elementary School, MA

Homer

H eroic brown dog
O ld but powerful
M y little baby boy
E veryone loves him
R eally cute

Alora Bouton, Grade 3
Penn Yan Elementary School, NY

If I Were a Frog

If I were a frog,
I would lay my teeny tiny eggs
On a bromeliad and swim until
My babies hatch.
I would teach them how to survive
In the pond.
After that I would
Find some tasty beetles
For breakfast.
Then my babies
Would splash around
In the pond.

Anupama Iyer, Grade 2
Heim Elementary School, NY

Taking My Time

When I take a test or quiz
I always have been
The last one
To finish it
I've always been taking my time
Like
When I eat food
Get ready for school
Write
Taking my time is better to me
Than rushing
And I like going slow

Joshua Garcia, Grade 3
Acushnet Elementary School, MA

The Ocean

The ocean is as blue as the sky.
We can hear the waves
We can hear seashells
Making the sound of the ocean.
The ocean is beautiful.

Daniel Levasseur, Grade 1
Hyman Fine Elementary School, MA

Are You, Am I?

Are you a butterfly in the sky?
Am I a skydiver in the blue sky?
Are you a crayon in a stinky shoe?
Am I a foot in a hook?
Are you a shoe in kung-fu?

Jonathan Sinclair, Grade 1
Buckley Country Day School, NY

Flowers

F lowers filled with
L ovely scent and pollen
O ther flowers smell like
W onderful body lotion
E very flower smells different
R everse the smell and that would be bad
S ometimes...

Ella Beattie, Grade 2
Hancock Village School, VT

Homework

Homework's really not so bad
In fact it makes me very glad
When I am done
I go and run
In the sun.

Alondra Casco, Grade 2
Public School 1 The Bergen School, NY

Be a Good Citizen

Be a good citizen
Clean up the Park
Turn off the lights and leave it kind of dark
Get some friends together
Do good deeds
That's surely what
The Earth needs
Recycle, volunteer, there's no need to fear
When a good Earth is definitely here
You should clean up litter
That's a no-kidder
You can help by leaving
Trash cans all over the place
That way people won't litter
if that's the case
We definitely need to conserve water
If we don't some people won't have it
Like your daughter's daughter
So it's your choice if you want to give a hand
Because the Earth needs cleaning
All over the land

Sage Cibak, Grade 3
Big Tree Elementary School, NY

Storm

Rain
Splashing
Down
Lightning shooting
To the ground
Streets flooding
Through the road
Bombs falling from the sky.
Gabriella Dziwura, Grade 1
Fulton Avenue School #8, NY

My Spring

Golden
Dandelions
Tickling my nose
Spring is here!
David Ron, Grade 1
Trinity Christian School, VA

Silent Mountain

Pure silent mountain
There is so much moss on it
It is beautiful
Zachary Weiss, Grade 3
Saw Mill Road School, NY

Water/Fire

Water
Calming, peaceful
Gushing, running, splashing
Rain, waves, flames, blazes
Burning, scaring, frightening
Blue, red
Fire
Connor Schramm, Grade 3
West Branch School, PA

Clouds

The fluffy pillow
makes me want to lay down.
Soft like a blanket.
Krystava Cabana, Grade 2
Killingly Memorial School, CT

Rocks

Rocks are cool and great
You can find rocks all over
Rocks are hard and soft
Destiny Foster, Grade 2
Fonda-Fultonville Elementary School, NY

Snowball Fights

Snowball fights
are full of delight
On the wintery, sparkling ground.
Then you get dressed (be sure to dress warm)
Then go outside
You could play in a storm!
When you come inside
Covered by snow
From head to toe
You enjoy a nice, warm HOT COCOA!
Taylor Bettencourt, Grade 2
Willis E Thorpe School, MA

My Mind

When my mind is blank
There's an expression that says
My mind is out to lunch
But sometimes I wonder
If my mind has gone to the bank
Or Ohio, or Washington D.C.
Or Texas, or Memphis, Tennessee
There are so many places
My mind could be
I could be in Alabama, or Florida
Or California
There are so many places
My mind could be
It could be in Alaska
Or in Boston, Massachusetts
Or in West Virginia, or possibly in Canada
Where I would like to be
Or Kansas, Oklahoma, or Mississippi
It could be in those places
But where it should be
Is with me!
Brian Walton, Grade 3
Lincoln Street School, MA

A Frightful Night
A ghost appeared in the pitch black night.
You could see, it clearly gave me a fright.

I froze in my steps as I started to cry.
You could see a tear drip out of my eye.

But then I awoke and started to scream
as I realized it was only a dream.

Jackson Aguas, Grade 3
Weston Intermediate School, CT

Spring
Beautiful flowers swaying in the field.
Soft wind blowing everywhere.
Cool leaves growing on the trees.
Smooth raindrops falling down on the ground.
Wet green grass moving on the ground.

Grace Di Giovanni, Grade 2
St Mary Magdalen School, DE

My Mom
My mom is loving and caring
She is always kind and sharing
And has a gentle bearing
Like the softness of a teddy bear.

My mom is very considerate
She always tries to make me happy
And never a little too shabby
Spoiling me dearly with toys and gifts.

My mom is always unselfish
She always meets my needs
With barely and heeds to her own health
Which worries me so and so.

My mom is my mom
Even though she might not be the best
She is indeed the greatest person in my life
I love my mom dearly
Because my mom will always be my mom.

Pranab Das, Grade 3
Public School 131, NY

Grass

Grass is long hair
for Earth.
It tickles your ankles.

A long hair brush
of silk scratches you
as you walk in it.

Getting longer each day.
Thin like paper
And slippery like a wet body.

Grass.

Marc Slezak, Grade 2
Buckley Country Day School, NY

Fish Hawk

A fish hawk flew
    out of the trees
Whispering something to me.
    I listen.
It says, "Listen to the wind."

Maeve Denshaw, Grade 1
Dartmouth Early Learning Center, MA

Shoes

I like shoes very much.
I love them with a matching clutch.
Ribbons, rhinestones, heels and bows,
I like shoes that show my toes.

In winter, I wear boots with fur.
In spring, it's rubber I prefer.
For summer, sandals are my thing,
And in the fall my cleats are king.

I like shoes when they're on sale.
I often order shoes by mail.
All sorts of shoes make my day,
Feel free to send some shoes my way!

Audrey Bloom, Grade 3
John Ward Elementary School, MA

My Fall

I love fall.
Falling leaves, blowing wind.
Frosty ground.
Coldness in the air.
While colorful leaves are falling.
Red, yellow down they go.
Just watch them flow.
In the coldness of the breeze
I love fall!

Sophia Bond, Grade 3
Center School, MA

Leprechaun Show

There once was a leprechaun Bow.
He wanted to mess up his show
He stood behind Bob.
Who was a big slob
After that he had to go.

Caroline Keane, Grade 3
St Rose School, CT

I Am

I am Morgan.
I am a girl.
I am eight years old.
I am sweet, loving, and talented.
I am a great illustrator.
I am on a soccer team.
I am a great reader.
I am nice and good.

Morgan Miller, Grade 2
St Mary's Primary School, MA

Snowboarding

I went snowboarding.
I stopped.
I felt something in my feet.
It was sticky.
It kept me from falling off.
I like snowboarding.

Mario Paniccia, Grade 2
Pomperaug Elementary School, CT

I'm Dreaming

In my dreams I am the mayor.
In my dreams I am riding a horse
On a saddle made of diamonds and gold.
In my dreams the horse is wearing a bridle
Made of gold and rubies,
And the horse flies over the sun.
The horse takes me to far away places
Like Egypt, Jordan and New York.
In my dreams the horse takes me back home!

Sheila Shaheed, Grade 3
Al-Rahmah School, MD

The Broom

Once upon a time there was a broom.
He was a very good broom.
He got his mother a fragrant bloom.
One day he did something bad,
He unscrewed the teacher's chair.
He knew he was doomed.
He was banished to his room.
Now he is filled with sadness and gloom.

Alex Cleaves, Grade 2
Walker Memorial School, ME

The Shark

Leathery skin just like felt
as fierce as a mutant alien
as fast as a Carrera GT
its 5 senses are like three superheros
as immense as a giant school bus
a great appetite of 50 humans
as careless of what to eat as a water filter

Demo Theofanopoulos, Grade 3
Buckley Country Day School, NY

Flowers/Plants

Flowers
Yellow, blue
Growing, blooming, smelling
I like beautiful flowers.
Plants

Thomas McGuire, Grade 3
Chestnut Street Elementary School, PA

Michelle

M ama's little girl
I 'm in 3rd grade
C ute and cuddly
H ates lima beans.
E ats a lot of chicken
L oves gym
L ove my family
E xtra special kid

Michelle Macaluso, Grade 3
Penn-Kidder Campus, PA

The Beach

The sand is warm,
the waves crash!
The seagulls speak,
they sing a special song!

I love the beach!
The sun is warm,
the sand is soft.
The sky is blue,
and the water is too!
Margaret Chamberlin, Grade 2
St Mary's Primary School, MA

Fall

F all is time for Halloween.
A pples are picked in fall.
L eaves fall in autumn.
L ots of birds migrate.
Hagan Aldridge, Grade 1
St Christopher's School, VA

The Dancing Hound

I have a hound,
he makes a loud sound.
His name is Fred,
his nose is red.
He likes to dig,
he dances the jig.
Liam Carey, Grade 2
St Stephen's School, NY

Lion-Turtle

You must be tall,
or he'll play with you as if you're a ball.
He has 6 spikes,
knows 7 Mikes.
He has 3 tails,
plays with pails.
He makes a great pet,
even though he hates to be soaking wet.
He's fun!
he could be your hun.
He's fast, because he's last.
He's not so big,
just the size of a baby fig.
It's a relief to know that
he's make believe!
Robert C. O'Neill, Grade 3
Seaford Central Elementary School, DE

Six

There are six colors in the rainbow.
There are six people in my family.
There might be six hangers in my closet.
There were six birds in my tree.
There are probably six leaves falling.
There will be six dots on my paper.
SIX SIX SIX SIX SIX SIX!!!!!!
Caroline Samsonik, Grade 3
Seton Catholic School, NY

Easter

What I got for Easter is a mystery you see!
Every egg had a secret.
Some had chocolate, and other good things!
Matthew Carlsen, Grade 2
St Mary's Primary School, MA

Spring

Beautiful butterflies flying in the sky
Wings of a bird flapping in the air
Perfect flowers blowing in the grass
Delicious water ice eating it in my backyard
Giant trees blowing leaves in the park
Grace Ruoff, Grade 2
St Mary Magdalen School, DE

Blue

Blue is the color of the beautiful sky
Blue is the color of a blue marker
Blue is the color of the wavy water at the beach
Blue is the color of a blue bird
Blue is the color of wet tears.

Annamaria Fazio, Grade 1
Buckley Country Day School, NY

If I Were

If I were the yellow sunshine,
And if you were a green tree,
I would let you drink me up,
And bask below me.
If I were a rough oyster,
And if you were a shining pearl,
You would rest inside me,
Until I would unfurl.
If I were a rocking sailboat,
And if you were the deep blue sea,
I would rest upon you,
While you gently rocked me.
If I were a skilled sculptor,
And if you were my lump of clay,
I would gently mold you,
And shape you all day.

Ben Maron, Grade 3
General John Nixon Elementary School, MA

Birds Singing

Birds singing in the air
Singing like they just don't care
Birds singing in the trees
Singing along with the bumblebees
Birds singing on the ground
everyone's heard that beautiful sound
Birds building nests up high
The baby birds will learn to fly
Birds making a pretty song
They're sometimes right where they belong
Birds singing in the air
Singing like they just don't care

Julia D'Entremont, Grade 1
Willis E Thorpe School, MA

A Surprise Trip

Where are we going?
I asked my mom.
My mom said to just stay calm.

Where are we going?
The zoo, Kentucky, the pool?
But then I found out that
It was the first day of school.

Madison Surmacz, Grade 3
Rossmoyne Elementary School, PA

Friends

F riends are friendly
R eally nice to each other
I nteresting people
E asy to get along with
N ice and kind
D ancing and
S inging all the time.

Annabelle Tang, Grade 1
Milton Fuller Roberts School, MA

Cat

Black, white, gray and fun.
Chasing a toy inside my house.
Quiet when he sleeps.

Victoria Ryan, Grade 2
Fisher Hill Elementary School, MA

Phase of the Moon

The full moon looks like
a big baseball
I can sit there all night
looking at it
when it is crescent
it look's like a sliver
and when it is half
it looks like a slice of watermelon
when the moon is new it disappears
From my view

Justin Beaudry, Grade 2
Tashua School, CT

Time

Time, time
Time flies by
It flies fast in your mind
It goes so fast
You can't keep track
Time, time
No one can beat it!

Leah Ford, Grade 3
Vivian E Hussey Primary School, ME

Fire

We like the fire.
Later it will grow higher.
More wood until the room
feels pretty good.
When the fire is low
the room blows cold.

Michelle Kokosis, Grade 3
Public School 2 Alfred Zimberg, NY

Ice Cream

Ice cream, ice cream, cherries
on top, ice cream
is so sweet
at night.

If you eat it at night,
you will be in a Sugar Shock.

Ice cream is so sweet to eat
and you will see how sweet, it really is.

Nicole Mansueto, Grade 3
Holy Rosary School, NY

Yahtzee

Lazy when he walks
Barks all night and sleeps all day
Paws at the front door
Has the name of a great game
Always wants your attention

Mackenzie Kearns, Grade 3
Memorial School, NH

Flag

F reedom to help us.
L ove to take care of our state
A nything to help us.
G iving help to make our country safe.

Allison Graham, Grade 3
Bradford Township Elementary School, PA

Spring

S now melting
P lanting flowers
R aindrops fall
I go outside
N ests are being built
G rass is growing

Terri Schneider, Grade 3
Chestnut Street Elementary School, PA

Shelby Cobra

Shelby Cobra
has it all.
289 won it all.
427 not at all,
Loud engine
big and small.
Very fast,
the headlight flashed,
let's all go to the cobra bash!

Jacob Elijah Palmer, Grade 3
Seaford Central Elementary School, DE

My Pet Kitten

My pet kitten is gray, black and white.
His name is Gobber.
He has markings like a tiger.
He purrs a lot and cuddles a lot too.
His fur is short and soft.
He is six month old.
He is the second best cat I ever had.
He was born on October 28th 2007.
I LOVE My Kitten Gobber.

Brandon Desmett, Grade 3
Bradford Township Elementary School, PA

Storm

Rain
Dripping down
Boom! Boom! Boom!
Pow! Pow!
And
The thunder
Is hitting
Your window
The rain
Say's, "boom!"
The thunder says
Plop
Plop
The thunder is Crunching
In
The air.
Joshua Harnisher, Grade 1
Fulton Avenue School #8, NY

Summer

Summer is fun,
Summer is cool,
All my homework is done,
And you get to swim in a pool.
The beach is fun,
In the hot hot sun,
We will bring snacks,
A whole ton,
I like sports,
I like to run,
You could wear shorts,
Make sure to have fun.
Dylan Biondo, Grade 3
Our Lady of Hope School, NY

Lion

A lion
In a sunny field
After a hunt
Has a trembling lip.
He had not caught anything.
Sam Lewis, Grade 2
St Christopher's School, VA

Animals

Goldfish, catfish, turtles, frogs
Rabbits, hamsters, parrots, dogs
Flamingos, horses, llamas, cats
Tarantulas, monkeys, snakes and rats

Turtles are reptiles, so are snakes
Both of them can live in lakes
Hamsters are little, horses are tall
Horses run, hamsters crawl

Monkeys swing, tarantulas are furry
Both of them move in a hurry
Frogs hop, rabbits too
Llamas, cats and rats chew

Some dogs are fast, some dogs are slow
Some birds fly high, others fly low
Some fish are fat, some fish are slim
Some have fins that help them swim

Goldfish, catfish, turtles, frogs
Rabbits, hamsters, parrots, dogs
Flamingos, horses, llamas, cats
Tarantulas, monkeys, snakes and rats
Ms. Alison Walsh's 2nd Grade Class
Henry Clay Elementary School, VA

Fishing

Fishing makes me think of fish.
Fish make me think of water.
Water makes me think of swimming.
Swimming makes me think of splashing.
Splashing makes me think of spring.
Spring makes me think of fishing.
Jake Coatoam-Oblinski, Grade 3
Cambridge Springs Elementary School, PA

Snow

Snow is white.
Snow is bright
And in the night
What a sight!
Jesus Reza Salazar, Grade 2
Public School 1 The Bergen School, NY

Pray

God takes good care of us.
I love Him very much.
I pray so I can go to Heaven one day.
I just pray.
Taylor Potts, Kindergarten
Agape Christian Academy, VA

Dads

Dads love you every way
Dads care for you every day
Dads are awesome
Dads are cool except
When they embarrass you at school.
Theresa Don, Grade 3
Center School, MA

I Dreamed

I dreamed
I was a Rockstar
on the stage with my guitar
singing a happy song
loudly
Daveona Lowery, Grade 2
Bensley Elementary School, VA

Marshmallows

they melt in hot chocolate.
they are gooey in s'mores
they are sticky in sweet potatoes.
they are sugary.
they are soft.
they are squishy.
Will Hodges, Grade 2
St John Neumann Academy, VA

Friends

Friends are like angels on earth.
They're here through it all.
They give me smiles and happiness.
Friends are sweet
Alexandra Cianfarani, Grade 3
St Madeleine Sophie School, NY

Venus

Venus
Hot, big
Circling, floating, moving
Craters, hot lava, round, second
Spinning, rotating, amazing
Heavy, red
Planet
Maxwell Horning, Grade 3
Brant Elementary School, NY

Rainbows

Sparkle in the sun
Shining like diamonds
Colorful as ten paints altogether
All the colors you see
So bright and cheerful
Beautiful and nice
It is a wonderful sight
Rain and sun make one
I love rainbows

Red for roses, on Valentine's Day
Orange for pumpkins, round and big
Yellow for lemons, sour and bright
Green for grass, tall and thin
Blue for a pool, with lots of fun
Purple for grapes, juicy and sweet
Violet for the night, dark and scary
I love looking at the sight
Stacey Li, Grade 3
Public School 48, NY

The Highest Flying Kite

I am a kite
I look down
at the ground
my points are as sharp as a knife
I fly like a bird
From the ground
the baseball on it looks as tiny as a fly
Mark Leonardi, Grade 1
St Rose School, CT

What I Can Do at the Beach

I can swim in the water.
I can lay on my towel in the sun.
I can find cool seashells.
I can make a sand castle.

Alyssa Bolton, Grade 2
Bensley Elementary School, VA

Salamanders

The salamander sits on a rock.
The sun is hot at twelve o'clock.

The salamander likes to stay cool
So he goes and dives into the pool.

Then the salamander eats a fly.
It tastes just like cherry pie.

Bryan Cotellese, Grade 3
St John Neumann Academy, VA

February

February
loving, snowy
ice skating, ice hockey, sledding
feeling good in February
second month

Lindsay Koppel, Grade 3
Evergreen Elementary School, PA

Trinity

Trinity was everyone's friend
But
Trinity had to move
To Rhode Island.
She was fun.
I was her first best Friend.
She felt like a sister
To me, but
Trinity
Had to
Leave.

Ahlyeea Stewart, Grade 2
Milton Terrace Primary School, NY

Girl from France

There once was a girl from France.
Who loved to water her plants.
She twirled and twirled,
Around the world.
And then her pants had ants.

Ludovica Palmieri, Grade 1
Mater Christi School, VT

Spring Is in the Air

The trees' leaves are coming back.
The grass is getting greener.
The flowers are blooming.
The birds are singing.
Spring is getting near.
The weather is getting warmer.
The sun is shining brighter.
The days are getting longer.
Spring is finally here.

Anthony Giacomarra, Grade 3
Our Lady of Hope School, NY

I Am Gold

Gold is the color of the sun.
Gold is a nice color for candy.
Gold is pretty on clothes.
Gold makes me happy.
Gold is the prettiest on eggs.
Gold reminds me of my teacher.
Gold is also the color of a pencil.
Some mountains are gold.
Gold is the color of my hair.

Allison McKenna, Grade 1
St Madeleine Sophie School, NY

Avocado

Avocados look green
Avocados smell sweet
Avocados feel bumpy
Avocados sound crunchy
Avocados taste buttery

Abhinav Venkatakrishnan, Grade 1
Richland Elementary School, PA

Gardens

Gardens can be veggies or flowers
Gardens can be fun for hours

Flowers to smell or food to eat
Growing a garden can be quite neat

You can grow things in beds or a pot
It's best to garden in summer when it's hot

You can plant roses or a tree
I don't care anything is fine with me

Plant in a greenhouse so they grow
Then put them in the ground with no snow

I'm learning more about plants
They are eaten by bugs and ants.

Dalen Sanders, Grade 3
Mary Walter Elementary School, VA

What Is School

S chool rocks my socks
C ookies at lunch
H ard homework
O n and off tests
O utstanding teachers
L essons learned each day

Alexia Madlinger-Williams, Grade 3
Helen B Duffield Elementary School, NY

The Rat and the Cat

The rat didn't like that cat,
and the cat hated that rat;
Boom, crash, bang, caboom!
Boom, bang, ouch!
Fly on the couch!
Run to the kitchen, kitty cat!
You're such a brat!
I hate you, kitty cat!
I hate you too, pretty rat!

Noah Dennis, Grade 3
Mohawk Valley Christian Academy, NY

School
S cience.
C lass
H undred chart.
O I like Art.
O I like music.
L unch.

Travis Lane, Grade 2
Bensley Elementary School, VA

What's in the Junk Drawer?
A candy cane that's gone bad
Battery that doesn't work
An empty tape holder
Old wire cutters
A night light that needs a new bulb
A hair clip that's broken
Phone charger that no one needs
An almost dried up marker

Hannah Overstreet, Grade 3
Nottoway Elementary School, VA

Season Are Sensational
Summer is super
Autumn is awesome
Winter is a whiz
and spring is sweet
All these seasons
Are some of God's best creations

Joseph Brunell, Grade 3
Trinity Christian School, VA

Baby Bird
I see a baby bird.
I see a baby bird.
I fell scared in my chest.
The bird is falling out of its nest
And into the field!
Oh no!
I hope the baby bird
Gets back to its herd.

Amanda LaCoy, Grade 2
Cornerstone Academy, MA

Caterpillars
They are fat,
Longer than a gnat.
They eat bright green leaves,
In the nice bright trees.
It turns into a red and black butterfly,
And then it says good-bye!

Catharina Hyeon, Grade 2
St Rose School, CT

Red
I have a red strawberry
covered in chocolate for lunch

My mom gave me a red heart

My dad has a baseball cap
with a big red "B"

I went to the park and saw a red train

I have some red shiny lipstick
I put on when I play rock star

Chloe Scharffenberg, Grade 1
Willis E Thorpe School, MA

The Forest
The trees, so many,
Always different
Changed by the rain
and the wind.
A sad kind of happy.

William Smith, Grade 1
Dartmouth Early Learning Center, MA

Water
W et
A quatic paradise
T he ocean
E els' home
R adiant beauty

Ken Nero, Grade 3
Heron Pond Elementary School, NH

Snow

Walking in the snow
Snow, snow, snow
it blows and blows
it glows and glows
it comes down
slow beautiful
snow.

Carlos Gutierrez, Grade 1
Public School 1 The Bergen School, NY

Emily

Emily…
    Hard worker, friendly, helpful
Emily…
Caring, nice, happy
Likes reading *Santa Paws, Our Hero.*
Emily has a dog named Cheerio
She respects and works well with other people.
Emily…
    My friend.

Cara Higginbottom, Grade 3
Robeson Elementary School, PA

The Sun

I like the sun
I call her "Miss Dunn."
She calls me "Very bright"
I call her "A sight."
I like it when she's red,
She likes the shape of my head.
I also like her yellow,
She says I'm a fellow.
She likes it in the daytime
I love it when it's playtime!
I like mud.
She calls me "Bud."
I always stink,
She says, "I'm pink."
I like it when she's big,
Because I'm a pig.

Griffin Dunn, Grade 3
Seaford Central Elementary School, DE

A Friend
There is a friend who lives near,
I think she's coming here.
There she is all in pink,
It was so bright I had to blink.
Isaac Voltoline, Grade 3
Craneville School, MA

Sounds
The sail whistled in the wind.
The dog howled in the night.
The boat cried through the water.
The bike zoomed through the woods.
The cart squeaked down the street.
Taylor Sommers, Grade 2
St Christopher's School, VA

Lambs
Lambs are as white as snow.
Their noses are as soft as velvet.
Ears as pink as petunias.
Eyes as delicate as a rose.
Lambs are adorable!
Audrey Sedensky, Grade 2
St Rose School, CT

The Little Red Plane
I like airplanes
They fly very high
I see them in the sky,
Oh my, I would love to ride.
Noah Dulaney, Grade 1
Nottoway Elementary School, VA

Soccer
S coring goals
O ften easy and hard
C olorful soccer balls
C oaches yelling
E very player counts
R unning to get the ball
Abigail Meyers, Grade 3
Leicester Memorial School, MA

Clueless
When I am clueless,
I am in a dream.
There are new people,
I have never seen.
Always new places,
Sometimes a new life,
Sometimes I am lost,
Sometimes I am falling,
Sometimes I'm just right,
Clueless is fun.
Catherine LeBlanc, Grade 3
James Russell Lowell School, MA

Ladybugs
Ladybugs
Zing zing
When they fly in the sky.

They have little polka dots.
Every summer they come back
And eat mosquitos
And fly all day long.
Gabriella Bloom, Grade 2
Buckley Country Day School, NY

Wintertime!
Winter, winter, winter,
Icy ground, cozy fireplace,
Big friendly, plump, snowman,
Small, fast, blue, sled,
These are just a few.

White winter, cold winter,
Hot creamy, chocolate cocoa,
Big heavy, warm coat,
Cozy mittens, too.
Freezing snowballs,
Towering snow forts,
Don't forget, delicious cookies,
Last of all, I like frosty winters!
Patrick Fenton, Grade 3
Stony Point Elementary School, NY

Winter

The winter's so cold
But the sun still shines
I won't complain, I won't whine.
I just wish spring was here
But it will come
So let's all cheer!

Kimberly Martinez, Grade 2
Public School 1 The Bergen School, NY

Cat, Hat, Rat

The cat wore a hat,
He ran to the rat,
The rat said, "Hey, why you wearin' that?"
And the cat refused to tell the rat
Why the cat was wearing
That strange hat.

Thea Nickolas, Grade 2
Cabot Elementary School, MA

About the Sea

The sea is flowing,
in the sunset.

The sea twinkles,
dolphins sparkle in the blue sea.

Their eyes sparkling from the gleaming moon.
Goodnight Moon!

Katie Walsh, Grade 2
St Mary's Primary School, MA

School

A B C D E F G
School is good for me.
H I J K L M N O P
Reading, writing, poetry.
Q R S T U V
Art, music, gym too
W X Y Z
Lots to learn, lots to do.

Alfredo Martinez, Grade 2
Public School 1 The Bergen School, NY

Sunset
I like the colors.
Inside the sky is orange.
God is watching me!
Angel Williams, Grade 3
Sacred Heart School, CT

Spring Beginning
Spring is beginning
Pretty buds ready to sprout
Sunshine all about
Sydney Feinberg, Grade 2
Guilford Lakes School, CT

Dogs
The furry beast had
hair standing like soldiers
when the stranger came
Alexa J. Shepherd, Grade 2
Killingly Memorial School, CT

Spring
Mud all over everything.
The warm sun shining on you.
Green grass growing in April.
Rain helping the flowers grow.
Flowers blooming in April.
Joanna Luck, Grade 2
Wells Central School, NY

The Turtle and the Hurdle
There once was a turtle
Who saw a hurdle.
He made a jump
And got a bump.
Colson Lugbill, Grade 2
Trinity Christian School, VA

Ninjas
Ninjas are so cool
They always carry a sword
So please, please beware!
Juan Casiano, Grade 3
Penn-Kidder Campus, PA

Reading
Reading
To learn new things
To read with my sister
To learn new words at school and home
Reading
Ryan Eddy, Grade 2
St Madeleine Sophie School, NY

My Trip to Ireland
I am going to Ireland to meet my mom's family.
They talk kind of funny
and I don't know what they are saying.
It sounds like their nose gets kind of runny
but I still love them because they are my family.
Samantha Walsh, Grade 2
Public School 205 Alexander Graham Bell, NY

Spring
Pretty flowers swaying in the field
Beautiful birds tweeting in the sky
Pink flowers growing in the meadow
Cold water ice freezing in my mouth
Colorful rainbows when they touch ground.
Anthony Ciampoli, Grade 2
St Mary Magdalen School, DE

The Crab
Clang! Bang!
I saw a huge, humongous, hungry crab.
I saw that silly old crab and said, "Hi!"
It chased me and I wanted to cry!
David Leskovec, Grade 3
New Freedom Christian School, PA

Kittens
Kittens are,
cute,
fun,
furry,
and funny!

I think they are happy and I am happy too!
Victoria Bleakney, Grade 2
St Mary's Primary School, MA

If I Were a Kapok Tree

If I were a remarkable kapok tree
I would spread out
My beautiful branches with joy
And offer a home to boa, dart frog, iguana,
Sloth, parrot and red-eyed tree frog.
I would invite them
To climb up my buttress roots
But I would warn them
Not to get hurt
By my spiky trunk.

Jordan Marshall, Grade 2
Heim Elementary School, NY

Going Golfing with My Cousins

I went golfing
with my cousins.
I played lots of games.
We played ball
I didn't fall.
Even though
I'm not too tall.

Edgar Ventura, Grade 1
Public School 1 The Bergen School, NY

Flowers on Hills

I see hills.
I see hills.
Hills covered with flowers, plants, and trees.
The hills would be a good home for bees.
Yea! Here come my friends.
Yea! Here come my friends.

Deepa Nandan, Grade 2
Cornerstone Academy, MA

Deevil

I have a sister named Deevil.
She was named that because she was evil.
She had to pay a fine,
She said, "But I'm turning nine!"
So she ran away to live in Anna Ville.

Julia Lemick, Grade 2
Oakdale Elementary School, MD

Colors

Roses are Red
Violets are purple
The sky is blue
The grass is green
Sunflowers are yellow
Garden snakes are gray
God's world is beautiful in all colors.

Mikala Goodemote, Grade 1
Calvary Chapel Christian School, NY

Tiger

Tigers are orange
Tigers move fast
Tigers live in the jungle
Tigers eat meat
Tigers are in the cat family

Luke Palermo, Grade 1
Richland Elementary School, PA

Stars

Stars, oh stars
You twinkle in the night
Like little glowing puffballs
You shine so long
You are great at night
You twinkle and twinkle and twinkle

Stars, oh stars
I love how you twinkle
You are so bright
You are a dot to the eyes
But a sun in the sky
You twinkle and twinkle and twinkle

Stars, oh stars
You are so far, light-years away
But yet I feel
You are so close to my heart
I will catch you one day
You twinkle and twinkle and twinkle

Pretam Nandi, Grade 3
Public School 69 Jackson Heights, NY

Dear Tooth

Dear Tooth,

I will be coming today at nighttime.
That is when everybody is asleep.
That's when I come.

Yours truly,
Tooth Fairy

Emma Bouchard, Grade 1
Glover Elementary School, MA

Frogs

Frogs are unusual,
They hide cause they're shy.

They don't have fur only skin,
Rain forests are where they win.

Frogs go on dirt,
But they do not flirt.

Frogs come in many sizes,
They display many colors.

They're on land and water,
Amphibians is what they are!

Bryan Canales, Grade 3
James Russell Lowell School, MA

The Beautiful World

Above, above
The sapphire sky
Below, below
The worms that all sigh
In the mountains, the mountains
The snowcaps up high
In the ocean, the ocean
The fishes swim by
Here ends my song,
The beautiful world.

Matthew J. Tobin, Grade 3
Spring Hill Elementary School, VA

Love and Care

Love is in all of us, and ready to be shared
Love is caring and sharing
To care is to say "I love you"
For caring is really another way of telling
Someone, allow me to be nice to you

Love starts with yourself and multiplies
on the way to every person
Regardless of color or race.
Regardless of birth place
Love means brotherhood,
as we carry out God's command

Jonathan Lewis, Grade 2
Great Oaks Elementary School, NY

Earth

E arth is 150 kilometers from the sun.
A round the Earth is one moon.
R otation takes one day around the sun.
T hird planet in the solar system.
H alf the Earth is lit at once.

Brave Hunter Williams, Grade 3
Brant Elementary School, NY

Leprechaun Fred

There once was a leprechaun named Fred.
He never ever got out of bed
He slept through that day.
His horse never got hay.
So he bumped his head on Ed.

Olivia Adams, Grade 3
St Rose School, CT

Money

I am money.
I buy things.
I feel sad when I'm given away.
I feel happy when I'm not on the ground.
I would tell my owner:
do not buy anything else with me.

Jalein Jenkins-Johnson, Grade 2
Bensley Elementary School, VA

Spring Joy
yellow
sun
shining
Spring is joyful!
Thomas Briscoe, Grade 1
St Rose School, CT

My Spring
The pink
rabbits are
hopping
spring is
here
Haley Silvernail, Grade 1
Trinity Christian School, VA

Summer
S ummer is fun!
U nder the trees!
M uch to do!
M orning birds chirping!
E veryone is having fun!
R iver rafting is awesome!
Yehuda Bukalov, Grade 3
Yeshiva Tifereth Moshe, NY

Witch
W itches are scary.
I do not like scary stuff.
T he witches fly on brooms
C ausing trouble.
H elp! It's Halloween!
Brooke Blakely, Grade 2
St Joseph School, NY

Dolphins
Sleek, playful
Jumping, swimming, helping
A joyful sea creature
Fun
Lauren Kim, Grade 3
Trinity Christian School, VA

Do You Like?
Do you like jelly?
Do you like fluff?
Do you like them to stick to your cuff?

Do you like bacon?
Do you like eggs?
Do you like when they run down your legs?

Do you like cookies?
Do you like cake?
Do you like to wait for them to bake?

Do you like cupcakes?
Do you like tea?
Do you like to eat with me?
Kaylah Stone, Grade 2
Hancock Village School, VT

My Room
This is where I sleep,
this is where I stay,
this is where I start and end my every day.

This is where I play,
this is my domain,
this is where I've been waiting to go all day.

I know I've said a lot,
but this isn't all I've got,
and I cannot stop yet anyway.

This is where I have all I need for me,
and if you haven't guessed yet,
my room is where I like to be.
Angelica Hoelzli, Grade 3
Willits Elementary School, NY

Lake Zoar
If you're athletic this is the place for you.
Just grab a bike and ride right through.
Take a break if you start to ache.
So have some fun you could probably even run.
Conor Murphy, Grade 2
Pomperaug Elementary School, CT

Leprechauns

Smart, greedy
Sneaking, tiptoeing, tripping
Very good at spying
Wee people
Sydney Maughan, Grade 2
Long Meadow Elementary School, CT

Clouds

Clouds are puffy
Clouds are light
Sometimes gray
Sometimes white
They float in the sky
See different things in them
Valentina Ciminera, Grade 3
Public School 2 Alfred Zimberg, NY

What Do Animals Know?

Animals know that winter is coming.
They can see their breath.
The air is getting colder.
It is hard to find food.
That's what animals know.
Kyra Lyons, Grade 1
Hyman Fine Elementary School, MA

Mice

Mice, mice where's your cheese?
Somebody stole it, they are mean!
Where did they put it, behind the tree?
Can you get it for me, me me?
Nick Cornay, Grade 1
Milton Fuller Roberts School, MA

The Man from Syracuse

There was a young man from Syracuse,
One day he was reading the news.
He fell off his chair,
Had a nightmare,
All because he was reading the news.
George Stultz, Grade 2
Oakdale Elementary School, MD

Friends

Friends are nice.
They like to play.
They always do things,
With their friends.

Friends are good.
Friends are friends.
Friends are nice,
All the time.
Cameron Drake, Grade 3
Mount Vernon Elementary School, PA

Ocean Dance

Dolphins,
seaweed, fish
and kites
dancing and swaying
calmly.
The kites fly
smoothly
gliding across the air.
Fish jumping everywhere.
Dolphins dance like ballerinas.
The seaweed moves its arms.

Suddenly,
day turns to night.
The lighthouse flashes.
Seaweed floats slowly.
Kites go home.
Fish lie down
and the dolphins fall fast asleep.
Erika Massaro, Grade 2
Dr Samuel C Eveleth School, MA

Pearl

I found a beautiful pearl.
I got it from an oyster.
I got the oyster from the ocean.
I got the ocean from the Earth.
Michelle Wisnewski, Grade 2
Buckley Country Day School, NY

Valentine's Day

V alentine's Day is
A wesome and so is
L ove because you get
E ven more candy
N ew, new ones
T oo
I t's so cool
N ow that we have
E ven more candy than I did
S o I love Valentines

D ay it's
A beautiful day
Y eah!

Brittney McMillen, Grade 3
Penn Yan Elementary School, NY

Pastries at the Fair

For breakfast I ate an eclair.
I ran like wind straight to the fair.
I had a delicious cupcake.
With a delicious chocolate shake.

Then I will make a tasty cake.
Then I had to go home and rake.
The last thing I saw was a spy.
With a delicious apple pie

Javier King, Grade 3
Bensley Elementary School, VA

Hawaii

So hot and sunny.
And the water is so cold.
With the coconuts
On the pom pom trees.
And the volcanoes.
With the warm sand.
And the cool jungles.
The amazing blue sky
With the tigers and lions.

Xavier Wolfe, Grade 2
Public School 2 Alfred Zimberg, NY

Papa, Papa

Papa, papa
Where are you?
Papa, papa
Tie my shoe.
Papa, papa
Don't go too fast.
Papa, papa
I am last.
Papa, papa
This is fun.
Papa, papa
I can't run.
Papa, papa
Let's play ball.
Papa, papa
Find my doll.

Camille Brockington, Grade 3
Bensley Elementary School, VA

Games

Fun
Jogging, action
Addicting, jumping, skating,
Running, watching, following, hopping,
School, walking, running,
Dull, sitting,
Boring

Jason Goodrick, Grade 3
Trinity Christian School, VA

Spring Is Here

Spring is here, so much fun.
I can play outside and smell the roses.
I will ride my bike on the sidewalk.
Home
Sun
Rain
Ice Cream
Robin's nest
Spring is here, I am so happy

Gene, Grade 1
Kanner Learning Center, PA

My Dog

When my dog jumps,
He does a twist.
He catches a ball.
He jumps down fast,
To give me the ball.
When he barks he barks so loud.
he barks at rabbits and ants.
when people come by he scares them away,
that is why people never stay.

Christian Kampas, Grade 3
Central Elementary School, PA

Aqua Blue

Aqua blue is like the sound of the ocean
water crashing on the hot sand.
Aqua blue is like the smell of a ripe
blueberry lollipop touching my nose.
Aqua blue is like the taste of a cold
refreshing Gatorade touching my tongue.
Aqua blue is like the feel of warm water
splashing against my toes in the pool.

Ryan Coccaro, Grade 2
Long Meadow Elementary School, CT

A Never-Ending Day

Silent breezes warm me in a naughty way
The juice of the sun is tastier than ever
The sun tries to leave in an unsteady way
The leaves leave me in a lonely way
but the stars stay with me forever
Today's a never-ending day

Robbie Doncourt, Grade 3
Lincoln Elementary School, PA

Rain/Water

Rain
Fast, slow
Filling, splashing, falling
Rain comes in spring.
Water

Toby Fox Jr., Grade 3
Chestnut Street Elementary School, PA

Spring

Spring is fun and beautiful!
Spring is sunny and rainy
Spring is lovely and swimmy
But most of all
Spring is love.

Lisa Price, Grade 1
St Rose School, CT

The Storm

Homework papers rattle
like a rattlesnake
in the grass
in a storm.
The storm stopped.
Now it is
raining like tears from
God and
Jesus in Heaven.
Lightning booming from
the Sky
down
to the
Earth.

Julian Coyle, Grade 1
St Rose School, CT

Christmas Spirit

Christmas Spirit
is in my heart.
I love Christmas
don't take it away.

Decorating the tree
and making cookies
for Santa. Reindeer
landing on my roof.

Santa leaving presents
under the tree.
That's why I love Christmas.

Benjamin Hall, Grade 3
Westall School, MA

Lemonade

Lemonade is yellow
It looks like a bright light.
It tastes like sweet lemons with sugar.
It sounds like falling rain when you pour it.
It smells like sweet sugar.
It makes me feel good.

Abby Bergman, Grade 3
Evergreen Elementary School, PA

December

December is so cold.
The wind does brow
There's also snow
But in the snow I'll play
Snow balls snow angels
Snowmen that will stay
Soon Christmas will be here
Solet's all cheer Hip Hip Hooray
Christmas is here!

Henry Oquendo, Grade 2
Public School 1 The Bergen School, NY

I Am Philip Pietruch

I am athletic and smart
I wonder about heaven in the sky
I hear bells ringing in the light
I see my future as being very successful
I am athletic and smart

I pretend there are no wars in the world
I feel my grandpa's hand
I touch my mom and dad's heart
I worry about being in war
I cry that I never saw my grandpas
I am athletic and smart

I understand life isn't fair
I say war stinks
I dream of world peace
I try respecting my sisters
I hope I live a long life
I am athletic and smart

Philip Pietruch, Grade 3
Stony Point Elementary School, NY

Flowers
Flowers are bright,
Flowers are colorful,
They're the most delicate thing you'll find.
For God's creation is a wonderful thing,
And the best of it is
Flowers.

Lillian Holley, Grade 3
Trinity Christian School, VA

Favorite
My favorite book's a fairy tale
with dragons twice my size!
There's kings and queens
and pure white steeds,
there's blue and berry pies.
And if you want to dare me to,
I'll show you my favorite day.
It starts with "toosd" and ends with "ay."
What is it?
Why, of course, it's Tuesday!

Zoe Dettelbach, Grade 3
Thoreau Elementary School, MA

Spring
S un is starting to come out
P eople are walking
R aining a lot
I 'm riding my bike
N ot freezing anymore
G rowing gardens

Lexi Walton, Grade 3
Chestnut Street Elementary School, PA

Butterflies
Butterflies make me think of kites.
Kites make me think of the wind.
The wind makes me think of tornadoes.
Tornadoes make me think of rainbows.
Rainbows make me think of colorful things.
Colorful things make me think of butterflies.

Megan Foister, Grade 3
Cambridge Springs Elementary School, PA

Clouds Are
Clouds are millions of soft,
White, fluffy pillows in the sky.
They all remind me
Of a white cat on a puffy bed.
I would love to go for a ride
On a funny shape cloud with a friend,
But, I know I can't.
I like to lie on the ground by myself,
Looking at the clouds go by...
One, two, three as I sigh.
Cassandra Arsenault, Grade 2
Richer Elementary School, MA

The Color of Blue
I am blue.
I rhyme with glue.
The sky is the color of me.
I am the color of jeans.
I am the color of a book bag.
I am the color of a blue bird.
I am in every season.
I am the color of a blueberry.
People say you are feeling
the color of me when you are sad.
I am the color of the sea.
Kiersten Becker, Grade 1
St Madeleine Sophie School, NY

Friends
Friends are cool.
Friends are neat.
Friends are really fun to make!
My friends are sweet.
My friends are neat.
Cheering up is what they do to me!
My friend, and I lend.
My friend made a poem
"Best of Friends Until the End."
I like my friends and they like me.
I have a big friendship tree.
Haseeb Waseem, Grade 3
Buckley Country Day School, NY

Spring
Beautiful flowers swaying in a field.
Birds tweeting and flying in the sky.
Bright flowers in the meadow.
Icy water ice melting in the cone.
Pointy grass grows in the ground.
Joseph E. Szczerba III, Grade 2
St Mary Magdalen School, DE

Kites
Dipping, diving,
gliding softly,
gently leaping
like a ballerina,
like leaves blowing
through the field,
like clouds

Kites in the sky
Jack Downing, Grade 2
Dr Samuel C Eveleth School, MA

Winter
Snow,
Snow,
Snow,
Cozy snow,
Icy snow,
Fast, gliding, green snowmobile,
White, warm, soft Santa,
These are just a few.
Sparkly snowflake,
Shiny frost,
Cold, icy, wintery snowman,
Sweet, warm, hot chocolate,
Colorful ornaments, too.
Tasty cookies,
Slippery ice,
Don't forget, beautiful Christmas trees
Last of all, best of all,
I like cinnamon gingerbread cookies!
Dante Restaino, Grade 3
Stony Point Elementary School, NY

March

March is here
So let's all cheer
Spring is near.

Lisbeth Gutierrez, Grade 1
Public School 1 The Bergen School, NY

Quetzal

He's the greenest bird you'll ever see.
With a touch of pink, how beautiful he is.
He's not a peacock.
Quetzal, Quetzal is his name,
To fly through the jungle is his game!

Wolf MackRosen, Grade 2
Dr Samuel C Eveleth School, MA

Winter Fun

Winter is just super fun!
But there isn't much warm sun.
Snowmobiles go,
And the only thing I can think of is snow!
Snowmen are fun,
But they can melt in the sun.
Since winter is fun,
For a snowman's hat, you can use a bun!
Every night is a pretty sight,
for that sight is very bright!
Winter is such a good sight,
I might get frostbite!
When you're cold, go for hot cocoa.
We'll see winter tomorrow!

Anthony Paolino, Grade 3
Penn-Kidder Campus, PA

Ducklings

Ducklings make me think of water.
Water makes me think of ponds.
Ponds make me think of a farm.
A farm makes me think of baby animals.
Baby animals make me think of spring.
Spring makes me think of ducklings.

Hadley Glenn, Grade 3
Cambridge Springs Elementary School, PA

Day to Night

Day
Bright, Alive
Thriving, Flourishing, Growing
Sun, Flower, Dark, Dead
Twinkling, Gasping, Heaving
Silent, Soft
Night
Erin Supko, Grade 3
Cabot Elementary School, MA

Summer Sun

Summer's sizzle
Sun fire balls
Sweat
Dripping
Down
On
Our
Head!!
Vincent Matarese, Grade 1
Fulton Avenue School #8, NY

Winter

Falling all around,
With fluffy snow
On the ground
Like a blanket that's cold
Freezes like ice
Turns to water
Licking it like ice cream

What can it be?
Snow — what else
Kristiana Lole, Grade 3
Public School 48, NY

Cranes

Cranes are beautiful.
Cranes can fly high in the sky.
Cranes are great creatures.
Christina Giglio, Grade 3
St Joseph School, NY

Underwater Dreams

The Princess awaits for her ball to begin
She flips her tail back and forth
calling in her guests
Everybody is having fun
except for her
Her prince is not here…
But wait…he comes swishing
through the coral reef
Megan S. Bardis, Grade 3
Public School 69 Jackson Heights, NY

A Very Warm Winter

This winter is a very warm winter,
The summer birds still come in to wake us up,
The butterflies don't migrate as early.
This winter is a very warm winter,
It hardly snowed at all,
But when it does,
It all melts that same day,
This has been a very warm winter,
We would all say.
Isabella Merchant, Grade 3
North Star Elementary School, DE

Friends

With my friend Sophie, I go to the movie.
With my friend Sophie, I am groovy!
With my friend Sophie, I eat a banana.
With my friend Sophie, I go to see Hannah.
Hope Cubbler, Grade 2
Trinity Christian School, VA

Winter

Winter gloves
Winter coat
Winter hat
Winter stoat
Winter sweater
Winter boots
Winter clothes
Hooray for winter
Toot, toot!
Anthony Rodriguez, Grade 2
Public School 1 The Bergen School, NY

I Dream
A low tapping of the fan in my room.
A dog on one side,
    a cat on the other.
Good dreams come to me.
Bad things float away
    like clouds passing an airplane.
Good things come.
Then I dream.

Maggie McCotter, Grade 3
Thomas Jefferson Elementary School, VA

Here Comes Spring
Here comes spring,
Here comes spring,
Budding flowers, spring dresses,
Here comes spring,
Here comes spring,
Chirping birds, butterflies in fields.
Here comes spring,
Here comes spring,
There it goes There it goes There it goes!

Samantha Livingston, Grade 1
Public School 167 Parkway, NY

Chocolate Bunny
My funny bunny likes to play games
My funny bunny like to play with my friends
He is a chocolate bunny
My friends might bite and eat him.

Emile Cunningham, Grade 1
Park Avenue School, NY

My Life
At first my life was twisted.
I never thought my life would be wasted,
thrown away.
It started to get better.
I got better and better at working
to get myself where I want to be.
I just want to be myself.

Kendall, Grade 2
Kanner Learning Center, PA

White

White is hard like marble and is as
wild as a Yeti
soft like paper
white is shiny like the moon and
strong like the white house
sounds like a windy day
white is as liquid as glue
and is as tasty as vanilla ice cream
on a snowy day
Demetri Lowry, Grade 2
Shady Grove Elementary School, PA

Chihuahua

Chihuahua
Cute, playful
Runs, eats, sleeps
She runs a lot.
Puppy
Lauren Bucciero, Grade 3
Granville Elementary School, NY

The Park

A park is a place
where we play
and have fun
it has water
slides and swings
and more fun stuff
people can play all day
oh, it is so good in the park!
Denyss Leon, Grade 2
Public School 2 Alfred Zimberg, NY

Dylan

Dylan is one of four boys.
He has fun playing with his toys.
Dylan is very tall.
He enjoys playing ball.
Dylan is always part of the team.
He loves ice cream.
Dylan Ioffreda, Grade 1
St Joan of Arc School, PA

Waves

whoosh
here comes a wave
splash
it soaks you
sitting down half-soaked
like a beach
then wham!
a big wave hits
super soaked
like the ocean
standing back
watching those naughty waves
Asa Mervis, Grade 3
Sinai Academy of the Berkshires, MA

My Friend Darcy

My friend Darcy
Cares for me all the time.
My friend Darcy
Helps me when I am hurt
All the time.
My friend Darcy
Plays with me all the time.
The most bestest friend
And nicest of all the friends
In the world.
Sophie Collins, Grade 1
Glover Elementary School, MA

Dinosaurs

Stegosaurus
Albertosaurus
Triceratops
Deinonychus
Sauropod
Protoceratops.
These are all names of dinosaurs
that lived years ago.
They all lived together
and shared the world alone.
Peter Ribbens, Grade 2
Tashua School, CT

Flowers

F lowers smell good
L ast time I went on vacation I had lots of fun
O range is my second favorite color
W inter is cold
E ggs are good for you
R aces are fun
S undays are great

Katie Koch, Kindergarten
Montessori Development Center, PA

Spoiled Brat

There is a spoiled brat,
she's going to be splat!
Because she is mean
to all that she is seen,
She gets her way
mostly all day,
and her birthday
is coming in May.
Spoiled brats get mad,
they might make another kid sad.
They make a lot of mess
they might even ruin their newest dress.
They think they are tough
so they don't take care of stuff.
If you ever see a spoiled brat,
please try not to knock her flat.

Tori Grimes, Grade 3
Seaford Central Elementary School, DE

Families

The important thing about families
is that they care about you.
It is that they have happiness for you.
It's like they love you so much.
It's that they play with you.
It's never like they're happy when you go.
But, the important thing about them
is that they love you!
And is that they care for you.

Ben Pratt, Grade 1
Glover Elementary School, MA

Spring!
Balls are bouncing!
Kids are pouncing!
Spring!
Fish are splashing!
Trees are swishing!
Spring!
Flowers are blooming!
The wind is swishing!
And trees are giving us shade!
Katherine Moran, Grade 3
St Rose School, CT

Cheetahs
Cheetahs eat meat
And cheetahs
Are cool!
Mckayla Dourant, Grade 1
Walker Memorial School, ME

Beautiful Sound
Chirp, chirp all around,
What is that beautiful sound?
Chirp here, chirp there,
Chirp almost everywhere.
I see something over there,
Tiptoe over if you dare.
Take a peak look and stare.
It's a bird to love and care.
Melissa Rebecca, Grade 3
Our Lady of Hope School, NY

Thunder
Thunder crashes really hard,
It is noisy and loud
And it comes from a cloud.
It comes after lightning,
It keeps coming and coming.
It becomes louder and louder,
Then softer and softer
And it keeps coming this way.
Justin Lin, Grade 2
Cabot Elementary School, MA

Spring
Lots of bees
Leaves on trees
Snow melting
Trees swing

Winds a-blowing
Flowers a-growing
Birds a-tweeting
Dogs a-barking

Apples growing
Rivers flowing
Fish swimming
Gardens growing

Spring is here
People cheer
People play
Every day

Raindrops fall one by one
Waiting for the summer sun
With winter gone and summer near
Spring is the perfect time of year
Maya Huckabone, Grade 3
Chestnut Street Elementary School, PA

Chocolate Ice Cream
One day I got chocolate ice cream,
it tasted so dreamy!
It was cold and sweet and so very creamy.

My it was tasty,
but maybe I'm too hasty,
as I ate it so quickly,
and my brain felt all prickly!

A brain freeze
How dreadful
I think I'll stop.
Well maybe some more
with some sprinkles on top!
Ann Fourquet, Grade 3
Seaford Central Elementary School, DE

Red

Red is when I'm hot.
Red is the color of a stop sign.
Red is the hottest color.
Red is the color of a fire engine.
Red smells like juice.
Red tastes like pepperoni.
Red sounds like a fire siren.
Red looks like lava.
Red feels like a stove.
Red is the color of cherries.

Ryan Kupetz, Grade 3
Evergreen Elementary School, PA

Feelings

Strangeness in the living room
Dancing in a circle
Loudness is in the hallway
Singing a jolly song
Shyness is in the closet
Doing her homework
Happiness is in the backyard
Feeding the animals
Shock is in his room
Being surprised by surprises
Anger is in the attic
Beating up a doll
Hunger is in the kitchen
Eating homemade bread
Love is near the fireplace
Planning Valentine's Day

Noah Duarte, Grade 3
Acushnet Elementary School, MA

I Love Spring

I love spring because,
It is nice outside
It is fun,
    warm,
        sometimes a little cold!
Lots of flowers grow.

Jacob Ducharme, Grade 2
St Mary's Primary School, MA

I Love Cocoa

Hot cocoa is so good
I always burn my tongue
And then I run and run
In my house
I get some water from a mouse!
Then I play with my dollhouse.
I get some more hot cocoa, too.
My mom said that I'm a hot cocoa girl
I said, "Phew" I love hot cocoa too.

Sarah Sweeney, Grade 2
Willis E Thorpe School, MA

Dogs

Dogs are so cute.
They're soft as a feather.
They're fun to play with.
They don't like the bad weather.

They go "Woof Woof."
They have a great smile.
There are different kinds.
They can run over a mile.

Catherine Lerose, Grade 3
Willits Elementary School, NY

Butterflies

The butterflies are flying in the air.
Butterflies are colorful.
Butterflies are beautiful.
Butterflies are cool!

Karianne Benoit, Grade 2
St Mary's Primary School, MA

Springtime

The sun is bright
children are playing
outside with their toys.
They are having fun playing
with their scooter, bicycle,
ball and hoola hoop.

Victor Rojas, Grade 2
Public School 122 Mamie Fay, NY

All About Space

Earth is green and blue.
The earth is in an air bubble.
Once meteors got the planet in trouble.
A meteor is a rock that is very fast.
The sun is made of yellow gas.
The sun is bright,
Like the moon at night.
A meteor blasts in space
I think its a dark place.

Paula Antar, Grade 1
Magen David Yeshivah School, NY

Leprechauns

Silly, small,
Golfing, singing, tricking,
Love to do shoe making
Little people.

Christopher DeRienzo, Grade 2
Long Meadow Elementary School, CT

Snow

The snow as silver as the moon on mid
summer nights sky with fresh warm air
and the scent of fresh fallen rain with
music in the air to blow away all that is
sad, and the nightfall as silky as a
white cat's fur and the elegant balance
of the stork and the silence of the lynx
when it's stalking its prey but still as
radiant as a new star in the midnight
sky beautiful flowing snow

Nick Popov, Grade 3
Thoreau Elementary School, MA

Spring

Spring is shamrocks in the wind
Spring is new green grass growing
Spring is springtime skiing
But most of all
Spring is gentleness

Grace-Marie Keane, Grade 1
St Rose School, CT

If I Were a Bird

If I were a bird I'd cross the ocean
If I were a bird I'd fly over a mountain
If I were a bird I'd get lost inside
If I were a bird I'd find my way home

Rose Thompson-Turcotte, Grade 3
Public School 69 Jackson Heights, NY

The Snowmen

It is winter. I like winter.
Do you like winter?
The trees are full of snow
Snowflakes are coming down slow
I built 2 snowmen with my brothers
Who came out to help? My mother.
Then when my little brother came in
He started to spin!

Molly Thibodeau, Grade 2
Willis E Thorpe School, MA

Hamsters

Hamsters are cute
hamsters are fuzzy
hamsters are pets
They spin on their wheels
and crunch on their vegetables
I like hamsters.

Matthew Mendez, Grade 2
Public School 2 Alfred Zimberg, NY

Friendship

Friendship is
Like a
Rollercoaster
You have
Your ups
And downs
It might go
Your way
Or it will
Turn around

Jayde Breault, Grade 3
Acushnet Elementary School, MA

Summer Is...
Summer is yellow.
It tastes like popsicles.
It smells like fresh cut grass.
Summer reminds me of kids playing
And sounds like bumblebees.
Summer feels like hot sun on your skin.

Gabrielle Vergerio, Grade 2
Curtisville Primary Center, PA

Spring Is...
Butterflies soaring through the sky
Skipping merrily outside
Having picnics at the park
Bike riding and jogging with my family
Going out for ice cream
Wind in my face
Inviting friends over
Watching the stars all night
Winter's gone spring is in!
That's what spring is to me

Liana Viola, Grade 3
Helen B Duffield Elementary School, NY

Woodpeckers
Woodpeckers make me think of birds.
Birds make me think of the sky.
The sky makes me think of air.
Air makes me think of trees.
Trees make me think of knotholes.
Knotholes make me think of woodpeckers.

Anevay Nichol, Grade 3
Cambridge Springs Elementary School, PA

Spring
Spring is pink.
It tastes like cotton candy.
It sounds like white doves.
It smells like fresh strawberries.
It looks like fluffy clouds.
It makes me feel happy and excited.

Elizabeth Long, Grade 3
St Clement Mary Hofbauer School, MD

Spring

Spring, spring is here!
I love spring, there's flowers
And green leaves on the trees.
The grass is so green.
It's so warm in spring.

Dale Plant, Grade 2
East Hill School, NY

Love

The most important thing
About my grandparents is
They love me.
They had surgery
And are fine.
I'm sorry they even
Had to have surgery.
They have a sofa
In their basement
And it can turn into a bed.
The basement has
About one-million toys.
For Christmas they
Gave me a
Razor scooter.
But the most important
Thing is they love me.

Miller Farley, Grade 2
St Christopher's School, VA

The Flag

Red, white, and blue
Are our country's colors
They wave like an ocean
When the wind blows around
It has thirteen stripes
And fifty stars
It's raised at dawn
It's lowered at dusk
It's always honored
In The U.S.A.

Carrie Shabe, Grade 3
Trinity Christian School, VA

Friends

A friend is nice
A friend is good
A friend will help
When she should.

Denisse Calixto Rosas, Grade 1
Public School 1 The Bergen School, NY

Boo

There once was a leprechaun named Boo.
He had a very bad flu.
He bought a harp.
It was very sharp.
He started to play it with his shoe.

Anna Brubaker, Grade 3
St Rose School, CT

My Cat Trouble

I have a cat
That is very fat.
Her name is Trouble
And she looks like a bubble.
She loves to play with bottle caps.
She also loves to take long naps.
She rides a skateboard and other cool tricks,
And then I reward her with Meow mix!!

Elena Cruz-Adames, Grade 2
Fox Chase School, PA

Robots

I think about my future
And what do I see?
Robots!
I see tons and tons of them
I see flying robots, swimming robots, and
Lots of them on moons
I see them running, walking, sliding
Jumping and digging
So now you see
I'm full with glee
and you can see that
What I see is
Robots

Jean-Claude Abiaad, Grade 3
Trinity Christian School, VA

My Cat
My cat sleeps on my bed
My cat sleeps on my head
She likes to purr and roll around
She makes me fall onto the ground
Bump, I go to the floor
Help I'm crawling out the door
My cat is crazy you can see
She thinks the bed is for her, NOT ME!!!

Leah Stribling, Grade 2
Mary Walter Elementary School, VA

What Is Pink?
Pink is the color of a sea horse,
Pink is the mother of a rose,
Pink feels like silk,
Pink sounds like a flower swaying in the wind,
Pink smells like a rose,
Pink is the little sister of red,
Pink is as soft as velvet
Pink is the nicest thing on Earth.

Carolyn Frank, Grade 2
Shady Grove Elementary School, PA

The Beach
The beach is a cool place.
People lay on the beach.
Some people stay for the sunset.
Families walk on the board walk.
The beach has a cool breeze
and footprints lay in the golden yellow sand.
The beach is a fun and happy place.

Amber Nuse, Grade 3
Robeson Elementary School, PA

Yellow
Yellow looks like flowers.
Yellow sounds like crackly leaves.
Yellow smells like lemons.
Yellow tastes like macaroni and cheese.
Yellow feels like sunshine.

Alex Johnson, Grade 1
St Christopher's School, VA

Skiing

I love skiing I really really do
I love skiing. How about you?
I love skiing with my dad.
I love skiing but sometimes I get sad.
I love skiing in the night.
But sometimes, I get a FRIGHT.

Carolyn Curtin, Grade 2
Willis E Thorpe School, MA

Planets

P luto is a dwarf planet
L and on Mars is red
A rocket is blasting off
N eptune is a blue planet
E arth has land and water
T he sun is a star
S tars are everywhere

Schuyler Cauley, Kindergarten
Montessori Development Center, PA

Bugs

Bugs bugs here and there
Bugs bugs everywhere
Please don't touch it!
Your mother says
But you do it anyway.

Suraya Lahlimi, Grade 2
Public School 2 Alfred Zimberg, NY

Breadsticks

Breadsticks on a plate
fresh and warm from the
oven at the dinner
table with steam
on each crispy
stick making clouds
of hot steam. And garlic
and crispy ends just
sitting there ready to be
eaten for dinner

George Lampman, Grade 3
Lincoln Elementary School, PA

Dad

Tall and brave
Swimming, yelling, running
In the navy
Dad

Tyler Kesselring, Grade 3
Nottoway Elementary School, VA

Easter

Easter is so fun
Eggs are lying everywhere
Baskets full of toys
The Easter bunny bringing
chocolate bunnies, candy, yeah!

Eric Fischer, Grade 3
Penn-Kidder Campus, PA

Peaceful Rain

Rain falling peacefully
Splashing outside
Making little dots on windows
Bouncing circles in puddles
Peaceful rain

Hanna Franklin, Grade 1
Dartmouth Early Learning Center, MA

Hare

H airy creatures of the
A rctic
R acing
E verywhere

Benjamin Hayward, Grade 3
Houghton Elementary School, MA

Flowers

Flowers flowers they grow in the rain
they start blooming in the spring
and get bigger in the summer
they can be all different colors
like red, purple, yellow and even pink.
Flowers are so beautiful!

Estefania Cleves, Grade 2
Public School 2 Alfred Zimberg, NY

Blue
Blue is the color
Of a beautiful blue jay
Chirping away in the blue morning sky
Jack Orlando, Grade 1
Buckley Country Day School, NY

Life Is So Great!
The skies are blue
Birds are chirping
The flowers are blooming
And trees are budding
Life is like nature
Never take for granted
What you have in front of you
Because just like when fall and winter come
And trees lose their leaves
And flowers lose their petals
We have no control
Of when our last day on Earth will be
So appreciate every day you have
With the ones you love
Like the petals on a flower
The leaves on a tree
Or the sweet sounds of birds chirping...
Blair Smith and Yuliana Maldonado, Grade 3
Oak Park Elementary School, PA

Flowers
F lowers are growing
L eaves grow on the trees
O utside playing are the people
W aterfalls for ducks to swim in
E very day people are out playing
R aindrops fall from the leaves
S pring brings cheer for everyone
Ashley Postlewait, Grade 3
Chestnut Street Elementary School, PA

My Cat Willy
Willy is my cat
Willy is special to me
I like him a lot
Savannah Bell, Grade 2
Fonda-Fultonville Elementary School, NY

Horses

Horses galloping, galloping
In the wind
My hair is flowing in the sky
Jumping over big logs going
Somewhere in midair
Fiona Russo, Grade 3
Center School, MA

Narnia

So full of action
half human and animal
wardrobe discovered
Luis Ortega, Grade 3
Sacred Heart School, CT

Clouds

Clouds float through the sky
like white fluffy cotton balls
that pour down wet rain
Rebekah King, Grade 2
Killingly Memorial School, CT

Stars

Shining shimmering stars
Marvelous light fills the room
Just in time
When I go to bed
Gently glittering
Good night!
Kelly Hwang, Grade 2
Tashua School, CT

The Pool

I went to the pool
I felt warm
I swam around
until I needed air
I got some air
and then I went
back in.
Cory Furrier, Grade 1
St Rose School, CT

Sky

The sky is blue and bitter like me
The sky is bright and shiny like me.
The sky is white and shiny like a marshmallow.
I see the sky in the morning and at night.
I see the sky all the time!
Why can't I feel you
Why 'O' Why?
Malik Habeeullah, Grade 3
Al-Rahmah School, MD

Bees

Bees make me think of pollen.
Pollen makes me think of flowers.
Flowers make me think of trees.
Trees make me think of the sky.
The sky makes me think of flying.
Flying makes me think of bees.
Chelsea Luikart, Grade 3
Cambridge Springs Elementary School, PA

Dogs

There was a small dog that lived in a can,
He barked and worried about large fans.
The dog was mean,
especially to cats.
He thought they were worthless,
and acted like brats!
He had better be careful,
this small little pup.
A cat is much meaner,
and may eat him up!
Corey Corbin, Grade 3
Seaford Central Elementary School, DE

Spring

S hort sleeves
P ink tulips
R abbits
I ce cream
N ew baby animals
G rowing plants
Lauren Gentile, Grade 3
Chestnut Street Elementary School, PA

Fluffy Dog

When I looked up in the sky,
I saw a cloud which was nice and high.
It looked like a white running dog,
Jumping over a big log.
When I saw it
I wanted to play,
in the bight sunny day.
When I tried to reach it
It was really too high.
Then I used a glider to soar up to the sky.
But when I touched the dog
It just felt like fog.

Amrit Padhi, Grade 2
Francis J Kane Elementary School, MA

Earth Is Wonderful

Earth is a planet
It is not like Mars.
Earth is like a sweet flower that can never die
This planet is wonderful.
Without Earth there would be no purpose
To people at all
This is an amazing
Planet
We have
Water, food, life, oil,
Plants and medicine on Earth.
It is like a butterfly
Giving light life to this planet
It is like a magnificent amusement park

Kenneth Wilson, Grade 3
Public School 30 R Hernandez/L Hughes, NY

If I Were a Snowflake

If I were a snowflake,
I would make the world white as can be.
I'd fall gently like rain.
People run around and around and
Have snowball fights with me.
I'd fall from the clouds.
It's fun!

Connor Dunn, Grade 1
Hyman Fine Elementary School, MA

Dogs

Dogs
Fluffy, soft
Running, jumping, catching
Swims, runs, plays, dives
Jogging, playing, rolling
Cool, awesome
Canines

Eli Tallchief, Grade 3
Brant Elementary School, NY

The Bat

Once there was a bat
Who got himself a hat.
He went upstairs
To get his wares.
When he came back,
He was with Mack.

Nerissa Baroni, Grade 2
Trinity Christian School, VA

Butterflies

grace
sparkle
whisper by
rainbows in flight
flower to flower
glide

Alexis Nanavaty, Grade 3
St Rose School, CT

Snow

Snow is a blanket
That shivers
On the cold ground
It is sprinkling
Down the sky
It will crumble on the ground
And blow like feathers
And swoosh and swoosh
Snow is a blanket

Peter Zimbalist, Grade 3
Willits Elementary School, NY

Snowflake, Snowflake

Snowflake, snowflake
Snowflake, snowflake
This is where
You belong
I want
Time with you
Before you go
Till next year.
I know I will miss
You very, very
Much.
But I also know I'll
Have a great time
In spring,
Summer, and fall.
But I like
You better
Than any season.
I can wait
Until winter
Is over!

Katie Duetsch, Grade 2
St John Neumann Academy, VA

The Happiest Time of Year

The happiest time of year is here.
Winter bells are a-ringing,
The cold may be stinging.
We gather around this cold winter day,
You'll feel cozy and gay.
Old St. Nick is coming,
Morning doves are humming.
He is coming with presents or coal,
And it will lift your soul.
Snowball fights we'll have,
Outside on this cold winter day.

Connor Shene, Grade 3
Trinity Catholic School, NY

Index

Index

Index